# PRINCES of the CHURCH

## A HISTORY OF THE ENGLISH CARDINALS

DOMINIC AIDAN BELLENGER
& STELLA FLETCHER

SUTTON PUBLISH

First published in 2001 by
Sutton Publishing Limited · Phoenix Mill
Thrupp · Stroud · Gloucestershire · GL5 2BU

British Library Cataloguing in Publication Data

A catalogue record is available from the British Library

ISBN 0 7509 2630 9

Dominic Aidan Bellenger and Stella Fletcher have asserted the moral right
to be identified as the authors of this work.

Typeset in 11/14.5pt Sabon.
Typesetting and origination by
Sutton Publishing Limited.
Printed and bound in England by
J.H. Haynes & Co. Ltd, Sparkford.

# Contents

# Foreword

I am very pleased indeed that Dom Aidan Bellenger and Stella Fletcher have written this history. The role of a cardinal has always been one of service to the pope in his ministry of pastoral care and of witness to Christ. Cardinals have come from very different backgrounds and are much influenced by the history of the times. The English cardinals are no exception. This book outlines brilliantly the distinctiveness of their lives, both here in England and in Rome. It is interesting to note how many of the English cardinals were resident in Rome and one of the fascinations of this book is the influence these cardinals had in the Vatican during the centuries since the Reformation.

The Church stands now at the beginning of the twenty-first century and I am conscious of following very many distinguished predecessors, not only here at Westminster but also those curial cardinals who serve the Church in a specific way in Rome.

I hope this book will be widely read, providing as it does a fascinating history of the role of the cardinal as well as a detailed history of the English cardinals.

Cardinal Cormac Murphy-O'Connor
Archbishop's House
Westminster
March 2001

# Introduction

'Like the immovable hinge, which sends the door back and forth, thus Peter and his successors have the sovereign judgement over the entire Church . . . Therefore his clerics are named cardinals, for they belong more closely to the hinge by which everything else is moved.'[1] Thus did the eleventh-century pope Leo IX (1049–54) describe not only the office which he himself enjoyed, but also that of his innermost circle of advisers, the Sacred College of Cardinals. Leo's fifteenth-century successor Eugenius IV (1431–47) was no less aware that the word 'cardinal' is derived from the Latin *cardo*, meaning hinge or pivot. In his assessment, 'as the door of a house turns on its hinges, so on the cardinalate does the Apostolic See, the door of the whole church, rest and find support'.[2] However, as Stephan Kuttner explained over half a century ago, the origins of the title which has come to be accorded to princes of the Church were by no means as straightforward as those two papal quotations might suggest.

Although cardinals came to be associated with the bishop and the churches of Rome, the term 'cardinal' was not initially an office confined to that city and its original meaning was distinctly different to its later one. Clerics in the Early Church were ordained to a particular post or 'title' for life and, if transferred to another place, were 'incardinated' into it: here the idea is not that of a hinge, but rather of a tenon wedging a piece of wood into a cavity. Such clergy were known not as 'titulars', but as 'cardinals'. This usage was accepted by Pope Gregory the Great (590–604) and employed in many dioceses in the western Church. It soon became a mark of honour. In 747 Pope Zacharias authorised Pepin the Short, king of the Franks, to designate the clergy of Paris as cardinals, to distinguish them from country priests. The designation of two of the minor canons of St Paul's Cathedral, London, as cardinals can be traced back to this practice: an otherwise curious survival of the term within the Church of England. The use of the title cardinal was restricted by Pope Pius V in 1567 to the cardinals of Rome. Whether as a 'hinge' or a 'tenon', therefore, the title of cardinal conveys notions of occupying a pivotal position and holding a complex structure together.

Personal ability could have been an incentive to incardinate a cleric and such men became close confidants of bishops, the pivot of their council or administration. In Rome the emergence of such a council was a prolonged process and the cardinals in the Roman Church began as liturgical functionaries. Priests attached to the various titular churches in Rome were asked to preside at liturgical functions at the shrines of the martyrs where pilgrimage churches were being built; these included the future basilicas of St Peter, on the Vatican hill, and St Paul, south of the city wall. When providing liturgical services there, priests became known as 'cardinal priests'. From the eighth century onwards the bishops of the neighbouring sees to Rome began to assist the pope in the liturgical services at his cathedral in the Lateran where, like the visiting priests at the basilicas, they became cardinals, in their case 'cardinal bishops'. The 'suburbicarian' dioceses which provided these cardinal bishops were Albano, Ostia and Velletri, Porto and S. Rufina, Palestrina, Sabina (with Poggio Mirteto) and Frascati (or Tusculum). In time these cardinal bishops provided a dean and subdean for the College of Cardinals.

The cardinalate came into its own during the reform papacy of the eleventh and twelfth centuries. Under Leo IX the cardinal bishops and priests became the central figures in the papal *curia*, or court, modelled on the *curiae* of secular rulers; this gave the cardinals a princely status when they met with the pope in formal meetings or 'consistories'. In the years 1050–1100 the cardinals became what amounted to a Church senate, an image first used by Peter Damiani (1007–72), a great ecclesiastical reformer and a promoter of papal power. As the senate the cardinals became crucial in the making of popes and at least notionally, as representatives of the Roman Church, took on the functions proposed by ancient canonical authorities who insisted that the election of any bishop should be made by the 'priests and people' of his diocese. The concept of the cardinalate was subsequently fleshed out by the great monastic reformer Bernard of Clairvaux (1090–1153), especially in his *De consideratione*, addressed to his disciple Pope Eugenius III (1145–53). Bernard saw their task as primarily a reforming one. Some writers even began to view the cardinalate as having a power autonomous of the papacy. In line with this the cardinals developed their own institutions independent of the popes and enhanced appreciation of their status was reflected in the ever larger households which served them.

It was, however, the election of popes which became the cardinals' defining role, a function which they acquired in the 1050s. *Licet de evitanda*, a decree of the Third Lateran Council (1179), remained the basis of papal elections throughout the period covered by this book. This insisted on a two-thirds majority of a quorum of two-thirds of the body of cardinals present at a 'conclave'. The fact that the papal election took place under locked conditions gives the name 'conclave' (with keys). The cardinals gave credibility to the pope's ecclesiastical independence and made possible his claims to the 'fullness of power'. By the end of the twelfth century the cardinals 'had become the Pope's essential collaborators in the government of the church as judges, guardians of the faith and political advisers'.[3]

The increasing scope of the papal administration led to the growth of a third rank of cardinals, the 'cardinal deacons'. In a Roman context deacons had organised the city's social services, the fall of the Roman Empire having left the Church to fill the void left in urban government. Although originally attached to the Lateran, the deacons eventually had a number of centres or *diaconia* for their activities; these *diaconia* duly provided the bases for the cardinal deacons. Cardinal deacons are officials of the Roman curia and before 1965 they were often not bishops.

Just as the term 'cardinal' evolved over a period of time, so also has the Sacred College evolved with regard to its size and the recruitment of its members.[4] Once the cardinalate became accepted as an exalted position, cardinals were jealous of their status and the income derived from it and tried to persuade popes not to dilute their authority by creating too many new cardinals. Sixtus V (1585–90) in 1586 and Innocent XII (1691–1700) made major reforms. Sixtus fixed the total number of cardinals at seventy, a figure which remained in effect until John XXIII (1958–63), and also attempted to internationalise the cardinalate with the 'official' representatives of the various Catholic nations. Innocent restricted the pastoral responsibility of cardinals in their titles to allow local clergy more effective pastoral care. In 1962 John XXIII decreed that all cardinals should be consecrated bishops. Paul VI (1963–78) imposed the age restriction, whereby cardinals over eighty take no part in papal conclaves.

The cardinalate is entirely in the gift of the pope. Usually all candidates are listed in a *biglietto* and named formally in a private consistory, but sometimes the identity of a cardinal is kept secret (often for political reasons, especially if religious persecution is a possibility) in the pope's 'heart' (*in pectore, in petto*). The new cardinal is invested in his office in a public consistory.[5] This is not a sacramental ceremony, but an inauguration.

'College' as well as 'senate' is a designation often attached to the body of cardinals. The cardinals acting together form a group not dissimilar to a cathedral chapter, or any other ecclesiastical college, but their role as 'senators' distinguishes them as successors to the senate of Imperial Rome and the Papal States (so long as they survived), as well as senators of the Catholic Church. From their senatorial rank came much of the colour of the office, 'the sacred purple', and the colour scarlet (red is too inexpressive a description) which characterises their dress.

The large red hat or *galero*, with fifteen scarlet *fiocchi* ('knots') on each side, survives heraldically, but has not been used at consistories since 1969. It often appears in works of art as a symbol of St Jerome (*c.* 345–420); although there was no such office at the time, he was by tradition made a cardinal by Pope Damasus (366–84) to whom he acted as secretary. From the Renaissance period onwards it was presented to the new cardinal at his public inauguration and never worn again. At his death it was taken from storage, carried before his coffin and then placed at the base of his bier. It was later displayed hanging from the vault of his cathedral or church. The symbolic cardinal's hat is a development of the *capello pontificale*, used by cardinals from the thirteenth century, with the distinctive shape of the *galero*, but without the fifteen tassels on either side. It was generally secured with a pair of tassels and was worn for travelling and on formal occasions, but not with liturgical vestments.[6] The new cardinals are now presented with a scarlet watered-silk biretta and *zucchetto* or skull cap. The following words, which underline the meaning of the cardinalatial scarlet, are used by the pope in the act of creating the cardinal:

In praise of God and in the honour of the Apostolic See, receive the red hat, the sign of the cardinal's dignity. For you must be ready to conduct yourself with fortitude, even to the shedding of your blood for the increase of the Christian faith; for the peace and tranquillity of the people of God and the Kingdom of Heaven and for the Holy Roman Church.[7]

In the nineteenth century cardinals' costumes attracted the attention of mildly anticlerical artists, especially in France and Germany, who portrayed eminences of various shapes and sizes, but always resplendent in scarlet, taking tea, drinking aperitifs or having their photograph taken. The alcoholic dimension has proved to be particularly inspirational in an English context, for the spiced wine known as 'bishop' becomes 'cardinal' if claret is substituted for port, while the distinctive cardinal's hat has been used in a number of pub signs.[8] Continuing this theme, the visitor to Archbishop's House, attached to Westminster Cathedral and the home of successive cardinals in the modern period, may be struck by the neighbouring hostelry called *The Cardinal*: its sign is currently a portrait of Cardinal Manning, an apostle of temperance.

In the secret consistory which followed the public act of creating the cardinal, there was performed a ceremony known as the 'opening and closing of the mouth'. The pope first told the new cardinal in the *aperitio oris* (the opening of the mouth) that he was to be 'heard' in consistories, congregations and all ecclesiastical gatherings; he was then told in the formula used for the *clausura oris* (closing of the mouth) that he was 'to keep the secrets of his office and to give wise counsel to the Pope'.[9] Following this each cardinal was presented with a new ring of office, traditionally a sapphire, and was formally assigned a Roman church which he held as titular. The arcane rituals, much simplified in recent years, reflect the great status of the cardinalatial rank and the dignity of cardinals as princes of the Church. On 10 June 1630 Pope Urban VIII decreed that members of the Sacred College were to be addressed as 'Eminence' and anyone else who used the title should henceforth cease. This was to distinguish clerical princes from those secular princes who were more frequently referred to as 'Highness'. The congresses of Vienna and Berlin confirmed that cardinals had a diplomatic status equal to 'princes of the blood' and therefore took precedence only behind emperors, kings and heirs to thrones. This protocol was ratified by the treaty of Versailles and remains in force today.

The papal court at Rome, following its return from Avignon, probably reached its pre-eminence in the period from 1450 to 1700. Papal authority shifted in a worldly direction. It was said of Urban VIII that 'he wished to be seen as a prince rather than as a pope, a ruler rather than a pastor'. In this period the papal monarchy became one of the most influential models for other royal households and the most spectacular court in baroque Europe, marked in its ceremonies by 'the exemplary public expression' of the religious calendar of Catholic Christendom.[10] In the High Middle Ages the cardinals had been true 'hinges' of the Church. In the sixteenth and seventeenth centuries they became gradually transformed into a courtly aristocracy with two main 'types' of cardinal emerging: 'the cardinal protector' acting as a defender of national interests in Rome and the 'cardinal nephew', who became known as the principal broker of political and religious patronage.[11] A period of stagnation in the eighteenth century was followed by a profound rethinking in the nineteenth and twentieth centuries, which shifted the emphasis of the papacy back towards its religious origins.

Into the world of consistory and conclave a select group of Englishmen, more than forty in total, have been admitted since the twelfth century and one of their number elected to the papacy. In contrast to the Celtic tradition, Rome and the English Church were closely associated from the outset, Pope Gregory the Great sending Augustine (of Canterbury) to convert the Anglo-Saxons in 596. The English connection may even be found in what must be the most enduring myth about papal Rome, that an Englishwoman, disguised as a cleric and with male lover in tow, was elected pope amid the political turbulence of the ninth century. The authoritative J.N.D. Kelly dismisses the stories of Pope Joan: 'It scarcely needs painstaking refutation today, for not only is there no contemporary evidence for a female pope at any of the dates suggested for her reign, but the known facts of the respective periods make it impossible to fit one in.'[12] The crucial period in Anglo-papal relations was not, however, the Anglo-Saxon one, but the years from the Norman Conquest to the death of King John. From that period onwards, despite the rupture of the Reformation, the English and Roman Churches have remained in creative dialogue.[13]

There have been at least three studies of the English cardinals published before this one. The first was a handsome two-volume account of the *Lives of the English Cardinals including Historical Notices of the Papal Court from Nicholas Breakspear (Pope Adrian IV) to Thomas Wolsey, Cardinal Legate* by Folkestone Williams, published by W.H. Allen (London) in 1868. Williams, delighting in intrigue and innuendo, is openly anti-Roman and presents a chronicle of plottings and poisonings. The volumes, bound in blue cloth, have handsome cardinals' hats on their spines. Dudley Baxter, a Catholic writer, dedicated his work *England's Cardinals*, published by Burns and Oates (London) in 1903, to 'England's Present Cardinal' (Vaughan) 'heir of St Augustine'. Bound in scarlet it proclaims the 'true seat of Catholic continuity in this country' to be

Westminster, not Canterbury. The third, *The Story of the English Cardinals* by Charles Isaacson, published in 1907 by Elliot Stock (London), is closer in tone to Williams with some hostile comments on the later cardinals (Isaacson goes up to Vaughan) to add to the stories of poisonings. Isaacson was an Anglican divine and a former fellow of Clare College, Cambridge.

The present work attempts a survey of the English cardinals, hoping to place them within the context of both European and English history. Not all of them were good or great, but by their exalted position they played a significant role in the development of the English Church and nation and embodied England's continuing role in European affairs. Although the basic function of cardinals in conclaves and consistories has remained largely unchanged down the centuries, the individuals who have held the office have been very much men of their times, as this multi-period study seeks to demonstrate. Thus we witness the evolution of the English cardinal from medieval theologian through Renaissance prince, early modern religious exile and nineteenth-century patriarch to twentieth-century servant of the people. The ecclesiastical, political and cultural emphases adopted in these pages have been thus dictated by the evolving role which English cardinals have been called upon to play.

# ONE

## *Medieval Christendom*

The trappings of the medieval papacy became increasingly magnificent and its spiritual and political claims grew more and more audacious. The reality of papal life during the period from 1000 to 1300 was less satisfactory. Papal reigns were short; the climate of Rome bred disease and its population was chronically hostile, especially to non-Romans. John of Salisbury, writing in the twelfth century, recollected how the English pope, Adrian IV, had reflected on the burdens of the papal office: 'no one is more wretched than the Roman Pontiff, no condition more unhappy than his . . . his duties alone would overwhelm him'.[1]

There was a great contrast between the physical reality of Rome and its spiritual status. By the twelfth century, when the office of cardinal emerged in a recognisable form, the population had dropped to some 20,000 from its height of half a million in the classical era. The city's economy depended on pilgrims coming to visit its 300 churches and its unparalleled collection of relics. In the tenth century the papacy had been controlled by powerful Roman families who fixed papal elections and commanded its revenues. The papal reassertion of power in the eleventh and twelfth centuries was always challenged by the Roman families, nor were the popes' problems confined to Rome.

The attempts of the papacy to be an international arbiter and to proclaim the superiority of the priesthood, the *sacerdotium*, over the

1

secular power, the *regnum*, led to constant conflict. Pope Gelasius I (492–6) had expressed the theory of the two authorities which led the world: 'There are two powers by which this world is governed in chief, the consecrated authority of priests and the royal power.' Until the emergence of a strong reformed papacy under Leo IX and most notably Gregory VII (1073–84) the task facing rulers was to reconcile the essential unity of the 'corpus Christi', as the Church was seen, with the duality of its earthly government and to define the frontiers between the two authorities. Gregory VII in his *Dictatus papae* (1075) made the explicit claim that the pope could depose the emperor. The conflict which ensued – often called the Investiture Contest, because so much dependent on who invested who with ecclesiastical authority – was to drag on for centuries. Gregory VII and high papalists who followed his lead, believed that the Christian world was a unity and local variations were not to be tolerated. Papal centralisation and the attempt to disseminate papal influence took several forms. Its chief instrument and motive force was to clericalise, even monasticise, the whole Church's leadership; the clergy began to see themselves more clearly as a race apart, owing direct obedience to the pope as 'universal ordinary'. This was assisted by a growth in the quantity and sophistication of canon law, the Church's own law, which in the twelfth century spread throughout Europe. Its mounting influence, apparent in England as elsewhere in Christendom, also coincided with the development of royal power and administration. The mirroring of papal curial reform in diocesan *curiae* and chanceries, the tightening of curial bonds through archdeacons, rural deans and episcopal visitations, show how the local Church was being transformed from within.

At times the local Church was visited by personal representatives of the pope, the legates. These legations increased in the eleventh century. Three kinds of legates emerged: *legati missi*, sent to accomplish a particular task, *legati a latere* (literally 'from the side of the pope) appointed for more wide-ranging or solemn functions, and *legati nati*, bishops of certain prestigious sees to whom legatine status was often given. In medieval England the archbishop of Canterbury often claimed this right. The calling of crusades to allow freedom of access to the Holy Places was a papal initiative aimed at uniting Christendom which was, in reality, on the road to dissolution. The papal crown was only the most potent symbol of what Ernst Kantorowicz sees as the imperialisation of the Church.[2] This imperialisation included the recruitment to the Roman curia of clerics from beyond Italy.

The long line of English cardinals began with Robert Pullen, whose name has been spelt in many different ways. Emden, whose prosopography gives such invaluable information on the lives of medieval English graduates, gives the following variants: Poldi, Polenius, Pollen, Pollet, Pulein, Puley, Pullan, Pullein, Pullenus, Pulley, Pully, de Puteaco.[3] Such a galaxy of nomenclature reveals the difficulties involved in putting together biographical details of the early cardinals, although, in the case of Pullen, a tentative *vita* and a theological overview have been attempted by Poole and Courtney respectively.[4] Pullen, it seems, was born of humble origins at a place unknown (Exeter has been claimed) sometime in the last quarter of the eleventh century. Like so many English cardinals he made his reputation as a teacher, perhaps at Oxford (at Oseney Abbey) or at Exeter in the cathedral school which had, at that time, a considerable celebrity. Poole favours Exeter, suggesting it is too early a date for an Oxford master and that there has been an understandable muddle between 'Exon' and 'Oxon';[5] Southern places him at Oxford as a forerunner of the university's future greatness.[6] In 1138 he became archdeacon of Rochester, but he was soon to resume his teaching career, this time in Paris, where in 1142 John of Salisbury, the English polymath who was to work in the papal court and to end his days as bishop of Chartres (but never a cardinal), attended his lectures. His non-residence at Rochester caused Bishop Asselin, appointed to that see in 1142, to call for Robert's return to duty. The archdeacon had friends in high places; St Bernard wrote to the bishop asking for the Englishman's continued residence in Paris.[7] Pullen was an opponent of Bernard's intellectual and personal rival Peter Abelard, and, in terms of monasticism, a proponent of the Anselmian tradition. Pullen's principal surviving work, the *Sententiarum theologicarum libri VII*,

3

was to be rapidly eclipsed by the deeply influential *Sentences* of Peter Lombard, a pupil of Abelard but also influenced by Pullen. A letter from St Bernard to Pullen reminds the cardinal of his responsibilities, both for the pope and for himself.

Watch over the pope carefully, according to the wisdom God has given you, so that in the press of business he is not circumvented by the craft of evil-minded persons, and led into decision unworthy of his apostolate. Act in a manner that becomes your position and the high dignity you have obtained. Labour prudently and manfully with the zeal God has given you, for his honour and glory, for your own salvation, and for the benefit of the Church; then you will be able to say with truth: 'The grace he has shown me has not been without fruit.' Heaven and earth are witness that hitherto you have faithfully and carefully devoted yourself to the instruction of many; but the time has come to work for God and do all that you can to prevent godless men from defying his law. Take particular care, dear friend, to be found a faithful and prudent servant of the lord, displaying dove-like simplicity in your own affairs, and in the affairs of the Church, the bride of Christ which has been entrusted to your care and loyalty; and the wisdom of the serpent against the cunning of that old serpent, so that in both God may be glorified. There are many things I want to say, but there is no need for a long letter when the living voice is at hand. In view of both your many occupations and mine, I have put my words into the mouth of the brother who brings this letter. Hear them as you would myself.[8]

Lucius II (1144–5) was another friend of St Bernard and a reforming pope who lost his life as the result of wounds received in an attempt to regain papal control of Rome. It was Lucius who created Pullen cardinal and appointed him chancellor at the papal court. From November 1144 to September 1146 Pullen was active at his post and enjoyed the support of the first Cistercian pope, Eugenius III (1145–53), a monk of St Bernard's Abbey at Clairvaux and a man of simplicity and holiness. From 18 September 1146 Robert Pullen's duties were performed by a subdeacon; no chancellor appears in the papal records until 17 December 1146 and it is then Pullen no longer. It is assumed that he died during this period. The place of his burial, like so much about the man, is not known.

The second English cardinal, Nicholas Breakspear, also became the only English pope, Adrian IV. His medieval biographers, who included Cardinal Boso and William of Newburgh (d. 1198) within thirty years of his death, and Matthew Paris (d. 1259), the St Albans chronicler who was biased towards his abbey and was a notable anti-Roman, have left his early life difficult to trace in detail. He was born perhaps as early as 1100 on the lands of the abbey of St Albans, by tradition at Bedmond in the parish of Abbot's Langley. His father, Robert of the Chamber, became a monk of St Albans and was buried in the chapter house of the abbey. Robert was a clerk in the king's chamber, a finance department which was becoming overshadowed by the exchequer. There is no solid evidence that Nicholas attended St Albans as a schoolboy and, given his later Augustinian connections, it seems more likely, as Poole suggested, that he was educated at Merton Priory in Surrey, where Thomas Becket had also been a pupil.[9] He then went to France, eventually becoming a canon of the house of Saint-Ruf, established at Avignon, but transferred to Valence in 1138. He was abbot there by 1147 and was noted as a reformer; this caused dissension in his own monastery but, according to the Augustinian chronicler William of Newburgh, it also brought him to the attention of Pope Eugenius III, who quickly made him cardinal bishop of Albano. Boso, more discreetly, suggests Breakspear impressed the pope by his conduct of his house's business and Matthew Paris mentions three visits to the papal court, each more successful than the previous. Whatever the reason, and the patronage of Robert Pullen was probably a determining factor (Pullen had strong Augustinian as well as Cistercian connections), by 1150 Breakspear appeared as a cardinal; he was probably appointed in December 1149. Breakspear's great work as a cardinal was his mission to Scandinavia where he was entrusted with the work of organising the Church in lands which had only become Christian in the second millennium. Arriving in

1152 he established an archbishopric at Trondheim in Norway and gave the Scandinavian churches a formal diocesan structure. To some, especially in Rome, he was seen as 'The Apostle of the North' and, on his return to Italy, he was elected pope on 3 December 1154, following the death of Anastasius IV. He took the name Adrian IV.

The five-year reign of the only English pope was marked by turmoil. As so often in the medieval period the question of ecclesiastical, and particularly papal authority was the centre of contention. In Rome Arnold of Brescia who, like the pope, was a canon regular, argued for a radical casting aside of ecclesiastical power, and attained great influence in the Roman commune. Adrian sought the help of the German king, Frederick Barbarossa, who, in turn, sought coronation from the pope. Frederick was crowned, but his relationship with Adrian mirrored in miniature the whole high medieval dispute about the precedence of power between the ecclesiastical and secular authorities, that dispute known as the Investiture Contest. Adrian's involvement in the politics of his native land are closely associated with his bull *Laudabiliter* (1155) which has been taken by some to mean that he gave Ireland to Henry II. The letter, the authenticity of which has aroused much debate, associates Henry II's conquest with reforming the Irish Church. An invasion of Ireland was discussed at an English royal council in 1155, after which John of Salisbury, then secretary of Theobald, archbishop of Canterbury, sought papal blessing on the intervention. The idea almost certainly came from Theobald in reaction to Canterbury's long-established control over the Irish Church, which was being challenged. *Laudabiliter* was later used as an argument against English intervention, on the grounds that the English kings had not fostered Church reform. The pope was an admirer of the Norman and Angevin involvement in Sicily as well as in England. Indeed, his mistrust of Frederick led Adrian, in the treaty of Benevento (18 June 1156), to recognise William I of Sicily as king of much of southern Italy, with special rights over the Sicilian Church, in exchange for William's acknowledgement of papal supremacy and an annual tribute. This was a switch of papal policy typical of a pope who was prepared to take resolute action as Vicar of Christ (he seems to have been the first pontiff to be so called) even if it antagonised his cardinals. Despite his intransigence, which he saw as part of his duty as pope, he was of an amiable disposition and, as his friend John of Salisbury suggested, he was able to listen to criticism, not always a characteristic of popes. He died on 1 September 1159, possibly of an acute sore throat (quinsy) or a heart attack and was buried in a magnificent third-century red Egyptian granite sarcophagus near the tomb of Eugenius III in St Peter's. Adrian's tomb, which recalls the porphyry of an emperor's tomb (and is indeed partly made of this material), is a statement of his status. The placing of porphyry quadrifógli in the pavement of Roman churches, which began during the Investiture Contest, is a similar imitation of imperial motifs.[10]

Boso, allegedly 'natione Anglus, Hadriani IV nepos',[11] was created cardinal deacon of SS. Cosma e Damiano in December 1155 by Adrian IV, one of eight new cardinals. Next to nothing is known about his early life and there is no evidence that he was, as has sometimes been asserted, a monk of St Albans Abbey. Indeed, it is probable that he was an Italian, a native of Lucca or Pisa who came to prominence through the patronage of the English pope, whose biographer he became.[12] Boso was chamberlain to Breakspear, one of the most influential figures in the curia and in charge of papal finances. He made the first attempt at a *Liber censuum*, or register of the different sources of papal income. Boso, who died in 1178, saw his chief task as laying the foundation of papal territorial power in Italy, something which he began under Adrian IV and continued under the great canonist Alexander III (1159–81) whose reign Boso chronicles as part of the *Liber pontificalis*. As Cardinal Orlando Bandinelli, Alexander III had been Adrian IV's closest admirer and, as pope, continued Adrian's pro-Norman and anti-German policies. Boso's account of Alexander's reign is dominated by the conflict between the pope and the Emperor Frederick Barbarossa, in which Pope Alexander emerges as an almost mythical figure.[13] Boso was promoted cardinal priest of S. Pudenziana by his patron Alexander in 1166.

The martyrdom of Thomas of Canterbury in his cathedral on 29 December 1170 put the English Church at the centre of the dispute between *regnum* and *sacerdotium*. The cult of the murdered archbishop spread rapidly throughout Europe and his companions, many of whom were quick to compile lives of the sainted primate, were given a prestige and celebrity which they would not otherwise have received. Herbert of Bosham, a Hebraist, theologian and scholar, was one of Thomas's clerks when the latter was chancellor of England (before 1157) and a close mentor, friend and letter writer throughout his archiepiscopate. He accompanied Thomas into exile, studied canon law with him under Lombardus of Piacenza at the French Cistercian monastery of Pontigny, where Thomas was exiled, and gives a first-hand account of this period in his *vita* of the archbishop, written in 1184–6, a somewhat prolix account full of Herbert's moralising views. He was not present at the martyrdom, much to his regret, as he had been sent by Thomas on a mission to France.[14] Some later writers have suggested that Herbert proceeded to Italy where he was given preferment and eventually became a cardinal; there is no evidence for this and it is probably drawn from a confusion between Herbert of Bosham and prelates of similar names (including Boso) or from a later patriotic desire to create another English cardinal. There seems to be no connection between the tomb recess in the south wall of Bosham church in Sussex and the putative cardinal.

The next generation of Plantagenet rule in England is generally associated with the *Magna Carta* of 1215 and the beginnings of English liberty. Again, a cardinal can be found at the heart of national affairs, for Stephen Langton's role in the sequence of events leading up to the signing of *Magna Carta* has received much attention. It would be a mistake, however, to associate Langton only with this event and only with English history.[15] He was a scholar with a European reputation long before he became archbishop of Canterbury and his French connections (as with so many medieval English cardinals) were the source of his influence. Langton was born, possibly as early as 1150, into the Lincolnshire gentry; his name has been linked to the village of Langton by Wragby, east of

Lincoln. He was a secular clerk who studied and taught at Paris, then the centre of European intellectual life, at a time when the teachers there were moving towards making themselves a corporation of masters, a university, rather than being an appendage to the cathedral school. Langton himself was a canon of Notre Dame and is credited with the composition of the sequence for the Mass of Pentecost, the *Veni, Sancte Spiritus*, a model of the austere and beautiful style he favoured. As a theologian, in a generation which had not yet rediscovered Aristotle, his speciality was the Bible and he is supposed to have provided commentaries on most of the Scriptures. In his search for an orderly presentation of the Bible he has been credited with the division into chapters which is still used today.

In 1198 Lotario, cardinal deacon of SS. Sergio e Bacco, aged only thirty-seven, was elected as pope and took the name Innocent III. A native of Anagni, south of Rome, he had studied at both Bologna and Paris. He became one of the greatest of medieval popes and presided over the Fourth Lateran Council of 1215, which codified many of the basic sacramental and theological teachings of the Church. He sought to reform the Roman curia and proposed a more austere approach to life in the pontifical court and a more exacting efficiency. He had a very high view of the papacy, but was also a defender of episcopal authority, hoping to limit the number and type of appeals to Rome and to encourage local reform through provincial and national synods. Into this reformed curia Stephen Langton was called in 1205 when he was appointed cardinal priest of S. Crisogono. The English chronicler Walter of Coventry suggested that Langton continued teaching theology in Rome. Roger of Wendover considered Langton as the *non-pareil* in the Roman court as far as learning and moral probity were concerned. His stay in Rome was, however, a short one.

A disputed election to the see of Canterbury, following the death of Archbishop Hubert Walter, led in 1207 to the appointment of Stephen Langton by the pope, who consecrated him at Viterbo on 17 June 1207. This act, seen by King John as an unacceptable use of papal power, led to a full-blown confrontation between king and pontiff and an interdict being placed on England. An interdict, the prohibition of the usual sacraments of the Church, was one of the fiercest weapons of papal power but, nevertheless, John remained intransigent and peace was not made until 1213, when the king finally capitulated. During this period Langton, barred from England, spent much time at Pontigny in northern France, Becket's retreat; it was used again by the later archbishop, St Edmund of Abingdon, who died there.

Langton's return to England and his claiming of his see was not a simple story of papal power triumphing over royal pretensions. Langton was certainly not Innocent III's poodle and the sending of papal legates to sort out the problems of the English Church and people did not meet with his approval. One of these legates was the Roman-born Pandulf, who died in 1226 as bishop of Norwich. He had been an influential member of the Roman curia, but never a cardinal. Langton's work of mediation in the tangle of jurisdictions, ecclesiastical, feudal and royal, which handicapped John's effective rule, reached some resolution in *Magna Carta* (15 June 1215), in the details of which Langton played an important, if not formative part. He approved the principles of government which the charter asserted and by giving the weight of his office to the rebels, he forfeited the support of the pope and was suspended from office between 1215 and 1218. Popes, aware of their own position, have consistently supported the political *status quo*. The new pope, Honorius III (1216–17), who succeeded Innocent III, sought harmony among the powers of Christendom to facilitate the launching of a crusade, called for by Innocent III at the Fourth Lateran Council. He encouraged the succession of the young Henry III to the English throne on John's death in 1216 and reinstated Langton.

Langton's last decade was dedicated to a reform of his province and diocese, with an eye to improving clerical discipline and pastoral care. His diocesan statutes of 1213–14, similar in many respects with those promoted by the English cardinal Robert Curzon while papal legate to the French Church, set the pattern for his wider reform programme promulgated at the Canterbury provincial council of Oxford in 1222, which became a model for much of the English Church. In 1220, to mark the jubilee of Becket's martyrdom, he presided over the translation of the martyr's body to a new shrine, amid scenes of great splendour and celebration, which included entertainment in a temporary 'palace' on a scale which was unprecedented, contemporaries reflected, since 'the time of Solomon'. He visited Rome the same year, taking with him a relic of his martyred predecessor, and managed to get the pope's support for his suggestion that during his lifetime there should be no resident papal legate in England. He also secured guarantees on the restriction of papal appointments to vacant benefices and on the precedence of Canterbury over York. Langton died on 9 July 1228 at Slindon in Sussex and his body was taken to Canterbury Cathedral where it lies buried in a simple stone coffin singularly placed half in and half out of St Michael's Chapel.

The fact that England was something of an appendage to France and that the culture of the English élite was essentially French is reflected in the career of England's next cardinal. Robert Curzon (or Courson or Coucon), a native of Derbyshire, was, according to Emden, possibly a student at Oxford but, as with Cardinal Langton, it was at Paris (where he was taught by Peter, precentor of Notre Dame) that he received his academic formation and secured a network which allowed him to progress in the Church's hierarchy. A fellow student of the future Innocent III (in Paris from 1180 to 1186), Curzon became a doctor of theology and was still lecturing in Paris in *c.* 1210. He had been appointed a canon of Noyon, by papal provision, in 1204 and a canon of Paris in 1209. On 9 June 1212 he was created cardinal priest of S. Stefano in Monte Celio by his friend Innocent III. He had one of the most challenging and exotic careers of any of the English cardinals, with his initial work as a papal judge delegate, which had begun long before he became cardinal, giving way to wide-ranging ambassadorial responsibilities. He was sent to France as papal legate in 1213, ostensibly to preach the crusade, but during his legation (which lasted probably until November 1215) he undertook the task of reforming and streamlining the French Church and regulating the syllabus at the

University of Paris. He was well prepared for his work by his academic expertise, expressed in his *Summa*, which was compiled between 1204 and 1208 and focused on the question of usury, so central to any consideration of Church benefices. This was reflected in the Church council held at Paris in 1213, which was paralleled by Langton's Oxford council. He drew up a code of statutes for the fledgling University of Paris in which, among other texts, Aristotle's *De metaphysica* and *De naturali philosophia* were proscribed. Curzon was a strong proponent of general councils as an instrument of Church reform and as an antidote to usury, very broadly interpreted, which he saw as the institutional Church's besetting sin. By way of a council he advocated a return to apostolic simplicity and an end to economic individualism and wealth creation: 'Thus would be removed all usurers, all factious men and all robbers; thus would charity flourish and the fabric of the churches again be builded; and thus would all be brought back again to its pristine state.'

Curzon courted more controversy by his attitude towards political and military events. The Albigensian crusade against the heretical Cathars of southern France was in full progress and was perhaps as much about imposing French hegemony (and language) on the dissident Languedocians as about religious uniformity. His preaching against the heretics of Toulouse received French approbation, but his severe criticisms of the French bishops and clergy led to his removal by Innocent III. He was accused, too, of showing an English bias, following the decisive French victory at Bouvines (1214), by arranging a five-year truce between King John and King Philip Augustus of France on 18 September 1214. He returned to Rome in time to be present at the Lateran Council of November 1215, but he was not allowed to remain *in curia*. Instead, his engagement with the crusade was reactivated. In 1218 the count of Nevers had asked Pope Honorius III to appoint a legate to accompany a body of crusaders sailing for Damietta in Egypt. On 28 July 1218 Curzon was sent not as legate, but to have spiritual charge of the crusaders. He died at Damietta on 6 February 1219.

Robert Somercote (or Ummarcote) did not venture so far from his native land but, like all the English cardinals in the medieval period, his career demonstrated both the importance of mobility for clerics destined for high office and the supranational culture to which they belonged. He was probably a native of the south of England, related to the Foliot family (which had given several bishops to the Church) and a kinsman or brother of Lawrence Somercote, a distinguished canonist and, like Robert, a papal subdeacon. He was educated at Bologna and held benefices in Kent and Norfolk. In 1236 he was made a papal subdeacon and in 1238 auditor of papal *literae contradictae*. In 1238 Gregory IX made him cardinal deacon of S. Eustachio. Gregory IX (1227–41) was a nephew of Innocent and, like so many leading churchmen, he had been educated at Bologna and Paris. He was made cardinal bishop of Ostia in 1206. Gregory was a consummate politician and also an encourager of new spiritual movements in the Church. He was, in particular, friend and patron of St Dominic and even more especially of St Francis, founders of the great mendicant orders. These two great orders of friars, founded to recapture the lost purity of the apostolic Church, were to become formidable weapons in the papal armoury. As centralised, mobile orders they could be used as instruments of papal reform much more easily than the older monastic orders with their tendency to localism. However, Gregory's pontificate was overshadowed by his conflict with Frederick II which reached apocalyptic proportions, with the latter calling for a general council to judge the pope and Gregory condemning Frederick as Antichrist. The pope died, having called an abortive council, and the conclave which followed elected Celestine IV, who reigned for only two weeks. There were then only twelve cardinals in the Sacred College but, as two of them were in prison, Celestine was elected by a rump of only ten men. Robert Somercote was one of these ten and was described by Matthew Paris as the most eminent of all the cardinals. There were reports that some expected him to become pope, a plausible possibility with so few candidates. It has also been suggested that he died, perhaps by poisoning, during the close confinement of the conclave, but he seems rather to have died during Innocent IV's pontificate, on 26 September 1241, and was buried in the church of S. Crisogono, built by Pope Honorius II's legate in England, Giovanni da Crema, where his epitaph can still be seen.

Folkestone Williams, in his *Lives of the English Cardinals*, makes much of the charges of poisoning. 'The prevalence of the crime of secret poisoning in Italy, more particularly among ecclesiastics', he writes, 'is not only a proof of the decadence of ordinary religious, but of ordinary social influences.' 'It was', he considered, 'regarded as an Italian practice.'[16] Fear of sudden death, whether by poisoning or illness, was a persistent feature of papal Rome and it is of interest that the next English cardinal after Robert Somercote, John of Toledo, was recruited for his medical expertise. John of Toledo is included by Folkestone Williams in his *English Cardinals*, but not by Isaacson or Baxter. The name is off-putting and background information on the man is very thin, but it seems almost certain he was English by birth and was often known as the English cardinal. Moreover, for thirty years he was at the centre of English ambitions and interests in Rome. He was supposed to have acquired his medical expertise at Toledo, in Spain, open as it was to Arabic medical knowledge, and was the reputed author of a number of medical treaties. He was also an authority in the field of alchemy. The science of optics, at the centre of so much medieval science, had its headquarters in Viterbo in this period, a city then used frequently by the papal court. John had gained from a renewed interest in papal health and the *prolongatio vitae* which began only in Innocent III's pontificate, who had inaugurated the annual alteration of the curia's summer and winter residences, established a residence for the papal doctor and kept in touch with medical ideas. John of Toledo benefited from this *milieu* and coming to Rome on business as the Cistercian abbot of L'Epau, in the county of Maine, he was soon made personal physician to the pope and cardinal priest of S. Lorenzo in Lucina (28 May 1244) by Pope Innocent IV (1243–54), a great jurist and convenor of the First Council of Lyon (1245), but also an exploiter of the system of papal provisions. Under the French pope Urban IV (1261–4), who was elected at a conclave of only eight cardinals meeting at Viterbo over a period of three months, John of Toledo, who was also known (presumably because of his Cistercian habit) as 'the white cardinal' (*Albus*) was created cardinal bishop of Porto in 1261.

John of Toledo was a cardinal *in curia* at a troubled time for the papacy, living as it was under the shadow of Frederick II, but nevertheless many Englishmen came to him, a number of them royal clerks seeking benefices. He acted in encouraging the canonisation of St Edmund of Abingdon, the model secular clerk, Oxford master and archbishop of Canterbury. On at least two occasions he gave valuable political services to the English Crown: in 1261 Henry III's stand against baronial domination was sustained by the cardinal's influence and by the diplomatic skills of Roger Luvel, royal clerk and cardinal's chaplain, and in 1257 when Henry's brother, Richard of Cornwall, became 'King of the Romans' (German sovereign) the cardinal exerted all his energy to get him elected to the senatorial office in Rome. Agostino Paravicini Bagliani's study of cardinalatial *familiae* in the years 1227 to 1254 includes Cardinal John's household, to which belonged a number of Englishmen, not only Luvel, but others including Henry of Evesham, William of Peterborough and a future bishop of Lincoln, Richard Gravesend.[17]

After thirty years as a cardinal John of Toledo died on 13 July 1275. This more or less coincided with the closure of the Second Council of Lyon which, in its constitution *Ubi periculum*, clarified the role of the conclave in the election of a pope to prevent protracted vacancies. By this document the cardinals were directed to assemble no more than ten days after the pope's death, at the place of his death, to stay together with minimal contact with the outside world, and to be liable to increasingly severe conditions the longer the election took: 'After an interval of three days, their discussion was to be stimulated by lessening their provisions; in five days they were to be reduced to a single meal a day; after that they must live upon wine and water.'[18]

Hugh of Evesham, created cardinal priest of S. Lorenzo in Lucina on 23 March 1281, was, like John of Toledo, a noted physician and it was to Cardinal John's own titular church that Hugh was appointed. It is possible he was called to Rome, where he lived until his death on 27 July 1287, as an expert on ways of combating the endemic Roman malaria. Although Evesham in Worcestershire had a Benedictine abbey, Hugh was a secular clerk, holding various rectories, including two in Yorkshire and the archdeaconry of Worcester. He was a canon of York and held the parish of Bugthorpe until his death. As an Oxford master he was a mediator to the terms of peace between the Irish and the northern scholars in 1267 and one of the five arbitrators who was appointed in 1274 to make peace between the northern and southern scholars. In 1269 he supported the Oxford Dominicans in their dispute over the observance of evangelical poverty – a judicious decision in terms of the Dominicans' political influence – but remained on good terms with the Franciscan Archbishop Pecham of Canterbury (never a cardinal), who had been his contemporary '*vel in curia vel in scholis*'. He became a king's clerk and in 1275 was referred to as having long served the king, Edward I, and his mother, Queen Eleanor of Provence. He was a candidate for the archbishopric of York in 1259 when his friend William Wickware was successful. As a curial cardinal, '*il nero*' (the black) as he was called, not only dealt with medical matters, but was also much preoccupied by English affairs; Archbishop Wickware sought his help in his disputes with the archbishop of Canterbury and the bishop of Durham in 1282. When Hugh died there were rumours that he had been poisoned. He was buried near the sacristy in his titular church.

In 1278 another Englishman, Robert Kilwardby, became the first of four English Dominicans to be given the red hat in just a quarter of a century; the others were Macclesfield, Winterbourne and Jorz. They were a distinguished group, but only Jorz remained a cardinal for very long. The predominance of Dominican appointments is in part due to the fact that, as David Knowles puts it, 'during the reigns of the three first Edwards the Preachers came to occupy something of the position filled by members of the Society of Jesus in the castles and palaces of the Counter-reformation'[19] by filling the role of royal confessors. In the papal court the master of the sacred palace (*Magister sacri palatii*), who served as the pope's personal theologian, was always a Dominican. Pope Benedict XI (1303–4), a

Dominican himself, created only three cardinals, all of them Dominicans, two of them English.

Robert Kilwardby's early career is obscure and even his distinctive surname belonged to two villages in the Middle Ages, one in Yorkshire, the other in Leicestershire. He became a scholar of grammar and arts and was probably a Paris master of the liberal arts in the years 1237 to 1245. 'The writings from this period', Osmund Lewry reminds us, 'form the earliest comprehensive witness to the teaching of the set books at Paris from one master.'[20] Following his entry into the Dominicans in 1245, Kilwardby began his study of theology and became a notable commentator on the Scriptures and a defender of the Augustinian tradition. He taught theology for many years at Oxford and continued his theological interests when elected provincial of the English Dominicans in 1261. The English Dominicans had grown rapidly and there were some 600 friars in the province. For the provincial of an international religious order, travel to Rome was not infrequent; Kilwardby and other men in similar positions were often used as messengers for the English Crown. Administrative burdens did not diminish his thirst for learning; in 1271, when consulted by the Master of the Order of Preachers on some philosophical questions, he replied with obvious relish and knowledge on 'the movements of the heavens, divine and angelic influence on physical realities, the bodily condition of the dead, human generation, the constitution of compounds from elements, the association of the planets with the days of the week; he also computes the distance from the surface to the centre of the earth'.[21]

The pope nominated him as archbishop of Canterbury in 1272, following another disputed vacancy, and he was consecrated on 26 February 1273. As archbishop he was assiduous in his episcopal and metropolitan visitations, but held aloof from national politics. Nevertheless, he presided at the coronation of Edward I at Westminster Abbey on 19 August 1274; the church had been rebuilt by Henry III and was resplendent in its Gothic magnificence. In 1276 he excommunicated Llewellyn of Wales for refusing to perform homage to King Edward. He was more at home presiding at the translation of the relics of St Richard of Chichester, who had been canonised in 1262, less than ten years after his death in 1253. Richard was one of several English medieval 'pastoral' bishops who were canonised. England, and especially the model secular cathedral chapter at Salisbury, played an important role in enhancing the status of the pastoral clergy. Kilwardby was much involved in the benefactions to Dominican house in London. His standing as the university's most distinguished elder statesman was crucial in his two visitations of Oxford in 1276 and 1277. During the second he delivered an attack on the Aristotelianism which had been introduced into the Dominican Order by Thomas Aquinas, by condemning thirty theses.[22] This corresponded to a similar condemnation which had just been made by Bishop Tempier in Paris. Sharp controversy followed these visits and some have seen his appointment as cardinal bishop of Porto and S. Rufina, by Pope Nicholas III on 4 April 1278, as a kind of superannuation. In this period cardinals resided in Rome and had to resign their bishoprics. He lived only until 10 September 1279 and was buried at the Dominican church at Viterbo.

William Macclesfield, the second Dominican cardinal, born in the Coventry and Lichfield diocese, had a distinguished academic career as a student and teacher at Paris and at Oxford, where he proceeded to his doctorate and was regent master of Blackfriars in 1300. He travelled to Rome on the affairs of his order and, as *definitor* of the English Province, attended the Dominican General Chapter at Besançon in 1303. He died at Canterbury on his way home. On 18 December 1303 he was created cardinal priest of S. Sabina, the titular church on the Aventine Hill which adjoined the residence of the Master of the Dominicans, before news of his death had reached Rome.

Walter Winterbourne fared little better. A native of the Salisbury diocese, he was probably not a doctor of theology and was not in the same intellectual league as Kilwardby or Macclesfield, but he was a skilled administrator and a trusted royal servant. He resided at various English Dominican houses and was at the king's court from 1282. He worked as an official of the office of the Wardrobe 'acting as an intermediary of the king in the issuance of writs and letters patent'.[23] As king's confessor from 1289 to 1304 he became one of Edward I's most trusted aides and accompanied him to Scotland in 1300. He was made cardinal priest of S. Sabina on 19 February 1304 and died at Genoa in the autumn of 1304 on his way to Rome. After burial in Genoa his body was later reinterred at Blackfriars, London.

The last of the English Dominican cardinals was Thomas Jorz, whose name has sometimes been modernised, misleadingly, to Joyce. His brother Walter was Archbishop of Armagh, though the family were not Irish, but probably of Nottingham origins and long settled in London. He proceeded to the degree of doctor at Oxford about 1292 and although not a great scholar, was seen by his order as a leader. He was prior of Oxford from 1294 to 1297 and prior provincial from 1297 to 1304. In this latter capacity he attended Dominican Chapters in Cologne, Marseille and Toulouse. He went to Rome on the business of his order on 1 January 1304. On 15 December 1305 he was created cardinal priest of S. Sabina by Pope Clement V (1305–14), a Frenchman who had served on a diplomatic mission to England in 1294. Cardinal Jorz busied himself as an agent in the curia for Edward I and Edward II and in obtaining benefices and privileges for his family, as well as in the more routine aspects of curial life. Thus, in 1307, Edward I wrote to Cardinal Jorz asking him to urge on the canonisation of Robert Grosseteste, the great and good bishop of Lincoln; later in the same year, the king consulted him on matters concerning French politics. Edward II also wrote several times to the cardinal as to various actions of the pope, and he also desired the canonisation of an English bishop, Thomas de Cantelupe of Hereford. In return for these diplomatic services an allowance from the treasury was made to the cardinal of 100 marks per annum.[24]

In the event Grosseteste was not canonised, but Thomas of Hereford was. Jorz died at Grenoble on 13 December 1310, on his way as papal envoy to the Emperor Henry VII, and he was buried at Blackfriars, Oxford. Jorz's activity as 'proctor' for English affairs in Rome reflected a growing trend in the thirteenth and fourteenth centuries. Lay and ecclesiastical appeals were heard in Rome, but it was not only ecclesiastical disputes which reached the pope, although even these were numerous; perhaps thirty cases of disputed elections of English bishops were taken to Rome between 1216 and 1264 alone.

The English cardinals discussed in this chapter were frequently drawn from the intellectual élites of their generation. They reflected the talent-spotting which has always been part of the process of ecclesiastical preferment, but many of them by birth and experience were unlikely princes of the Church. They were special advisers, internal trouble-shooters, theological experts, skilled canon lawyers, increasingly bureaucratic rather than saintly. As far as English cardinals in the High Middle Ages were concerned, the cardinalate was no empty honour, but a dedicated and hard-working calling where the prospects were often blighted by the stalking horse of premature death.

# TWO

## *Avignon and Conciliarism*

Between the death of Thomas Jorz in 1310 and the promotion of Simon Langham in 1368 there were no English cardinals. Thereafter, a large proportion of the Englishmen who were or appear to have been raised to the cardinalate in the later fourteenth and early fifteenth centuries were not permitted to use their eminent titles in their native land. Both of these facts were symptomatic of crisis, the cardinals' collective crisis of identity serving as a microcosm of the economic, social, political and ecclesiastical crises of the time. It all began with the weather.

Late medieval Europe experienced a mini ice age after centuries of general warmth. Agricultural expansion ceased, harvests failed and the population became more vulnerable to disease. The Black Death, or bubonic plague, arrived in Mediterranean ports in 1347: between a third and half the population of western Europe died from it in the next few years. France and England were further weakened economically and socially by Edward III's lengthy military campaigns, which in turn occasioned the Florentine banking crisis of the 1340s. Social upheaval came in the wake of plague as the workforce used its scarcity value to demand first higher wages and then increased political power and representation. Uprisings occurred in town and country alike: the Jacquerie in France (1358), the Peasants' Revolt in England (1381) and the revolt of the wool workers, the Ciompi, in Florence (1378). If secular hierarchies, their

21

theories and practices, could be attacked and found vulnerable, why not ecclesiastical hierarchies too? The anticlerical cleric John Wycliffe had a receptive audience in his native England, where his followers were known as Lollards, and became a major source of inspiration to the Hussite rebels in early fifteenth-century Bohemia. The papacy was particularly vulnerable to attack.

That there were no English cardinals between 1310 and 1368 can be interpreted as a reflection of the gallicisation of the papacy during the period when the popes were based in Avignon, a period which also witnessed the first phases of the Anglo-French Hundred Years War. When the archbishop of Bordeaux, a city then under English rule, was elected pope in 1305 and took the name of Clement V, he thought it wise to remain in southern France for a while in order to negotiate a peace between the French king Philip the Fair and Edward I of England. This resolve was confirmed when the rich and powerful Knights Templar were arrested on the order of the French king in 1307, accused of the most scandalous and sacrilegious practices. A general council, which met at Vienne in 1310, was summoned to deal with the crisis which resulted from the arrests. Thus the origins of the Avignon papacy are easily explained. No diminution of papal authority was intended: there were challenges to be met in France and the popes were on hand to meet them.[1] Another advantage was that, contrary to popular perception, the city of Avignon itself was not directly subject to French control. French popes created French cardinals who, in turn, elected French popes, seven of them between 1305 and 1378. It was Benedict XII, the former inquisitor Jacques Fournier, who began to build the fortress-like Palais des Papes – perhaps as much a defence against the mistral wind as against the threat of imperial armies coming from beyond the Alps – and thereby created the impression that the bishops of Rome were to be absent from their diocese for the foreseeable future. The palace was dramatically enlarged by the Benedictine Clement VI, who created an impressive court and employed some of the leading artists of the day. If being spiritual leaders of western Christendom meant tapping into the most vibrant cultural currents of the time, then the popes in Avignon were very well placed to do that. If it meant organising a pan-European administrative machine which enjoyed ease of access to the major centres of population in the Low Countries and northern Italy, as well as to France, Spain and Germany, then it was not possible for the popes to be better situated than they were in Avignon. It was, therefore, something of an inconvenience that they happened to be the successors of St Peter and bishops of Rome, an inconvenience of which they were reminded by luminaries as diverse as the poet Petrarch and St Catherine of Siena. An abortive return to Rome was made by Urban V in 1367, after the warrior Cardinal Albornoz brought the papal states back to something approaching order. Gregory XI finally took the papacy back home to Italy, but the consequences of creating a largely French curia and then transporting it to the other side of the Alps only emerged after his death in 1378. Fearing the Roman mob, the cardinals wanted a quick conclave and hastily elected the wrong man. A delicate touch was needed and Bartolomeo Prignano, though legitimately elected as Urban VI, was no diplomat. Rebel cardinals broke away instantly and elected Robert of Geneva as their alternative pope. This anti-pope, 'Clement VII', took up residence in Avignon and western Christendom was soon split between the 'obediences' of the Roman pope and the Avignonese anti-pope. France naturally headed the Avignon obedience, reason enough for England to side with distant Rome. The Church was in serious crisis.

The papal schism and, more particularly, possible solutions to it loomed large in the careers of the English cardinals of the period.[2] One option was for one side to admit it was in error and stand down. The Roman popes, Urban VI, Boniface IX, Innocent VII and Gregory XII, were convinced of their legitimacy so unlikely to give way. The Avignon anti-popes, 'Clement VII' and especially the intransigent Catalan 'Benedict XIII', were temperamentally unsuited to such a compromise. Another option was for both popes to abdicate and for their sole successor to be elected by the Roman and Avignonese cardinals combined. This was favoured by the University of Paris and formed the basis of conciliar thought, the steadily evolving view that the Church was in dire need of root and branch reform, that popes could not be trusted to bring about such reform of themselves and others and that a general council of the Church represented the only way forward. Such a council met at Pisa in 1409 and elected the archbishop of Milan as Alexander V. This might have proved a lasting solution, had Alexander not died within a matter of months. The Pisan council then elected Baldassare Cossa, 'John XXIII', but the validity of his election was not accepted by many of the secular powers. Indeed, Gregory XII and 'Benedict XIII' were still alive, creating the even greater scandal and confusion of there being three papal claimants. The most general of general councils was required to resolve this dilemma: it met in the German city of Constance between 1414 and 1418. Conciliarism did not disappear with the election of Pope Martin V in 1417 and he respected the decision made at Constance that councils should meet on a regular basis. However, widespread enthusiasm for the conciliar ideal soon waned and the council which met at Pavia and Siena in 1423–4 was something of a damp squib. The council which met at Basel from 1431 was a different affair entirely and rapidly became a focus for those who were discontented with the anti-conciliar policies of Eugenius IV, Martin's successor and Gregory XII's nephew. For a while the Basel assembly provided the secular powers with a useful counterweight to the pope, but relations between these alternative sources of ecclesiastical authority steadily deteriorated, with Eugenius repeatedly trying to dissolve the council and the Basel fathers responding by summoning pope and cardinals to appear before them as the supposedly superior body. When in 1439 the council attempted to depose Eugenius and replace him with their own anti-pope, 'Felix V', their cause was decisively discredited. Naples, Scotland and other states which had supported the council were persuaded to make their peace with Rome. France did so in the form of the Pragmatic Sanction of Bourges (1438), by means of which the popes waived their claim to appoint to vacant French benefices and lost control over the Church's temporal wealth in the kingdom.

Simon Langham (d. 1376) was a beneficiary of the Black Death.[3] His origins have been traced to Rutland, but nothing is known of him for certain until 1339–40, by which time he was a Benedictine monk of Westminster Abbey. He studied at Oxford in the late 1340s, but failed to graduate, a result for which the plague was presumably responsible. Clerics were a particularly high-risk group at times of plague and the Westminster community was rapidly halved in number. In consequence, Langham was appointed prior on 10 April 1349 and elected abbot as soon as the following 27 May: a small but telling indication of the turmoil caused by the plague. No less a sign of the times was the anti-papal legislation enacted by the English parliament during the following decades, for the four Statutes of Provisors (1351, 1353, 1365 and 1389) asserted English independence from the French-dominated papacy during the first half of the Hundred Years War. These statutes dealt with the contentious issue of appointing candidates to vacant benefices: should they be 'provided' to such vacancies by the pope or, alternatively, elected by cathedral chapters or appointed by the king or another lay lord? The English Crown was very far from exceptional in wanting to limit papal powers in its land, for variations on the theme are to be found in many states in the late medieval period. In England, the conflict of jurisdictions was underpinned by the 1353 and 1393 Statutes of Praemunire which forbade Englishmen taking legal suits to any non-English courts or foreign powers, which in practice meant the papacy. These combined additions to the statute book could be invoked with greater or lesser rigour, or even conveniently overlooked, depending on the circumstances in which the English Crown found itself. Appointments to bishoprics were at issue, but a bishop who was elevated to the cardinalate should have remained unaffected by the statutes, for the tradition was that he resigned his see and resided at the curia thereafter. In 1361 Langham, who had proved himself to be a strong disciplinarian at Westminster and was appointed treasurer of England in 1360, was elected to the bishopric of London, but provided by Innocent VI to that of Ely: interestingly, it was the Ely promotion that stood. Provision to the archbishopric of Canterbury followed in 1366, again with Edward III's approval, by which time Langham had also been chancellor of England for three years. When Urban V made him a cardinal in September 1368 Langham did indeed resign Canterbury and was with the pope at Montefiascone, north of Viterbo, by May 1369 and resided in Avignon from late 1370. Langham's indisputable financial and organisational competence recommended him to the popes just as much as it had to King Edward, and Gregory XI showed his commitment to resolving the Anglo-French conflict by appointing Langham as joint-legate to France, England and the Low Countries in 1371. His fellow countrymen preferred the military option and were in no mood to negotiate, so by April 1373 Langham was back in Avignon and remained there until his death three years later. He was a severe critic of pluralism, but this was nevertheless the means by which he rapidly acquired a vast fortune: this was bequeathed to Westminster Abbey and allocated towards the rebuilding of the nave.[4]

Of Simon Langham's status as a cardinal there is no doubt, but questions remain about the status of those Englishmen who were created cardinals during the papal schism of 1378 onwards. The popes in Rome and anti-popes in Avignon sought to score points off each other by employing what Ludwig von Pastor, the historian of the papacy, called 'a liberal use of the hat'.[5] Urban VI created sixty-three cardinals from states belonging to the Roman obedience in a bid to outnumber the 'Clementine' cardinals who retreated to Avignon. 'Clement VII' reacted with thirty-eight new cardinals of his own. 'Benedict XIII' continued the trend with twenty-three, as did the Pisan pope 'John XXIII' with forty-four. That the cardinalatial office was diminished in value was as nothing compared to the utter confusion created. William Courtenay (d. 1396), son of the earl of Devon and grandson of the earl of Hereford, had been successively bishop of Hereford and of London and was archbishop of Canterbury when Pope Urban raised him to the cardinalate on 1 August 1378, at the very outset of the schism.[6] As England was one of Urban's more significant anti-French supporters and Courtenay was a cousin of John of Gaunt, the most powerful man in England during Richard II's minority, he was an obvious choice, but he refused to acknowledge the honour. He was able to exercise greater authority in England than he could have done at the itinerant curia and in the service of an unstable pontiff and did indeed do so in his initiatives to counter the theological and social threats posed by Lollardy.

In spite of Courtenay's refusal to accept a red hat, England remained loyal even to so violent and unstable a pope as Urban VI. That the kingdom was consistently devoted to Rome throughout the schism has been described as 'characteristic of English conservatism or, perhaps, of English inertia'.[7] England's next cardinal might easily be regarded as a conservative, in that he was a curialist who conspicuously advocated papal claims against the intellectual assaults of Marsilius of Padua and William of Ockham, but inert he most certainly was not. Adam Easton (d. 1398) was a Norfolk man who became a Benedictine monk at Norwich Cathedral Priory, studied at Gloucester College, Oxford, and soon came to the attention of his fellow black monk Cardinal Langham.[8] Easton may well have journeyed to Italy with Langham in 1368. His was the first name in a list of beneficiaries in Langham's will, perhaps indicating that he was the cardinal's secretary; as executor of the will he was responsible for ensuring that Westminster Abbey received the legacies of its former abbot.[9] Easton followed in his patron's footsteps by urging the pope to issue anti-Wycliffite bulls, but this was only part of his defence of the Church in general and the papacy in particular at a time when those institutions were exceptionally vulnerable. His *Defensorium ecclesiasticae potestatis* was dedicated to Pope Urban, naturally enough, and completed by December 1381, when Easton was made a cardinal. Yet even so staunch a papalist could not remain unmoved by the pope's behaviour and Easton was among those cardinals who proposed the calling of a general council to 'limit his despotic power'. This was during the winter of 1384/5 when the curia was uncomfortably quartered at Nocera near Perugia. On 11 January 1385 Easton and five other cardinals were summoned before the pope, accused of plotting to kill him, tortured and imprisoned. At that stage Easton had just one English benefice, the deanery of York, and of this he was deprived. He wrote to the English Benedictines who, in turn, petitioned

Richard II to intervene. The army of Charles of Durazzo, king of Naples, forced the curia to flee from Nocera and after some meandering, it next settled in Genoa. When forced to move again Urban decided to kill the prisoners as a matter of convenience. The other five cardinals were indeed killed, but Easton's life was saved, perhaps thanks to entreaties by his order and his king, though the cardinal himself maintained that it was due to the intercession of the visionary Bridget of Sweden (d. 1373), whose cause he championed thereafter. The loss of his cardinalatial dignity was a small price to pay, but this was restored by Boniface IX at the start of his pontificate in 1389. Bridget of Sweden's canonisation followed in 1391. The last phase of Easton's life may well have been passed in 'dignified leisure', perhaps devoted to the writing of some of the numerous works which have been attributed to him, but which have not survived. Among other achievements, he is understood to have learned Greek and Hebrew in order to make a translation of the Old Testament. He died in 1397 and is buried in his titular church of S. Cecilia, in the Trastevere area of Rome. A little ironically for one who was so ardent a papalist, the arms of England are prominent on his tomb.

Langham, Courtenay and Easton were all staunch upholders of orthodoxy against the teachings of the Oxford theologian John Wycliffe, but some measure of Wycliffe's brief popularity can be gained from a consideration of the early career of Philip Repyngdon (d. 1434), whose later promotion to the Sacred College has been a matter of dispute.[10] In 1382, in sermons at Brackley, Northampton-shire, and at Oxford, Repyngdon, an Augustinian canon of St Mary de Pré, Leicester, expressed his support for Wycliffe's rejection of transubstantiation. As a result he was invited to a disputation with Oxford divines on 7 June that year and was duly suspended from preaching by the chancellor of the university. The brevity of Repyngdon's Lollard phase is confirmed by the fact that his formal excommunication by Archbishop Courtenay led to him abjuring his heresy before the primate on 23 October and in Oxford the following month. The popularity of England's native heresy was similarly short-lived. In the 1370s Wycliffe had a powerful advocate in the person of John of Gaunt, because antipapalism was then useful to the Crown, but when Repyngdon invoked the duke's name in his support Gaunt denounced Repyngdon and others as 'devils' who held and taught odious opinions. That rebuff notwithstanding, the key to Repyngdon's later advancement was his friendship with Gaunt's son, Bolingbroke, whose deposition of the legitimate king, Richard II, in 1399 made him a usurper with an unstable power base and in need of whatever friends he could muster. By 1399 Repyngdon had been abbot of his house at Leicester for five years; within months he was Henry IV's confessor, his '*clericus specialissimus*', a royal councillor and chancellor of his old university. When Henry Beaufort was translated to Winchester in 1404, Repyngdon filled the vacancy at Lincoln and even became known as a zealous persecutor of Lollards. A letter written by Repyngdon to Henry in 1401 is often cited as evidence of the nature of their relationship. It expresses his distress at what he saw as the complete breakdown of law and order in England. He had hoped for great changes under the new king but, on the contrary, it seemed that violent crime and the oppression of the poor were now worse than ever: he urged Henry to take action.[11] Another vignette is provided by the piously lachrymose Margery Kempe of Lynn. With her husband she resolved to take a vow of chastity for which she required the permission of a bishop. The see of Norwich being vacant, they travelled to Lincoln and were warmly received by Bishop Repyngdon, though the fact that he asked her to write down the details of her extraordinarily vivid spiritual life may suggest a degree of scepticism on his part. Margery was greatly impressed by his charitable giving to the poor, but less so by his recommendation that the Kempes make a pilgrimage to Jerusalem the better to prove themselves. As Christ Himself pointedly told Margery: 'Daughter, say to the Bishop that he dreadeth more the shames of the world than the perfect love of God.'[12]

Gregory XII raised Repyngdon to the eminence of cardinal on 19 September 1408, but the title is not used in English sources. The confused circumstances of the schism did lead to a relaxation of the rule whereby cardinals automatically resigned their bishoprics, but that in itself cannot be the complete answer. The problem hinges on the annulment of all Gregory's acts after May 1408, part of the process whereby it was hoped that the schism could be resolved. In 1419 Repyngdon resigned his see and was granted a pension by Martin V: the timing suggests that he was defending ecclesiastical independence from the secular authorities by expressing disapproval of Henry V's opposition to Bishop Henry Beaufort of Winchester being made a cardinal.

In view of the fact that Thomas Langley (d. 1437) and Robert Hallum (or Hallam, d. 1417) were made cardinals not by a legitimately elected pope acting under pressure, but by the frequently vilified 'John XXIII', their claim to the title ought perhaps to be rather more tenuous than that of Bishop Repyngdon. However, when John promoted them in order to seek English support in 1411, the Council of Constance had yet to be called and he had yet to be proved the most disposable of the three papal claimants. Henry IV opposed their promotions. Nevertheless, Langley and Hallum merit consideration not only because of their significance as English diocesan bishops and servants of the Crown, but also because they played active parts in the conciliar process at a time when the carefully constructed image and even the reality of Henry V gave England increased significance on the European stage.

Langley was a Cambridge-educated northerner whose early patron was John of Gaunt and who remained a conspicuously loyal adherent of the House of Lancaster, serving as Henry IV's keeper of the privy seal and as chancellor to Henry IV, Henry V and Henry VI.[13] In the latter capacity he opened a number of parliaments with loyal orations and thereby helped to secure subsidies for the Crown, even when war-weariness began to set in at the end of Henry V's reign. His diplomatic experience included a mission to Paris in 1414, a year prior to the Agincourt campaign. Durham was his sole bishopric and he is buried there in the cathedral's Galilee Chapel. The Oxford-educated Hallum is buried neither in his native Lancashire nor in his cathedral at Salisbury, but in front of the high altar in the cathedral at Constance, where he had led the English delegation to the council for two years.[14] Whereas Langley was a political prelate, Hallum was a model churchman and a model conciliarist, defending more general ecclesiastical rights and privileges vis-à-vis secular governments, as opposed to more narrowly papal ones. Indeed, no other English bishop of his generation was so committed to the ideal of reform. Gregory XII provided him to the archbishopric of York in 1406, but relations between England and Rome being then at one of their lower ebbs, in the aftermath of the execution for treason of Archbishop Richard Scrope, Henry IV objected and Hallum received Salisbury by way of a compromise in 1407. He was consecrated by the pope himself. At Salisbury Hallum found himself surrounded by an erudite, reform-minded chapter, among whom was the notable scholar Richard Ullerston. Hallum took as his role model Osmund, the eleventh-century bishop of Salisbury, and reinvigorated the campaign to have him declared a saint. Osmund was finally canonised in 1456.

The English delegation sent to the council held at Pisa in 1409 numbered about thirty-five men, either senior ecclesiastics representing themselves or proctors representing the king, bishops, religious houses and the universities. Langley, Hallum and Ullerston were among their number. However determined they were to resolve the papal schism, when one compares Pisa with Constance, the former does appear as something of an exercise in how not to organise a general council. Did it lack canonical authority because it had not been convened by a pope? How could its decisions be implemented with the secular powers still so divided in purpose? What incentive was there for any power to support its popes, Alexander V and 'John XXIII'?[15] The bishops of Durham and Salisbury clearly made an impact on the Pisan gathering, which did their own careers no harm, while Hallum emerged from the experience all the more convinced of the need to reform the Church in both head and members. This was the conviction that he took to Constance in 1415.

The council of Constance was summoned by 'John XXIII' and Emperor Sigismund and was the high-water mark of conciliarism. Its objectives were the eradication of heresy, reform of the Church – which included limiting the number of cardinals in the Sacred

College to twenty-four – and resolution of the papal dilemma. In his capacity as king of Bohemia Sigismund was most interested in the defeat of heresy, for Jan Hus's followers had rejected not merely the teachings of the Church but also the social order headed by the king. As Hus's inspiration came from Wycliffe's writings, reasoned Sigismund, England had a particular responsibility in this matter. To this end he cultivated Henry V and sanctioned the English delegation voting as a separate 'nation' at the council, rather than as part of the German nation. The non-German Latin nations wanted a new pope with undiminished authority, an option which was highly unlikely to lead to far-reaching reform. England's independence from the German nation, on the other hand, doubled the number of nations committed to reforming the Church before moving to a papal election. Some members of the English delegation were not as devoted to this policy as Bishop Hallum; nor were Henry V's motives unmixed, for he considered Sigismund the most valuable ally possible in his anti-French strategy. In 1415 the council condemned Wycliffe's ideas and Hus's body to the flames, 'John XXIII' was formally deposed, Gregory XII agreed to abdicate in the interests of Church unity, but the Anglo-German reformers were then thwarted by Henry's renewal of hostilities in the late summer, leading to his famous victory at Agincourt on 25 October. Sigismund, who had been in Spain, endeavouring to persuade 'Benedict XIII' that his cause was hopeless, tried to mediate between France and England. He received short shrift from the French and the Order of the Garter from Henry, precipitating a renewal of Anglo-German friendship once the emperor returned to Constance in 1416. Hallum, who delivered a number of important sermons during the council, was particularly fulsome in his praise of Sigismund.

Deadlock over the rival claims of papal election and reform of the Church was finally broken in the second half of 1417. An early sign of movement was Henry V's decision to press for a papal election.[16] On 18 July instructions were sent to the English representatives at Constance that they were to execute the king's policies rather than follow their own. That same day Henry Beaufort, bishop of

Winchester, announced his intention of going on pilgrimage to the Holy Land, a declaration which can only have been a cover for a planned intervention at Constance, not least because Beaufort was an experienced diplomat who stood the greatest chance of mollifying Sigismund over the defection of his English allies. On 23 July Beaufort resigned as chancellor and was replaced by Thomas Langley. Conveniently for Henry and for Beaufort, Robert Hallum, the champion of thoroughgoing ecclesiastical reform and of episcopal leadership rather than papal centralisation, died at the castle of Gottlieben, near Constance, at the beginning of September. No less conveniently, Gregory XII died in October, before Beaufort reached Constance, removing another obstacle to a papal election. The tide was turning against reform and in favour of quick results, though the sequence of events could easily be twisted to give the impression that Beaufort personally broke the impasse and therefore deserved to be elected pope. With Sigismund's approval an electoral college made up of cardinals and the national delegations duly elected the Roman patrician Oddone Colonna as Pope Martin V, one of whose first papal acts was to acknowledge the support he received from the English by raising Beaufort to the cardinalate on 18 December. Martin also made him legate *a latere* in England for life and allowed him to retain the bishopric of Winchester *in commendam*.[17] By this apparently friendly gesture Martin actually reignited English hostility to papal provisions, a running sore in Anglo-papal relations throughout the fifteenth century.

With one exception, Henry Beaufort (d. 1447) enjoyed every advantage that nature and late medieval society could bestow.[18] He was an astute politician who built up a supporting network of able associates, a statesman of remarkable ability who served his king extremely well in times of war and of uncertain peace, and a careful administrator who garnered substantial wealth from ecclesiastical and secular sources and put it at the disposal of his country. The 'exception' was legitimate birth.[19] His father was John of Gaunt, duke of Lancaster, third son of Edward III and his mother was Katherine, widow of Sir Hugh Swynford. At the time of Beaufort's birth – *c*. 1375 – Gaunt was married to his second wife, Constance of Castile. Katherine bore him four children, John, Henry, Thomas and Joan, the eldest of whom was born in the year of Sir Hugh's death and seems to have been illegitimate twice over. These children took the name of Beaufort from one of Gaunt's French lordships. Gaunt's marriage to Katherine took place in 1396 and the Beauforts were legitimised the following year. John Beaufort, the eldest son, was highly favoured by Richard II, who made him earl of Somerset and arranged his marriage to Margaret Holland, daughter of the earl of Kent and one of Richard's maternal relatives. In consequence, Somerset initially opposed his half-brother Bolingbroke's usurpation of the Crown in 1399. However, once it was clear that Richard's cause was lost, Somerset became as loyal to Henry IV as he had been to Richard, serving as chamberlain of England, admiral of the same and captain of Calais prior to his death in 1410. Thomas Beaufort, duke of Exeter, was no less of an asset to the House of Lancaster, being particularly valued by his nephew Henry V. A second generation of Beauforts identified themselves with the Lancastrian cause, though the military careers of John Beaufort II, duke of Somerset, and Edmund Beaufort in the latter stages of the Hundred Years War were marred by financial scandals.

Like Thomas Wolsey a century later, Beaufort's political vision was one which encompassed the whole of western Europe. Unlike Wolsey, he had family contacts who could be called upon to facilitate his diplomacy. The fact that his mother's family was from Hainault appears to have enhanced his appreciation of the significance of England's trading links with the Low Countries. That region steadily came under the control of the Valois dukes of Burgundy, whose increasing independence from and, indeed, hostility towards France made them invaluable allies after Henry V's renewal of the Anglo-French war. When his niece, Isabel of Portugal, daughter of King João I and Philippa of Lancaster, became the third wife of Philip the Good, duke of Burgundy, Beaufort made assiduous use of this dynastic connection in the interest of English trade and foreign policy. Another niece, Joan Beaufort, married James I of Scotland, a connection which the cardinal used to help neutralise the threat on the northern border so that English arms could be directed towards the continent.

Henry Beaufort, who appears to have been Oxford-educated, was bishop of Lincoln from 1398. He supported Bolingbroke's claim to the throne and was a member of the party which accompanied Joan of Navarre from Brittany to become Henry IV's queen in 1402. Henry and Joan were married by Beaufort in Winchester Cathedral, shortly after which Beaufort was appointed chancellor, an office he held for two years before resigning it when William of Wykeham's death led to his translation to the see of Winchester. He retained this bishopric, the richest in England, for forty-two years. The rise of the Beauforts was tempered somewhat in 1407: Henry IV confirmed their legitimation but Archbishop Arundel, the then chancellor, ensured that they were excluded from the royal line of succession by insisting on the insertion of the words '*excepta dignitate regali*' in the royal decree. The Beauforts reacted by becoming increasingly associated with a faction surrounding the prince of Wales, the future Henry V. As power slipped from the hands of the ailing king, Bishop Beaufort may have suggested that Henry abdicate in favour of his eldest son. When Henry V duly succeeded in 1413 there was no doubt that Beaufort was the king's principal minister.

In the domestic politics of Henry V's reign, Beaufort succeeded Arundel as chancellor in 1413, resigning that office four years later in order to head for the Holy Land, via Constance. He did not return to England until 1419, though he participated in Anglo-French negotiations along the way. Although he did not hold governmental office during the later part of the reign he made a significant financial contribution to Henry's war effort, with particularly generous loans in May 1421.[20] When death from dysentery saved the king from what was rapidly proving to be an unwinnable war, Beaufort was named as one of the infant Henry VI's guardians. Henry V's brother John, duke of Bedford, became protector in England and regent in France, but the pressing practicalities of the French war left another brother, Humphrey, duke of Gloucester, to govern England. Beaufort's loans to the Crown continued on an almost annual basis throughout Henry VI's minority, though Gloucester's increasing animosity meant that Beaufort no longer dominated the domestic scene. He was chancellor again in 1424–6, but took any opportunity he could to assist Bedford on the diplomatic front or to seek a role further afield. A useful indicator of Beaufort's domestic priorities can be found in the orations which he delivered as chancellor at the opening of parliaments. Law and order feature highly: by April 1414 Sir John Oldcastle's Lollard revolt had been defeated, but sedition was still a threat, so Beaufort took as his text 'He hath applied his heart to understand the laws'. Henry V's stunning military success at Agincourt provided Beaufort with his theme for the 1416 parliament: the king's just war must be supported through to its victorious conclusion. Financial support was duly provided by that parliament and another campaign was mounted in 1417. If one looks for the origin of the myth-making associated with Henry V, one might reasonably conclude that Bishop Beaufort was the king's chief 'spin doctor'. When Beaufort addressed the Leicester parliament of 1426 triumphalism was no longer appropriate, for there was already discord among the young king's uncles. Henry VI was himself present to hear the chancellor deliver an un-compromising message based on the text 'Children listen to your father. Do what I tell you if you want to be safe.' Did the young monarch appreciate its significance? One of the secrets of Beaufort's success was his careful placing of consistently loyal supporters in the lower chamber of parliament. A key figure was his cousin Thomas Chaucer, Speaker of the Commons in a total of five parliaments. Another was John Stafford, bishop of Bath and Wells and treasurer of England. Thanks to Stafford's complicity Beaufort was able to maintain his 'stranglehold' on royal finances.[21]

Henry V's refusal to accept Beaufort as a cardinal in 1417 is striking not only because the king refused to allow respect for his kinsman to blind his vision where perceived acts of rebellion were concerned, but also because it highlighted thorny questions about benefices which had lain dormant prior to the papal election. Archbishop Chichele of Canterbury led the opposition to Beaufort being made a cardinal and to his being permitted to retain the bishopric of Winchester, citing the convention that cardinals ought to be based at the curia and to resign their bishoprics upon promotion. An English cardinal in Rome might have suited Henry's purpose very well, but Pope Martin was no less determined that a cardinal legate was required to enforce papal authority in England. Henry's will proved the stronger on this occasion, but Martin responded by ensuring that men of his choice were appointed to a number of English bishoprics, including John Kemp to London, in 1418–19. It was the English anti-papal legislation which was at issue, for Henry made no attempt to block Martin's appointments to benefices in English-occupied Normandy.[22]

The legislation was still in place when Henry died and the more aggressively anti-papal stand adopted by Henry VI's minority government, under Humphrey of Gloucester's leadership, made Beaufort's position ever more difficult. Gloucester was adept at the deployment of literary propaganda and it was he who now developed the reputation of his late brother to suit his own purposes.[23] Thus it was that Humphrey had himself presented as the natural heir to the great warrior-king, whose legacy could best be honoured by further heroic exploits in war against the French. As Humphrey came to personify a war party within the English élite, so Beaufort, with his command over the royal finances and his natural bent for diplomacy, came to accept the futility of the conflict and to head the peace party. It is hardly surprising that Humphrey invoked the name of Henry V in his opposition to Beaufort, telling how the king had exclaimed 'that he had lief set his crown beside him as to see [Beaufort] wear a cardinal's hat'.[24] English domestic government was paralysed in the mid-1420s by the first of Gloucester's concerted attacks on Beaufort, order being restored only when the duke of Bedford intervened to effect a reconciliation. Anglo-papal disputes came to a head once more in 1426: Martin dispatched to England the highly respected Cardinal Giuliano Cesarini in the hope of persuading Humphrey, Chichele and their colleagues to repeal the Statutes of Provisors. Cesarini reported back to Rome on the contrast between the popularity of the archbishop's anti-papalism and Beaufort's isolation as possibly the pope's only friend in

England. It was on 24 May that year that Beaufort was finally and unequivocally promoted to the Sacred College and shortly afterwards that Chichele, who had failed to ensure the repeal of the Statutes, was temporarily suspended from the legatine powers which he enjoyed as archbishop.[25] Martin's victory was confirmed when he appointed Beaufort's nephew Robert Neville to the see of Salisbury, in spite of well-founded objections that this young man of twenty-two was not a suitable candidate for the position.[26]

In 1418 Beaufort had successfully avoided controversy at home by undertaking a pilgrimage to the Holy Land. A decade later he sought political refuge and perhaps political rehabilitation by accepting a papal commission to raise a crusading army for war against the Bohemian Hussites.[27] It was to this end that Martin appointed him legate to Bohemia, Hungary and the German states in March 1427. Days later, in Calais, he wore his cardinal's hat for the first time. By August he had ample evidence of the strength of Hussite forces and the inadequacy of the crusaders, who were not even inspired by the legate's dramatic unfurling of the papal banner near Tachov on 4 August. Recalling his nephew's famous victory at Agincourt, he declared that 10,000 English archers could have succeeded in battle against the Bohemians. In that spirit plans were soon afoot for Beaufort to undertake another military campaign against the Hussites the following summer. His army was indeed to be raised in England, in spite of the difficulties which the government was finding in recruiting men for the ongoing war in France. The king's council gave Beaufort permission to preach the crusade and recruit troops, but not to raise taxation; the financial support had to come from Rome. Humphrey of Gloucester's faction continued to quibble about Beaufort's status: a legate could only be admitted to the country at the king's invitation, so Beaufort's capacity could only be that of a cardinal without legatine authority. What makes this episode particularly interesting is the ease with which Beaufort diverted his men from the Bohemian crusade to assist Bedford's beleaguered troops in France. This was the period of Joan of Arc's brief, remarkable appearance on the military scene when the tide suddenly turned in favour of Charles VII, disinherited under the terms of the treaty of Troyes in 1420, by which his mentally incapacitated father, Charles VI, named Henry V as heir to the French throne. It was to maintain the terms of that treaty that first Henry and then Bedford committed English resources season after season, securing a reasonable degree of control over the duchy of Normandy, but otherwise being dependent on their Burgundian allies and on divisions among the French. Regardless of the less romantic reality, Joan's presence was said to have inspired the raising of the siege of the strategically located city of Orléans in April 1429, as well as the English defeat at Patay two months later. Within days of that defeat Beaufort's force of some 2,000–3,000 men was committed to the French conflict and prevented Paris from falling to Charles. The operation was so smooth and the political dividend for the cardinal potentially so great as to prompt well-founded speculation that Beaufort had been scheming at papal expense all along and always intended to employ the men in France. Not surprisingly, the pope was horrified to learn that the troops he had funded were being employed to fight fellow Christians.

If the second Hussite crusade was never anything more than an elaborate ruse, it worked perfectly. Beaufort's star was once more in the ascendant, for he was soon restored to the king's council, loaned money to the Crown more generously than ever, and reasserted his authority by taking a prominent part in Henry VI's coronation as king of England on 6 November 1429. Beaufort and Bedford were the young king's godfathers and together organised the twenty-one-month expedition which was designed to make a reality out of his claim to the French throne. It was Beaufort himself who presided at Henry's second coronation, on 16 December 1431, the tenuousness of the English claim being underlined by the fact that it took place in Paris, whereas Charles VII made sure that he had tradition on his side by being crowned at Rheims on 17 July 1429. It was also Beaufort who presided over the king's council in France and held that office at the time of Joan of Arc's trial and execution in Rouen, capital of English-held Normandy. While many of England's nobles accompanied their king on this rather less than glorious campaign for the hearts, minds and wealth of Frenchmen, Humphrey of

Gloucester was left to govern England, scheming to discredit Beaufort by any means he could. In 1429, for example, he sought to have the cardinal suspended as chaplain to the Order of the Garter, an office traditionally held by the bishops of Winchester. Humphrey's temporary seizure of Beaufort's movable wealth at Sandwich in February 1432 suggests that the duke's motivations were not altogether idealistic, though he consistently based his arguments on the incompatibility of Beaufort being a cardinal and holding an English see and of being exempted by the pope from Archbishop Chichele's jurisdiction. Beaufort's position as cardinal and bishop did create a precedent in England: Humphrey can hardly be blamed for not anticipating the sequence of cardinal archbishops of Canterbury in his own century, let alone subsequent variations on this Anglo-papal theme. For as long as Bedford lived, Humphrey's attacks on the cardinal could be thwarted, but Bedford's death in September 1435 set the seal on English fortunes in France as well as on Beaufort's own political fortunes in England. Philip of Burgundy had long recognised the futility of the English cause in France, contrasting it with the resurgence of the French under Charles VII and staged his dramatic defection from his erstwhile allies during the peace congress held at Arras in September 1435. Beaufort felt this betrayal very keenly and led the English delegation out of the congress.

Although he was never far from the centre of political power in England and continued to be the state's chief creditor, Beaufort's later years were spent in relative retirement from public life. His financial management remained astute to the end of his life, prompting charges of avarice, though the bequests made in his will suggest that he was no less pious than many of his contemporaries and expressed that piety by putting his wealth into building projects to honour his own memory and that of his dynasty, in addition to others which provided practical charity for those less fortunate than himself. Henry VI's foundations of Eton and King's College, Cambridge, each received £1,000 and smaller bequests went to a number of religious houses with which the cardinal was associated, but Beaufort died at Wolvesey Palace in Winchester and it is to his long-held see that we should look for extant signs of his transient earthly glory. At nearby St Cross he founded an Almshouse of Noble Poverty for thirty-five brethren and three sisters of good birth but limited means: it is among the most notable architectural projects of fifteenth-century England. His Purbeck marble chantry stands in Winchester Cathedral, though the striking polychrome effigy is a copy of the original and dates from the 1660s. In that chantry the monks of St Swithun's were to say daily masses for the cardinal's soul and remember those of his parents, together with Henry IV and Henry V: even in death Beaufort identified himself as a Lancastrian.

In the public sphere many of Beaufort's policies and priorities did indeed live on in the person of Cardinal John Kemp (or Kempe, d. 1454).[28] Lacking Beaufort's illustrious birth, Kemp could not cut so princely a figure nor allow himself to be cast as quite so obvious a papalist when in England. An Oxford-educated man of Kent, Kemp received his doctorate in canon law in 1414 and held, thereafter, a sequence of high offices in both State and Church: chancellor of English Normandy (1417–22) and keeper of the privy seal (1418–21), chancellor of England (1426–32, in succession to Beaufort, and again from 1450); bishop of Rochester (1419–21), Chichester (1421), London (1421–5), archbishop of York (1425–52) and of Canterbury (1452–4). Kemp made little attempt to present himself as a pastorally minded prelate and proved distinctly unpopular in his neglected northern province; his priorities were very obviously political and diplomatic. So closely allied were Beaufort and Kemp that the latter refused to attend council meetings in 1425 at the time of Gloucester's first serious attack on Beaufort. When Kemp lost the chancellorship in 1432 he adopted the pretext of ill health, which did indeed blight him in later years, but it was actually due to Gloucester's opposition. In 1441 Kemp was among the judges who found Gloucester's wife, Eleanor Cobham, guilty of treason in attempting to use witchcraft to determine the date of Henry VI's death and consequently of her husband's accession.

In December 1439 Pope Eugenius created seventeen new cardinals. They included the former Orthodox bishops Isidore of Kiev and Bessarion of Nicaea, whose promotion was designed to cement the agreements made in Florence in 1438–9 to reunify the eastern and western Churches in the hope that Christendom would unite to break the Ottoman stranglehold around Constantinople. They also included three men whose lives were seriously affected by the Anglo-French conflict: Kemp, the former Norman chancellor who served as a diplomatic envoy on many occasions and was one of the leaders of the English delegation at Arras in 1435; Guillaume d'Estouteville, a Norman whose family fled their estates and remained loyal to Charles VII and who accumulated vast wealth as a curial cardinal prior to his death in 1483; and Louis de Luxembourg, archbishop of English-held Rouen from 1436 until his death in 1443, who became closely involved with the English government and a valuable ally of Beaufort in particular.[29] Had Beaufort and Kemp been curial cardinals England would never have been so well represented in the Sacred College. That Kemp was no more a curial cardinal than Beaufort compounded the problems identified by Gloucester and Chichele. The latter, especially, was acutely conscious of the question of precedence. When the archbishop of York and the bishop of Winchester were both cardinals, but the archbishop of Canterbury was not, who should take precedence? Neither unreasonably nor unsurprisingly, Eugenius ruled in favour of his two cardinals.

By the time Kemp succeeded John Stafford at Canterbury in 1452, Chichele having died in 1443, the final English defeat in France was only months away and the descent into civil war not far beyond that. Beaufort and Gloucester had died within days of each other in 1447, which was also the year that Nicholas V succeeded Eugenius IV. As chancellor in 1450 Kemp had dealt with Jack Cade's revolt against the poor governance of the realm. The final descent into governmental chaos was brought about by Henry VI's protracted bout of complete amnesia from August 1453 to December 1454, during which his wife, Margaret of Anjou, gave birth to their only child, a boy to whom Kemp was godfather. By the time Henry 'recovered his wits', Kemp had been dead for nine months.

# THREE

## *Renaissance and Reformation*

No princes of the Church were more princely, either in blood or in manner, than those cardinals who lived during the fifteenth and sixteenth centuries. From Portugal, Poland and Naples the sons of kings were called to join lawyers, theologians and men of letters in the Senate of the Church, as the Sacred College was still often called and fittingly so in that classicising age. English royal blood, in varying degrees of dilution, coursed through the veins of Cardinals Henry Beaufort and Thomas Bourchier, grandson and great-grandson of Edward III, as well as those of Reginald Pole, arguably the last of the Plantagenets, while princely magnificence was cultivated to perfection by the humbly born Thomas Wolsey. Similarly in the Italian states, papal dynasticism blurred the boundaries between the clerical and secular élites, as the examples of the Medici and Della Rovere families neatly illustrate, each supplying two keepers of the Petrine keys and becoming rulers of dukedoms in consequence.

Breaking free from the shackles of conciliarism was only one of various interconnected priorities for the renascent papacy of the fifteenth century. Secular powers continued to threaten the calling of general councils to reform the Church in head and members, but those calls rang increasingly hollow as the papacy reasserted itself and did so by playing those secular states at many of their own games. The city of Rome itself, economically poorer but otherwise relishing its independence during the popes' absence in Avignon, presented the most immediate challenge to papal authority. If the Colonna Martin V had difficulty controlling the city, what hope was there for popes of non-Roman, even non-Italian, origin? As late as 1453 there was an attempt to overthrow papal government and create a Roman republic, inspired by ancient example, while faction-fighting, led by the baronial families of Orsini and Colonna, blighted Roman life throughout the fifteenth century and even contributed to divisions within the Sacred College. It was partly to impose order on the city that the Renaissance popes, taking their inspiration from the grandeur of Rome's imperial legacy, undertook policies of urban regeneration. Some of these developments were associated with the jubilees presided over by Nicholas V in 1450 and Sixtus IV in 1475. Pilgrims had not ceased to visit Rome while the popes themselves were at Avignon, but pilgrimage to Rome could now be harnessed as part of an overarching policy of anti-conciliarist centralisation. Papal building projects became ever more magnificent, culminating in the rebuilding of St Peter's Basilica under the direction of Bramante and Michelangelo. For Julius II, Leo X and Clement VII in the early sixteenth century, Raphael and other masters frescoed the walls of the Vatican with images of papal primacy and authority, though the political reality beyond those walls told a rather different story.

Beyond the city walls of Rome lay the Papal States, stretching across the Italian peninsula and as far north as Bologna. Within those states each city, together with its subject territory, was ruled by a papally appointed vicar, but these small states and their rulers also took advantage of papal absence from Italy, consolidating power in their own hands. Reimposing papal control was a high priority for the Renaissance popes, but expelling the previous vicars and installing their own kinsmen or favourites often caused as many problems as it appeared to solve. Julius II's expulsion of the Baglioni from Perugia and the Bentivoglio from Bologna in 1506 was the apogee of this policy and would have been a greater triumph had Italy not become the battleground of Europe, for bringing the Papal States under subjection became overshadowed by war on a much larger scale.

In 1494 Charles VIII of France staked his dynastic claim to the kingdom of Naples, thereby ushering in what was perceived as a new phase in Italian political experience. Charles's successor, Louis XII, staked a similar claim to the duchy of Milan in 1499. Spain responded to the French challenge in Naples; the emperor and the Swiss endeavoured to counter French expansionism in northern Italy. Squeezed between these theatres of war, the popes found themselves subject to powers well beyond their control and none more so than Clement VII, held captive by Emperor Charles V after imperial forces famously laid siege to and then sacked Rome in 1527. The cultivation of secular powers by means of dynastic marriages with members of the papal families and the politically astute creation of cardinals were policies developed by the fifteenth-century popes and eagerly embraced by their beleaguered successors in the early sixteenth. Clement VII's arrangement of the marriage between his niece Caterina de' Medici and the future Henry II of France was perhaps the most obvious playing of the dynastic card, but virtually all the Renaissance popes promoted their kinsmen and women by means of judicious marriages, lay office-holding or fast-track ecclesiastical careers and the secular powers aided and abetted these practices. Cries of 'Nepotism!' issue more readily from the pages of post-Reformation historiography than they did from the mouths of contemporaries.

Nevertheless, clerical abuses did exist, as much at the Roman curia as anywhere in western Christendom. Benefices were held in plurality and promised to others while their occupants yet lived. Bishops were frequently absent from their dioceses, as lesser clergy were from their livings. Popes were well aware of these problems before Erasmus and others voiced concern about them and they made piecemeal attempts at reform, such as that initiated by the perhaps improbable reformer Alexander VI in 1497, but a more co-ordinated policy was evidently required and, as events proved, that necessitated the calling of a general council – at Trent, between 1545 and 1563. The Council of Trent was also, of course, one of the Church's responses to the Lutheran challenge, a reminder that the definition and maintenance of orthodox belief was ever a papal priority, though one which became obscured by the practical problems faced by the popes in the Italian peninsula. Faith and politics overlapped in another sphere, one which constantly preoccupied the Renaissance popes, that of a crusade to counter the very real threat posed by the western expansion of the Ottoman Empire in the Mediterranean and through the Balkans. Christian forces held out at Belgrade in 1456 and the Hospitallers valiantly defended Rhodes for decades, but the trend was against them, with the fall of Constantinople in 1453, the temporary Turkish occupation of Otranto in southern Italy in 1480–1 and their decisive victory over the Christians at Mohács in Hungary in 1526. Pius II, who died at Ancona in 1464 while waiting in vain for crusaders to join him, was not the only pope to be conscious of the severity of the Ottoman threat, but the powers of western Christendom repeatedly failed to heed papal calls for unity of purpose and of action.

A continent away from Constantinople, what part did England play in papal policies and priorities in this period? England mattered as a potential recruiting ground for what turned out to be abortive crusading schemes. It mattered as an age-old thorn in the side of French kings, a useful counterweight to French ambitions in Italy after 1494. It mattered also as an exporter of Wycliffite heresy in the fifteenth century and importer of Lutheranism and Calvinism in the sixteenth. On the other hand, it contributed relatively little to papal finances compared, say, to French-speaking lands and it did not send armies into Italy. Throughout this period England featured more prominently in papal calculations only when Englishmen, including English cardinals, rejected insularity and sought to make a greater impact on the wider European stage.

Paul III was the only Renaissance pope to create more than one English cardinal. No Englishmen were promoted to the Sacred College by Nicholas V, Calixtus III, Pius II, Sixtus IV, Innocent VIII, Pius III, Adrian VI, Clement VII or Julius III, all of whom were Italians with the exception of the Catalan Calixtus – Alfonso Borja – and the Dutchman Adrian. Conciliar ideals about fairer representation for the various 'nations' were abandoned and the increasingly Italian character of the College was an accurate reflection of papal preoccupations with peninsular affairs. This trend was temporarily reversed by Alexander VI, the second Borgia pope, who promoted large numbers of his fellow Spaniards, but also many Frenchmen and other non-Italians. The overall size of the College tended to increase steadily throughout the period. As the pope's natural counsellors, the majority of cardinals continued to be based at the curia when they were not representing him as legates, and just as the popes rebuilt the Vatican and became ever more firmly entrenched there, so the cardinals participated fully in the physical creation of Renaissance Rome, building ever grander palaces for themselves and their households, an evolution which can be traced from the relative simplicity of the fifteenth-century Palazzo Capranica to the overwhelming nobility of the Palazzo Farnese, built for the future Paul III. As in previous centuries and in the fifteenth century arguably more significantly than ever before, cardinals' households were miniature versions of the papal household. Prior to the foundation of seminaries for the training of priests, a Counter-Reformation initiative, cardinals' households were the natural homes in Rome of the cardinals' fellow countrymen. Ambitious young clerics attached themselves to the households of influential cardinals, who in turn found papal employment for these clients and ensured that they received further financial support from often distant benefices. The securing of major benefices for favoured clients was one of the most important occupations of a curial cardinal in this period, especially when the client was the preferred candidate of a secular prince or power. The Sacred College became increasingly politicised, especially when popes placated princely families by creating cardinals from among their ranks. This undermined and compromised the College's effectiveness as the pope's advisory body and, by the end of the fifteenth century, the popes accepted that the principal secular states should each have a cardinal protector to act in their interest in much the same way that the religious orders had had for some time.

In the fifteenth century it was claimed, with some justification, that 'a cardinal away from the curia is like a fish out of water', yet non-residence at the curia became the norm for English cardinals, none of whom were based there between the death of Adam Easton in 1397 and the promotion of Christopher Bainbridge in 1511. Nevertheless, at the same time as curial cardinals were becoming statesmen, so statesmen were becoming non-curial cardinals. Wolsey's contemporaries included Francisco Jiménez de Cisneros, the austere and learned Franciscan reformer who was regent of Castile in the 1510s, Cardinal Antoine Duprat, chancellor of France, and the imperial chancellor Cardinal Mercurino de Gattinara. Duprat and Gattinara were Wolsey's exact counterparts in government. The careers of Cardinals Georges d'Amboise, Matthäus Lang and Matthäus Schiner also serve to underline the point. Cardinal-ministers became a prominent feature throughout the states of western Europe.

Prior to Henry VIII's break with Rome, English interests there were served by a succession of ambassadors, 'orators' and proctors, many of whom became closely associated with the English hospice in Via di Monserrato, founded in 1398 and later to become the Venerable English College. Medieval practice had been to send embassies of short duration and for particular purposes, but fifteenth-century Europe experienced a diplomatic revolution and late fifteenth-century orators such as John Shirwood, bishop of Durham, became highly experienced curial operators, possibly more at home in Rome, culturally and politically, than they were in England. It was in this world of increasingly specialised diplomacy that the cardinal protectors were formally acknowledged, the first of whom for English affairs was the highly respected Sienese Francesco Todeschini Piccolomini, who also specialised in German business and was pope for twenty-six days in 1503, taking the name Pius III. The later protectors included Giulio de' Medici, who had no direct experience of England and was elected pope as Clement VII in 1524, and Lorenzo Campeggi, the legate who sat in judgement with Wolsey on Henry VIII's divorce case and probably felt he had rather too much English experience. Anglo-Roman communication was also facilitated by the agents and representatives sent out by the papacy. Those who went to England with legatine status were generally resented by the ruling élite. Those whose task was to collect papal taxation generally fared rather better, particularly in terms of their own ambitions. Giovanni Gigli was papal collector and nuncio in England from 1476, was sent to Rome as Henry VII's orator in 1490 and was made bishop of Worcester in 1497. Both the oratorship and the bishopric were inherited by his nephew Silvestro the following year. Silvestro Gigli's career was matched and eclipsed by that of Adriano Castellesi, another papal collector 'turned' by Henry VII and employed by him as his proctor at the papal court. With Henry's support Castellesi became bishop of Hereford in 1502, a cardinal in 1503 and bishop of Bath and Wells in 1504, thereby ensuring himself at least a footnote in histories of the English cardinals.[1]

Thomas Bourchier (or Bourgchier, *c*. 1410–86) was archbishop of Canterbury for an unprecedented thirty-two years and a cardinal for over eighteen, but made little impression outside England and not much more on later generations of his fellow countrymen. Posterity has permitted him to be overshadowed by his more controversial contemporaries, including Richard III and the 'kingmaker' Richard Neville, earl of Warwick. Bourchier is depicted as a passive figure, responding to the turbulent events of his time rather than determining them, a pliant cleric who crowned the first Yorkist king, Edward IV, in 1461, Edward's consort Elizabeth Woodville in 1465, Richard III – 'albeit unwillingly' – in 1483, the first Tudor king, Henry VII, in 1485 and finally united the Houses of Lancaster and York by celebrating Henry's marriage to Elizabeth of York in January 1486, just two months before his own death.[2]

The cardinal's mother, Anne, was the granddaughter of Edward III through her father Thomas of Woodstock, duke of Gloucester, making Bourchier the highest-born English ecclesiastic of his generation. The fact that his father, William Bourchier, count of Eu, died in 1420, reinforced the significance of Thomas's maternal inheritance. The future cardinal was clearly no intellectual, his Oxford education being unremarkable in everything, save that he went on to become chancellor of the university between 1434 and 1437. Neither personal merit nor personal initiative accounted for

Bourchier's rapid promotion through the ecclesiastical ranks. In 1433 he was Henry VI's – that is Beaufort's – candidate for the bishopric of Worcester, vacant after the death at Basel of Beaufort's ally Thomas Polton, regardless of the fact that he had yet to attain the canonical age. 'Nighness of blood' to the king was all that mattered. Eugenius IV provided Thomas Brouns to Worcester, refusing to be swayed by Bourchier's illustrious backers. The difference of opinion was neatly resolved in 1435 when Brouns was translated to Rochester, a poorer see, and Bourchier, just of age, succeeded him at Worcester. No less contentious was the means by which Bourchier was translated to Ely in 1443. Papal support for the move came as early as 1436, but the king's council opposed it and the diocese was 'administered' (held in plurality) in the interim by that English ally Cardinal Louis de Luxembourg, Archbishop of Rouen.[3]

High birth alone virtually guaranteed the sort of honours that Thomas Bourchier had thrust upon him and which he evidently accepted as natural for a man of his status, but the more precise timing of a person's office-holding, whether in Church or State, came to depend increasingly on his factional allegiance. At no time was this more obvious than during the 1450s, when Henry VI, the tool of favourites even in his periods of lucidity, became mentally incapable of ruling and the governance of the realm was twice assumed by his kinsman and rival, the anti-Lancastrian Richard, duke of York. Here the career of Henry Bourchier, count of Eu, Viscount Bourchier and earl of Essex (d. 1483), sheds some light on that of his brother, the cardinal. Henry was a close associate of the House of York and became treasurer of England during York's second protectorate (1455–6). When York's son became Edward IV in 1461 Henry Bourchier's loyalty was rewarded with the earldom of Essex, after which he repeatedly served as treasurer and was one of Edward's most valued councillors. His brothers William, Lord FitzWarin, and John, Lord Berners, were no less loyal to the Yorkist cause.

Cardinal Kemp's death in 1454 coincided with England's entry into a particularly isolationist period. The final defeat in and withdrawal from France occurred in 1453, preceding the first battle of St Albans in 1455 and the other armed encounters between the supporters of the House of York against those loyal to Henry VI and Margaret of Anjou. This distant dynastic struggle was of little consequence in Rome, but Pope Pius II came to favour the Yorkist cause in around 1460, even against an anointed king. Pius was briefed by his legate Francesco Coppini who, in turn, got his information from York's right-hand man Richard Neville.[4] Thomas Bourchier's continued ascent of the ecclesiastical ladder still owed nothing to favour in Rome, which he made no obvious attempt to cultivate, but everything to factionalism in England. It was during York's first protectorate (1454) that he filled the vacancy left by Kemp at Canterbury and there can be no doubt that he was the duke's candidate. The office of lord chancellor followed briefly during the second protectorate. In 1459 York lost the initiative and was exiled to Ireland; his son Edward, earl of March, together with the earls of Salisbury and Warwick, fled to Calais. When the earls returned to England to make their bid for the crown in 1460, Archbishop Bourchier ensured that their retinues had safe passage through Kent and that they received financial support from the clergy of the southern province, then conveniently meeting in convocation. It was, however, left to Warwick's brother, George Neville, bishop of Exeter since York's first protectorate, to win Londoners over with a splendid oratorical performance. The Nevilles and the Bourchiers were among the small group of nobles who finally made the earl of March king, as Edward IV, early in 1461.

Under its first Yorkist king, England began to emerge from self-imposed isolation. Edward's sister, Margaret, became the third and final wife of Charles the Bold of Burgundy, 'the great duke of the West', underlying the importance of English trading links with the Low Countries. The king was also well served by a succession of able proctors at the Roman curia. George Neville, chancellor from 1461 and archbishop of York from 1465, was of the opinion that the new regime should be honoured by the creation of an English cardinal and that he was the most obvious candidate for the post.

A man of great political ability, of genuine learning and culture, and a master of the art of patronage, Neville was a significant force in the land, while maintaining valuable contacts in Rome. Yet the Neville brothers reckoned without their young protégé establishing his own political agenda, including the rejection of their pro-French, rather than pro-Burgundian, foreign policy. Edward turned on these overmighty kingmakers. George Neville was deprived of the chancellorship in June 1476; three months later Paul II raised Bourchier to the Sacred College at the king's request. Paul created a number of admirable curial cardinals on that occasion and possibly calculated that he could throw away one hat in the hope of winning over England's dynamic young king for crusading purposes. It was said that Edward sent the pope's letter to the archbishop of York to show how decisively the latter's ambitions for a red hat had been thwarted. Thomas Bourchier became a cardinal not because he was a trusted servant of the king, for he held none of the high offices of state, nor because he would be a valuable advocate for England at the curia, for he never went to Rome, but simply because he was not George Neville. Previous English cardinals had had their titles disputed in England: not so Bourchier, who represented no threat whatsoever to the Crown. The Nevilles' final bid for power came between 1469 and 1471, when they joined forces with the king's disaffected brother George, duke of Clarence, drove Edward into exile in the Low Countries and brought back the hapless Henry VI as a puppet king. Bourchier was apparently responsible for the reconciliation between Edward and Clarence, which precipitated the Nevilles' defeat in the battle of Barnet and George Neville's exile in the English territory around Calais.

One further episode of national importance featured Cardinal Bourchier in something between a starring role and a walk-on part. Edward IV died unexpectedly in April 1483. His brother Richard, duke of Gloucester, gained control of the minority government of Edward V and prepared for the coronation. The dowager queen, Elizabeth Woodville, fled into sanctuary at Westminster Abbey, accompanied by her numerous daughters and younger son, Richard, duke of York. Gloucester insisted that the boy join his brother in the

Tower of London, calling upon Bourchier to bring this about. Our source is the Italian agent of the Italian bishop of the French see of Vienne:

> When the queen saw herself besieged and preparation for violence, she surrendered her son, trusting in the word of the cardinal of Canterbury, that the boy should be restored after the coronation. Indeed, the cardinal was suspecting no guile, and had persuaded the queen to do this, seeking as much to prevent a violation of the sanctuary as to mitigate by his good services the fierce resolve of the duke [Gloucester].[5]

As is all too well known, the two boys were lodged in the Tower and 'began to be seen more rarely . . . till at length they ceased to appear altogether'. Bourchier's passivity is striking in so highly charged an atmosphere, but on this occasion it was in all probability the passivity of old age.

Bourchier's mission to Westminster merits him an appearance in Shakespeare's version of the usurpation crisis, itself based on Thomas More's account.[6] Three scenes later the villainous Richard of Gloucester makes a seasonal appeal for strawberries from the bishop of Ely's garden at Holborn. The bishop was John Morton (*c.* 1420–1500), to whose household the youthful More was attached in the 1490s. Whatever the origin of the strawberry incident, the reality was that on Friday 13 June 1483, three days before the young duke of York was released from sanctuary, the lord protector, Gloucester, called a meeting of the king's council. To be more accurate, he called two meetings: those councillors who represented less of a threat to the protector's ambitions met at Westminster to discuss plans for Edward V's coronation; those who remained most loyal to the memory of Edward IV were summoned to the Tower. There Lord Hastings, the lord chamberlain, was accused of conspiring against Richard and was beheaded on Tower Hill without any semblance of a trial. Archbishop Thomas Rotherham of York, Bishop Morton of Ely and Lord Stanley were all arrested in this *coup*, though Stanley was soon released and the

University of Cambridge successfully interceded on Rotherham's behalf. Morton was sent to Brecon in the custody of Henry Stafford, duke of Buckingham. There is a certain irony in Morton being identified as a close associate of Edward IV, for in his early career he had been a notable Lancastrian.

In contrast to the noble Cardinal Bourchier, Morton was of humble Dorset birth and steadily rose to the top by his own industry, ability and ambition. In 1452 he crowned his academic career at Oxford with a doctorate in civil law. As was customary for those clerics destined for high public office in fifteenth-century England, he was financially supported by a large number of temporarily held minor benefices. Although excluded from Edward IV's pardon of Lancastrian supporters in 1461, briefly detained in the Tower (from which he escaped), attainted[7] and exiled in 1464, Morton's legal mind proved to be sufficiently supple to accommodate itself to the Yorkist regime, and the Yorkists recognised the value of having him on their side: soon after the Readeption (1470–1) his attainder was lifted and he was appointed master of the rolls. The bishopric of Ely followed in 1478. Again in contrast to Bourchier, Morton gained considerable experience of politics and diplomacy outside England. As a Lancastrian he shared Margaret of Anjou's French exile in the 1460s; as a somewhat unlikely Yorkist he undertook negotiations with Edward's IV's brother-in-law Charles the Bold (1474) and helped to draw up the Anglo-French treaty of Picquigny (1475), for which service he received a sizeable French pension. As his sphere of activity was not limited to England, it was only natural that he sought refuge in the Low Countries after falling foul of Richard III and being attainted a second time. The details of his journey from captivity in Brecon to exile in Flanders in 1484 remain mysterious, though it is significant that his flight from captivity coincided with Buckingham's rebellion against his erstwhile patron. Was Morton responsible for turning Buckingham into a rebel or did the duke react first and win the bishop over to his way of thinking?

The episcopate was as divided over Richard III's usurpation and the legitimacy of his rule as was any portion of England's ruling élite. Richard himself had spent much of his life in the north and was particularly close to the Neville family. The only bishoprics to become vacant during his brief two-year reign were given to northerners: St David's and Salisbury to Thomas Langton, Durham to John Shirwood. Langton and Shirwood were also distinguished as Cambridge graduates, whereas most of the high office-holders in the fifteenth century were Oxonians, and by having extensive Italian experience, either as students or as proctors at the Roman curia.[8] In October 1484 Richard requested that Pope Innocent VIII honour Shirwood with a red hat, recommending him in particular for his command of both Latin and Greek. The request was bound to go unrealised, for Innocent had been in office less than seven weeks, was very much the creature of Cardinal Giuliano della Rovere, whose interests were essentially French, and, moreover, accepted the election capitulation which demanded that he would not permit the Sacred College to exceed twenty-four in number. Innocent's only creation of cardinals occurred in 1489, when six Italians and two Frenchmen were promoted.

Bishop Stillington of Bath and Wells avidly supported Richard's cause, for it was he who publicised the story of Edward IV's pre-contract with another woman, thereby invalidating his marriage with Elizabeth Woodville and rendering all their children illegitimate. Among the anti-Riccardian bishops was, quite naturally, Elizabeth's brother, Lionel Woodville, bishop of Salisbury and chancellor of Oxford University, who sought sanctuary at Beaulieu in Hampshire. Another was Peter Courtenay of Exeter, who went into exile in Brittany with the man who came to embody both latent Lancastrian hopes and active opposition to Richard: Henry Tudor, son of Lady Margaret Beaufort and stepson of Lord Stanley. Here was the key to Morton's political resurrection. The details are again shadowy and have been the subject of much conjecture, but it seems that, in Flanders in 1484, Morton heard that a deal was about to be struck between Richard and the duke of Brittany, whereby the Bretons would surrender Henry Tudor to the English, thus depriving the anti-Riccardians of their figurehead. Morton informed Henry of the danger hanging over him and did so by means of Margaret Beaufort's agent Christopher Urswick. Urswick arranged for Henry to seek safety in France. In spite of the fact that Henry was on French soil, Morton in Flanders and Margaret Beaufort obliged to keep a low profile in England, they were rapidly forming the nucleus of an alternative regime, each of them as 'supple and wily' as the other two, but not entirely devoid of principle or policy. The policy that united them may well have been devised by Morton: that Henry Tudor should marry Edward IV's daughter, Elizabeth of York, as it was rumoured that the widowed Richard III was planning to do, thereby terminating the dynastic squabbles which had blighted English political life for so long. A papal dispensation was required for such a marriage between persons related within the prohibited degrees of affinity and this practicality doubtless accounts for Morton's presence in Rome between January and May 1485, for the necessary dispensation was granted with suspiciously convenient rapidity. Not only that, but Innocent obligingly added that the new king's rebel subjects in Ireland were excommunicate.[9]

The English political nation soon gathered around the victor of Bosworth, even Bishops Shirwood and Stillington taking part in Henry VII's coronation. Morton was the obvious figure to be Henry's lord chancellor and after a couple of more than worthy stopgaps (Rotherham and Alcock), he was appointed on 6 March 1486. Cardinal Bourchier's death at his manor of Knole on 30 March created an attractive opportunity at the very outset of the Tudor era. Again, it was a Morton-sized vacancy. John Alcock succeeded him at Ely, with the latter's nephew Robert Morton stepping into Alcock's episcopal shoes at Worcester. That the chancellor served his famously parsimonious king well during the remaining fourteen years of his long and eventful life is amply attested by the fact that the perfectly common sense formula for extracting money from taxpayers should be known as 'Morton's fork'.[10]

Thomas More remembered Morton as a consummate statesman. Without the benefit of personal recollection, others have seen him as 'impossibly ubiquitous and malign'.[11] Such might have been the judgement passed on many a political trimmer, but for the last seven years of his life Morton foreshadowed Wolsey's achievement by being both the king's chief minister and a cardinal, a combination designed to blacken him in the eyes of post-Reformation Englishmen, even more so in that he was promoted by that most notorious of Renaissance popes, Alexander VI, a man whose own reputation suffered because he was a Spaniard, a foreigner, in Italy. Rodrigo Borgia, the vastly experienced vice chancellor of the Church, was elected pope in August 1492. The addition of thirteen new cardinals to the Sacred College in September 1493 provided the pontiff with an opportunity to cultivate most of Europe's major secular powers: the Emperor Maximilian, Charles VIII of France, Ferdinand of Aragon, Henry VII of England, László of Hungary and Jan Olbracht of Poland, the republic of Venice and the duchies of Milan and Ferrara. It is true that Alexander's son Cesare Borgia was also added to the College on this occasion, but a number of others were undoubtedly appointed on merit.

Even apart from the Borgias, clerical dynasticism is popularly associated with the Renaissance papacy and not without cause. Paul II was a nephew of Eugenius IV, the tip of an extensive Venetian clerical dynasty; Pius III was the *nipote* and obvious heir of Pius II; Julius II was a nephew of the seriously nepotistic Sixtus IV; Clement VII was a cousin, albeit illegitimate, of Leo X. Similar patterns can be traced throughout the hierarchy, one such example being in the family of Thomas Langton, already mentioned as bishop of St David's and Salisbury, but who was also translated first to Winchester in 1493 and then to Canterbury in 1501, though he died before reaching his primatial see. Langton's nephew Christopher Bainbridge (*c.* 1462–1514) owed his ascent of the ecclesiastical ladder entirely to his uncle's patronage and duly expressed his gratitude by requesting that the pope grant an indulgence to pilgrims visiting Langton's chantry at Winchester. In various ways Bainbridge's career paralleled that of his patron: both were from Appleby in Westmorland; both undertook further studies in Italy – Bainbridge was in Ferrara in 1487–8 and gained a doctorate in civil law at Bologna in 1492; both served their monarch in Rome – Langton was king's proctor in 1484, Bainbridge held the same office from 1509. Like his uncle, Bainbridge received bishoprics in rapid succession: Durham in 1507, followed by the archbishopric of York in 1508. However, the nephew eclipsed his uncle by being raised to the cardinalate in 1511. For a man who enjoyed such prominence, Bainbridge is frequently overlooked by English historians, perhaps because his episcopal career was relatively brief, but more probably because he resided at the curia continuously from 1509 and never once set foot in his archdiocese. For the first time since the death of Adam Easton (1397) there was an English cardinal in more than name only.[12]

When Bainbridge was sent to Rome in September 1509 it was with a specific mission from the government of the new king, Henry VIII. The powers of western and central Europe had been flexing their military muscles in northern Italy for a decade, most recently by uniting in the League of Cambrai (1508) and exacting revenge on the republic of Venice, which had built up its land empire at the expense of neighbouring states in the course of the fifteenth century. Venetian forces were defeated at the battle of Agnadello (14 May 1509), Pope Julius placed the republic under an interdict, by which its citizens were deprived of the sacraments and France was left as the dominant power in the region. In a bid to check French expansionism, Bainbridge's task was to persuade Julius to lift the interdict and to join England and Venice in an anti-French coalition. When Julius turned on the French, the Venetians saw that Bainbridge was rewarded with a number of minor benefices in the Veneto. Active hostility towards France was a constant feature of Bainbridge's Roman career, a hostility extended to France's Scottish allies: news of the Scottish defeat at Flodden (1513) was perhaps the most welcome that ever reached him in Rome. Although sent on a diplomatic mission, Bainbridge was by nature no diplomat. He was sent to operate among the subtle schemers observed by Machiavelli, among whom the Englishman felt that none were more subtle than the French. What the cardinal of England lacked in cunning and duplicity, he made up for in loyalty and commitment to his king. It was perhaps his forthright manner which appealed to Julius II, 'the warrior pope', who not only named him first among the nine new cardinals appointed at Ravenna on 17 March 1511, but made him legate to the papal and Venetian armies on the same day. Those armies were then poised to fight French forces to the south and west of Ferrara, so the choice of foe might have been calculated to appeal to Bainbridge. The odds were against him succeeding in driving the pope's 'barbarian' enemies out of Italy; he tried to refuse the appointment. Julius's will and his authority were stronger and Bainbridge was sent to deal with troops demoralised by heavy rain and lack of food. The campaign was a disaster; the legate could not hope to emerge from it with any credit. By the end of 1511 Bainbridge was in Rome, in time for the May 1512 opening of the Fifth Lateran Council, a papal counter-offensive in response to the French-sponsored council which met at Pisa in 1511–12. Nine cardinals defied the pope by throwing in their lot with the Pisan assembly. Bainbridge stayed in and around Rome until his death in July 1514, taking part in the annual cycle of ceremonial activities, though not without earning criticism from Paris de Grassis, the papal master of ceremonies, who objected both to his English liturgical practices and to his failure to respond to big occasions with Italianate prolixity. In March 1513 Bainbridge did what no English cardinal had done since Simon Langham in 1370 and voted in a conclave. As there were no anti-French cardinals likely to win, Bainbridge's vote went to a man who was not a cardinal at all, while he in turn received the votes of the sometime proctor Adriano Castellesi, of the Venetian Marco Cornaro and possibly that of the Spaniard Jaime Serra. The election of the Florentine Cardinal Giovanni de' Medici as Pope Leo X did indeed signal a change in papal policy towards France. Leo sought to pardon those cardinals who had taken part in the council at Pisa, a move to which Bainbridge was resolutely opposed, not least because he had profited from the confiscation of their benefices.

Whereas Henry VII had encouraged Anglo-papal diplomacy and consequently enjoyed a trouble-free relationship with Rome, English relations with the papacy were allowed to lapse into comparative confusion in the early years of Henry VIII's reign. Giulio de' Medici was appointed cardinal protector after Bainbridge's death in 1514, but there is no indication that Bainbridge had been formally acknowledged as protector, even though he presumably did the job in practice. The rise of Thomas Wolsey, Bainbridge's dean at York (1513–14), contributed to the confusion, as the former preferred to avoid his own archbishop in his dealings with Rome. When Wolsey began to campaign for his own red hat he used Castellesi to promote his cause. Thereafter he favoured the proctor Silvestro Gigli, a man to whom Bainbridge took a violent dislike, convinced that he was working for the king of France rather than the king of England. This fits neatly with Wolsey's plans for an Anglo-French treaty, such as that in 1514 which was cemented by the short-lived marriage between Louis XII with Henry's sister Mary: death spared Bainbridge the news of this. Metaphorically speaking, the irascible, but unquestioningly loyal cardinal had been stabbed in the back. In reality, the cause of his death was said to have been poison, that convenient cover for medical incompetence so beloved by contemporary and subsequent conspiracy theorists. Suspicion centred on Gigli, but he enjoyed both diplomatic immunity and papal favour. A disaffected familiar of the late cardinal, one Rainaldo da Modena, claimed to have purchased poison in Spoleto and put it in Bainbridge's soup at Corpus Christi, 15 June. The cardinal was indeed ill at that time, but soon recovered and did not die until 14 July, possibly of altogether unrelated causes. Rainaldo went on to implicate Gigli as the instigator of the plot and then took his own life. Gigli dismissed Rainaldo as a lunatic, but Bainbridge's level-headed secretary Richard Pace remained convinced that Gigli should be prosecuted. Like any good detective, Bainbridge's biographer urges us to ask who benefited from the cardinal's demise? Gigli certainly did, as it left him the sole English representative in Rome, but it was Thomas Wolsey who became the next Archbishop of York.[13]

In spite of the fact that he never voted in a conclave or met with the pope and his fellow cardinals in consistory, the figure of Thomas Wolsey (c. 1475–1530) has come to epitomise – in English eyes at least – all that it meant to be a Renaissance cardinal.[14] Had England retained a tradition of cardinal-ministers, as France did with Cardinal Guise in the sixteenth century and Cardinals Richelieu and Mazarin in the seventeenth, Wolsey might have attracted a little less attention. His rise to eminence proved that lowly origins did not prevent exceptional ability from being recognised and allowed to realise its potential in an ecclesiastical career and that the secular authorities readily cultivated talent which it was prudent to have working for them rather than against them. The son of an Ipswich tradesman, his ability was indeed recognised early in life and by the age of fifteen, according to his own recollection, Wolsey was known at Oxford as 'the Boy Batchelour'. His early career was associated with Magdalen College, of which he was a fellow by 1497. One advantage which Wolsey did not enjoy was that of a highly placed kinsman, the key to Bainbridge's success. What Wolsey did enjoy was the best available substitute: the patronage of Bishop Richard Fox. Fox pursued higher studies in the Low Countries – where Wolsey later gained his first experience of diplomacy – attached himself to the cause of the exiled Henry Tudor and was duly rewarded with a succession of bishoprics, membership of the king's council, the keepership of the privy seal and the king's unfaltering support. In his venerable old age Fox was only too willing to bow out of public life and leave the reins of government in the hands of his vigorous protégé. Wolsey had experience of life at court from 1505, but it was only with the accession of Henry VIII in 1509 that his fortunes improved considerably.

Glancing across the courts of early modern Europe, one can see how many a minister became all-powerful because his king was young, inexperienced and perhaps temperamentally or intellectually unsuited to the demands of government: the examples of Lerma and Olivares in seventeenth-century Spain might be added to those of the cardinal-ministers in France. Wolsey's monarch was young, but out of his minority; relatively inexperienced, but eager to remedy that shortcoming, particularly if it involved war against the French; he was also temperamentally suited to the grand occasion, but not intellectually suited to the inglorious minutiae of quotidian administration. Wolsey astutely observed Henry's strengths and weaknesses, perceiving how he could make himself invaluable. His attention to detail, whether in foreign or domestic policy, filled the days which Henry devoted to hunting and other courtly pleasures,

61

and his organisation of a brief but astonishingly successful French campaign in 1513 brought Henry the instant glory he craved and brought Wolsey both his king's gratitude and the bishopric of Tournai. Until that point Wolsey had held the post of king's almoner, but was in effect acting as his secretary. Thereafter, major benefices came thick and fast: the bishopric of Lincoln in 1514, vacated just seven months later, after Bainbridge's death facilitated his promotion to York; Bath and Wells from 1518, Durham from 1523 and Winchester in 1529. In terms of quantity, Wolsey's total matched Kemp's five bishoprics. The difference was that Kemp held no two simultaneously, whereas Wolsey retained his archbishopric while holding the other sees *in commendam*. Among Wolsey's contemporaries in the Sacred College this practice was by no means unusual. Richard Fox had also been successively bishop of Bath and Wells, of Durham and of Winchester, so the parallel must have been particularly satisfying to Wolsey, even though his governmental responsibilities meant that he was a non-resident bishop until the last few months of his life. He attained the highest offices in Church and State in the second half of 1515, his appointment as lord chancellor coming three months after Leo X overruled the objections of curial cardinals by raising the Englishman to their status. Wolsey remained the dominant force in English government, Church and law for the next fourteen years.

Though more than competent in all spheres of government, it was in foreign policy that Wolsey took particular delight. As a Venetian ambassador explained: 'Nothing pleases him more than to be called the arbiter of the affairs of Christendom.'[15] By the early decades of the sixteenth century the incorporation of smaller states, such as Brittany, into larger ones, such as France, together with generations of dynastic intermarriage, had left power in western Europe in relatively few hands. The Emperor Charles V, elected to succeed his grandfather Maximilian in 1519, had been the chief beneficiary of dynastic marriages, ruling the German-speaking lands, the Low Countries, the Spanish kingdoms, together with the kingdom of Naples and, from the 1520s onwards, the duchy of Milan: too vast an inheritance for practical purposes, but nevertheless regarded as a serious threat by the more compact and unified kingdom of France, surrounded as it was by Hapsburg lands. From 1515 the French king was Francis I. As Wolsey perceived, Henry VIII's England was ideally placed not only to maintain a balance of power in western Europe, but also to champion the ideal of peace. Though accused of various underhand and duplicitous practices, Wolsey steadfastly maintained that his objective was peace between Christians. In doing so he demonstrated that his thinking was in line with that of his contemporary, Erasmus, the most famous of the Christian humanists. Even as kings and princes invited him to grace their courts, Erasmus chided them with his combination of eloquence and acerbic wit because they would not cease making unholy war against one another. Erasmus was no less critical of the Church, particularly under the leadership of Julius II, and was the leading proponent of reform of religious orders. It was a message the secular princes were keen to hear when it suited their anti-papal and anticlerical motives, but one for which Charles and Francis had little use after the rise of Lutheranism equated religious reform with political revolt. Erasmus was still the intellectual darling of Christendom in 1520 when Wolsey pulled off one of his greatest *coups* in the cause of peace, the extravagant summit meeting between Henry and Francis at the location near Calais known as the Field of the Cloth of Gold. A temporary palace was constructed, a marriage was planned between the dauphin and Henry's daughter Mary, peace between England and Scotland was even on the diplomatic agenda, while the kings and nobles indulged in many chivalric feats of arms. The English cardinal presided over the organisation of the entire event and, indeed, at a Solemn High Mass attended by both kings, the papal legate, three other cardinals and twenty-one bishops. The episode was all the more extraordinary because of Henry's preference for an alliance with the emperor, his wife's nephew, and abiding hostility towards Francis.[16]

The imperial option, which conveniently favoured English trading interests in the Low Countries in combination with traditional Francophobia, was so widely preferred in England as to give the impression that Wolsey was the only person who wanted an Anglo-

French *rapprochement*. In the cardinal's grand design the Field of
the Cloth of Gold was but a beginning and Wolsey hastily made an
Anglo-imperial agreement afterwards, in order to keep the emperor
convinced of his good intentions. Buoyed by this success, in 1521
Wolsey chaired a conference at Calais with the aim of securing peace
between the warring French and imperialists. Cardinal Duprat
represented Francis, the imperial delegation was led by the
Chancellor Gattinara, and the Venetian Gasparo Contarini acted as
the papal observer. Duprat and Gattinara did not share Wolsey's
idealism and the negotiations rapidly ground to a halt. Wolsey broke
the deadlock by going to Bruges to negotiate a bilateral Anglo-
imperial agreement with the emperor himself. By this means Charles
thought that he had persuaded England off the diplomatic fence and
into arms against France, but Wolsey carefully promised no English
action for two years, by which time any number of diplomatic and
military twists might have taken place. Rather like the mercenary
soldiers of the period, who were said to fight half-heartedly in order
to fight another day, so Wolsey was a natural diplomat who always
left himself the option of negotiating another treaty and avoiding the
unpredictability of open warfare. When time finally ran out for
Wolsey in the late 1520s it was connected with the one important
diplomatic link which he had rather neglected.

'Itt is necessari for the Kyngis Grace to have oon or ii yff nede
were cardinals and residents in the courte of Rome boithe for
knowliege of all thyngs that shall succede here and also for the
creation of popis', wrote Richard Pace to Wolsey in September
1514.[17] Although Cardinal Giulio de' Medici was England's cardinal
protector after Bainbridge's death and had the great merit of being
Leo X's cousin and right-hand man, his real commitments were to
his family and to his native Florence. In the longer term England
suffered from the lack of its own curial cardinal. It also suffered
because of the high-handed tone which Wolsey adopted in his
dealings with the papacy. In 1518 Cardinal Lorenzo Campeggi was
sent as legate to England to preach a crusade against the still-
menacing Ottomans. Wolsey objected that precedent was against
foreigners enjoying legatine authority in England. Campeggi kicked

his heels beyond the Channel for six weeks while Wolsey haggled with Rome over joint legatine powers for himself. The English cardinal was already used to dealing with kings and emperors and determining the fates of nations; surely the pope would also recognise that it was in his interest to place his trust in Wolsey. He did not. Giulio de' Medici wrote to Campeggi on 6 October 1518:

> With great displeasure has His Holiness learned that Wolsey has set aside the proposal of a five years' truce, because he does not wish to leave the final position of affairs in the hands of the Pope. No Christian – far less a Cardinal – should venture to express himself in that way, and least of all Wolsey, who has received so many honours and favours from the Holy Father.[18]

In the light of England's subsequent relations with the papacy there is a certain irony in the fact that the rise of Lutheranism initially brought them closer together and, in effect, bought Wolsey more time in which to work out his grand strategy. It was in 1521 that Henry VIII presented his anti-Lutheran defence of the seven sacraments, the *Assertio septem sacramentorum*, to Leo X, thereby earning himself the title *Defensor fidei*. Leo died on 1 December that year and the rivalries between the Holy Roman Emperor, the Most Christian King of France and the English Defender of the Faith were duly played out in the contest for the papal tiara. The conclave took place in January 1522. Wolsey is often assumed to have entertained papal ambitions himself, a natural enough interpretation in Rome where so many of the cardinals did precisely that, and the only two conclaves in which any such ambitions might have been realised were those of 1522 and 1523. In reality, Charles V initiated the idea of Wolsey's candidature by promising his support and Henry eagerly pounced on the notion. Wolsey himself was not enthusiastic.[19] The 1522 conclave resulted in the election of Charles's former tutor Adrian of Utrecht, on the face of it as 'political' an appointment as Wolsey's would have been. Each pontificate was something of a reaction against the previous one: Giovanni de' Medici – Leo X – was the self-proclaimed 'doctor' (*medicus*) of the Church, healing the wounds inflicted by Julius II's sword; Adrian VI in turn reacted against the cultural splendours of Leo's court and presided over a brief interlude of dull simplicity and austere faith which was not to Roman tastes. Come the conclave of 1523 Wolsey and Giulio de' Medici were considered to be *papabile*, but the overwhelmingly Italian College played safe and elected the Florentine. A return to the Medici meant a return to pro-French policies in Rome, but whereas Erasmian peace and unity among Christians had been popular with princes at the time of Leo's election in 1513, that phase had now passed. Charles V and Francis I had both been enthusiastic supporters of ecclesiastical reform along Erasmian lines, but both ultimately rejected that approach when Lutheran-style reform became allied with political revolt and the overthrow of traditional hierarchies. Wolsey remained idealistic about the benefits of peace, but his policy was sidelined as Charles, Francis and Henry grew ever more belligerent. On 24 February 1525 Francis was captured at the battle of Pavia and spent almost a year as Charles's prisoner in Madrid. Calls for peace fell on increasingly deaf ears, but Wolsey persevered by negotiating with Francis's mother, Louise of Savoy, and adopting an anti-imperialist stance as a counterweight to the emperor's military dominance. Wolsey's fear of imperial might was borne out in May 1527 when Rome itself was besieged and sacked by imperialists, forcing Clement VII to seek refuge in Castel Sant'Angelo and then to become Charles's prisoner. Henry VIII demanded that this outrage be avenged. Accompanied by a massive retinue, Wolsey went to Amiens to discuss coordinated responses with Francis. Along the way he pointedly celebrated Mass at the altar of the martyred St Thomas Becket at Canterbury: the Church would not be cowed by royal bullies. Wolsey championed papal independence from secular control and proposed that all cardinals who were free to do so should make their way to Avignon to administer the Church during the pope's unfortunate confinement. Francis himself was friendly enough, only too ready to capitalise on Charles's unpopularity and signed an Anglo-French treaty on 18 August, but there was no support for the Avignon scheme, which looked suspiciously like a recipe for schism.[20]

Roberto Acciaiuoli, the Florentine ambassador to France, made a study of Wolsey at Amiens in 1527:

> Although the cardinal displays publicly a somewhat exaggerated and ostentatious pomp and state, yet his talk, bearing, and manner of transacting affairs show a truly large and enterprising mind. He is a man of attractive character, full of noble and lofty thoughts. I do not remember since the days of Alexander VI to have seen anyone who filled his position so majestically; but, in contrast to the Pope, it must be stated that the Cardinal's life is without blame.[20]

According to other sources Wolsey fathered two children by a Mistress Larke: Dorothy, a nun, and a son known as Thomas Winter, acknowledged by the cardinal as his 'nephew' and supplied with a stream of rather lucrative benefices. As depicted by Acciaiuoli, Wolsey was at the height of his magnificence, though the height of his power as the 'arbiter of Christendom' had passed in 1519–21. Wolsey's princely magnificence and, indeed, munificence was most obviously displayed in his building projects: at Bridewell, his first London house, from 1510; at York Place, the archbishop of York's official London residence, from 1514; at Hampton Court, also acquired in 1514; at The More, Rickmansworth, and Tyttenhanger, near St Albans, both of which came to him as commendatory abbot of St Albans from 1522; at Durham Place, London, and at the bishop of Winchester's manor of Esher; at Southwell and at Cawood Castle, south of York.[21] Wolsey was also the last of a line of pre-Reformation bishops to found a university college, the most recent example of which was Richard Fox's Corpus Christi College, Oxford, in 1517. Within a decade Wolsey had acquired a neighbouring site for his own considerably more ambitious foundation, tellingly named not in honour of Christ or a saint but of himself: Cardinal College.[22] Like William of Wykeham's colleges at Winchester and Oxford, or like Henry VI's foundation of Eton and King's College, Cambridge, Wolsey began to build a Cardinal College in his native Ipswich to act as a feeder school for his Oxford project.[23] It seems, though, that Ipswich was designed to be merely the first of many such schools. All of which amounted to greater patronage of architecture and education than the king undertook and easily dwarfed the activities of any other builders and patrons, contributing to the resentment felt by the nobility at what they perceived as Wolsey's overweening pride.

The first sign of noble discontent was heard in the boasting of Edward Stafford, duke of Buckingham, son of the 1483 rebel duke, who made the mistake of attacking the king's minister and staking his own claim to the throne. He was executed for treason in 1521. There followed a subtle undermining of Wolsey's authority in a series of poems by the aged John Skelton, the best known of which opens with an attack on Wolsey setting himself up as a second king:

> Why come ye not to Court
> To which court?
> To the king's court,
> Or to Hampton Court?
> Nay, to the king's court.
> The King's court
> Should have the excellence
> But Hampton Court
> Hath the pre-eminence!
> And York's Place
> With my lord's Grace!
> To whose magnificence
> Is all the confluence,
> Suits and supplications,
> Embassades of all nations.
> Straw for Law Canon,
> Or for the Law Common,
> Or for the Law Civil!
> It shall be as he will.[24]

Thus encouraged, by the mid-1520s the dukes of Norfolk and Suffolk were proclaiming themselves to be the natural counsellors who should displace the base-born cardinal and restore a natural order.

When Henry became anxious about his lack of a male heir and expressed grave doubts about the validity of his marriage with his brother's widow, Wolsey's opponents at court were to be found forming a faction around the figurehead of Norfolk's kinswoman and Henry's mistress, Anne Boleyn. That Anne and her immediate family were enthusiastic about the Lutheran texts seeping into England in spite of official prohibitions was all the more convenient for those determined to ruin the cardinal. In May 1527 Wolsey and Archbishop Warham of Canterbury set up a secret court to try the legality of Henry's claim for an annulment of his marriage to Catherine, but Wolsey's attention was soon distracted by the Sack of Rome and his departure for Amiens offered the Boleyn faction an ideal opportunity for scheming against him in his absence. The annulment could only be granted by the pope and would not be forthcoming as long as Charles V remained the dominant power in Italy and pledged himself to defend the honour of his maternal aunt, Catherine. Henry's legal case was weak and was, arguably, weakened further by his growing alienation of Wolsey. Ever his master's loyal servant, Wolsey explored the legal options himself, found fault with Catherine's case and a subtle means of undermining it, but Henry wanted quick results and had no time for subtleties.[25] Wolsey's isolation was increasingly obvious: the pope's incapacity for independent action, together with the cardinal's own neglect of curial diplomacy, made assistance from Rome unlikely; Henry's determination to be rid of Catherine, together with the anticlericalism of the Boleyns and noble opposition created a formidable alliance against him in England.

The legatine powers acquired by Wolsey in 1518 had been repeatedly amplified by the Medici popes and confirmed for life in 1524. The demand arose for Wolsey, as legate, to try the divorce case in England. He bowed to this pressure. Cardinal Campeggi, who had been England's protector and bishop of Salisbury since 1524, returned as legate in September 1528 and their joint legatine court sat at Blackfriars from 18 June 1529. The high drama of

Catherine's single spirited appearance in court came early in the proceedings, but by late July legal technicalities meant that a result – any result – was no nearer than ever. Campeggi adjourned proceedings on 31 July and they were never resumed. The king had demanded more of Wolsey than the law permitted him to deliver. Although Henry showed belated signs of appreciating his minister's consistent devotion and incomparable management of affairs, he was finally persuaded to ruin the cardinal in October that year.[26] First Wolsey was indicted for *praemunire* on account of having acted as papal legate in England, in spite of the fact that the king wished him to do so, and then he was demanded to surrender the Great Seal. Petty vindictiveness by his persecutors was not matched by any loss of dignity on the cardinal's part. During the year of life that remained to him, he lived quietly at Esher before devoting himself to the care of the previously neglected northern province. The interception of his correspondence with Rome provided the basis of a treason charge and he was arrested at Cawood Castle on 4 November 1530. Disregarding his poor state of health, Wolsey began the journey south, but death met him at Leicester Abbey on 29 November, saving him from the indignity of standing trial and his enemies from exacting a final revenge.[27]

Among those who defended the absent Catherine at Blackfriars was the man who became England's next cardinal: John Fisher, bishop of Rochester (d. 1535).[28] Although Fisher was executed just twenty-two days after being made a cardinal by the Farnese pope, Paul III, and most certainly never functioned as a cardinal, his career can be interpreted as a microcosm first of how the Renaissance 'new learning' fed into the ideal of ecclesiastical reform and then of how that idealism came to grief on the rocks of more militant Protestantism.

Fisher's early education was in his native Beverley, but virtually his entire career was associated with the University of Cambridge, whether as a student in the 1480s, as fellow of Michaelhouse from *c.* 1491, senior proctor (1494–5), vice-chancellor (1501–2), the first Lady Margaret Reader in divinity (1502), president of Queens' College (1505–8), or chancellor from 1504. To the last office he was re-elected for life in 1514. As senior proctor he came to the attention of the king's mother, Lady Margaret Beaufort, who thereupon 'resolved' that he should be her spiritual guide.[29] By the time she died in June 1509, just twenty days after her son, Fisher had channelled her enthusiasm for bettering the education of preachers, teachers and, by extension, the laity, into the foundation of the readership of which he himself was the first holder and, more significantly, the refoundation of Godshouse as Christ's College (1505) and St John's Hospital as St John's College (1505–11). This unprecedented concentration of royal patronage at the university was intended as a spur to evangelism, but it was also a vote of confidence in English scholarship, for among Fisher's contemporaries were John Colet, dean of St Paul's, regarded by Erasmus as a model Christian humanist, William Grocyn, William Latimer and Thomas Linacre, notable Greek scholars and outright polymaths, while the younger generation boasted the talents of Thomas More. It was to this circle of scholars that Erasmus was attracted during his three English sojourns. In this company Fisher felt disadvantaged by his lack of Greek, though posterity has tended to overlook this on account of his hospitality towards Erasmus: thanks to Fisher's patronage and Lady Margaret's munificence the Dutchman was appointed to a chair of Greek at Cambridge in 1511. Fisher and Erasmus later drifted apart, not least because the Englishman's theology was a little too traditional and his philosophical vision rather less than all-encompassing.

The nature of episcopal office and the mode of life appropriate to a bishop was a popular subject for Christian humanists throughout Europe. The Venetian Ludovico Barbo and the Florentine St Antoninus were among the role models for bishops who rejected the temptations of both court and curia, resided in their dioceses, provided pastoral leadership and encouraged high educational standards among their clergy. It was in 1504 that Fisher received what turned out to be his only bishopric, that of Rochester, and four years later that he resolved to reduce his Cambridge commitments in order to spend more time in his diocese. His reconstructed itinerary suggests that Fisher was as good as his word, though the proximity

71

of Rochester to London permitted him to combine episcopal residence with a role in affairs of state. Even his foray to the Field of the Cloth of Gold in 1520 need not have taken him away from his diocese for more than a month and projected pilgrimages outside England were simply never realised.[30]

The subject of personal piety has not loomed large in our account of the English cardinals thus far, but it cannot be overlooked in the case of Fisher.[31] That Fisher's doctorate was in theology, rather than laws, predisposed him to publish on theological matters, which in turn facilitates an investigation of his personal piety. His chosen course of study may also have acted as a brake on his advancement in public office. Fisher belonged to a generation of theologians and preachers whose works were disseminated by the presses, as those of the late fifteenth-century episcopate had not been. His sermons on the Penitential Psalms were printed by Wynkyn de Worde in 1509, after having been delivered before Lady Margaret Beaufort the previous year. In 1511 Fisher was her natural choice to preach at Henry VII's funeral in St Paul's, his text on that occasion also appearing in print. With the passage of time the bishop's literary output became more controversial in nature. His *De unica Magdalena* of 1519 was a rapid and conservative response to Jacques Lefèvre d'Etaple's discussion of the Gospel Maries and conclusion that three different women had become conflated into the one figure of Mary Magdalen. Lefèvre was the more eminent scholar; his works provided inspiration for a generation of French evangelicals, including Guillaume Briçonnet, bishop of Meaux, and Francis I's sister Marguerite d'Angoulême, but Fisher was anxious to prevent orthodox believers being upset and confused by innovative ideas. *Evangelisme* was the principal expression of Erasmianism in France, thoroughly biblical, committed to ecclesiastical reform, but no less devoted to unity among Christians and so not in danger of breaking with Rome. Until 1534 French evangelicals enjoyed their king's support, but that was withdrawn after the distinctions between *Evangelisme* and Lutheranism became increasingly hard to discern. Erasmus thought that Fisher had been too hard on Lefèvre, but just as Christian humanism has come to be regarded as a harbinger of the Reformation, so Fisher's criticism of Lefèvre can be seen as a trial run for his anti-Lutheran writings in the 1520s and 1530s. These were interspersed with tracts in defence of Queen Catherine, making it abundantly clear that the parties in the divorce case were to be identified with the reformers and the conservatives in the Church, even though it was Henry VIII who had at least co-authored that defence of the seven sacraments and Catherine who had been a patron of the humanist educator Juan Luis Vives. Fisher's last works, *A Spiritual Consolation* and *The Wayes to Perfect Religion*, were written for his half-sister during his imprisonment in the Tower and present a reassuringly serene conclusion to what, since 1527, had been a period of turmoil and distress, but it is to an earlier period that we should turn to discover Fisher's model of piety. Writing to Bishop Fox in 1526, he recalled his relationship with the Lady Margaret and explained that he 'learned more of what leads to an upright life from her rare virtues than I ever taught her in return'.[32] In June 1511 he delivered her 'month's mind' sermon and reflected on how:

. . . her ears hearing the word of God and the divine service, which daily was kept in her chapel with great number of priests, clerks and children, to her great charge and cost; her tongue occupied in prayer much of the day; her legges and feet in visiting the altars and other holy places, going her stations customably when she was not let; her hands in giving alms to the poor and needy, and dressing them also when they were sick, and ministering unto them meat and drink.[33]

Characteristics of late medieval English spirituality, most famously expressed in the works of mystics such as Walter Hilton and Richard Rolle, have been discerned in Fisher's thought.[34] The principal custodians of that tradition in Fisher's day were to be found in the Carthusian order, whose Charterhouses at London and Sheen were among the most intellectually and spiritually vibrant religious communities of early sixteenth-century England. Also notable were the Bridgettines at Syon and the Observant Franciscans at Greenwich.

Because Fisher was the only member of the episcopate to be executed for his opposition to religious innovation and the royal divorce, it is easy to think of him as a solitary elderly reactionary, but he enjoyed consistent support from the likes of Richard Reynolds at Syon and William Peto at Greenwich, together with the network of sympathisers for whom they acted as figureheads. Peto (or Peyto, d. 1558) was a Warwickshire man who became a fellow of Queens' College, Cambridge, during Fisher's time as president and was provincial minister of the English Observants from 1522.[35] On 31 March 1532 the king visited the Greenwich community and heard Peto preach on the dangers of evil counsel. One counsellor then growing high in the king's favour was Thomas Cromwell, trained in matters of state by Wolsey, who became Henry's chief minister in the early 1530s and masterminded the legislation which severed the English Church from Rome. After the sermon a heated argument arose between Peto and the king about Henry's proposed marriage to Anne Boleyn. The friar's temerity earned him a short spell of imprisonment and he was living in exile by the time Henry and Anne were married by the new archbishop of Canterbury, Thomas Cranmer, in January 1533. That Peto was a reluctant cardinal for the last ten months of his life (June 1557 to April 1558) makes him a singularly appropriate figure to highlight alongside Fisher.

From 1532 successive pieces of legislation put the bishop of Rochester on a collision course with his king: some prevented English ecclesiastical wealth being taxed by Rome; the Act in Restraint of Appeals (1533) barred Catherine, or any other English subject, from having a legal suit tried in Rome; the Succession Act (1534) declared Princess Mary to be illegitimate and Anne Boleyn's daughter Elizabeth to be Henry's heir; the Act of Supremacy (1534) marked the decisive breach with Rome by declaring Henry to be Supreme Head of the Church in England; and the Treason Act (1534) confirmed the Act of Supremacy by making it a treasonable offence to deny Henry that title. The first offence for which Fisher was tried and found guilty, in March 1534, was misprision of treason. This arose from his sympathy with the nun Elizabeth

Barton, known as the 'holy maid of Kent', who told Henry to his face that he would soon cease to be king if he rejected Catherine and married Anne. Like the chancellor, Thomas More, Fisher refused to take the oath required by the Act of Supremacy, thereby denying Henry his new title. As soon as the Treason Act was passed both were automatically guilty of that capital crime. Fisher was much the more ardent papalist of the two and was staunchly committed to defending the pope's rights, privileges and spiritual authority.

Martin V had sought to humble Cardinal Beaufort by reminding him that a cardinal's red robes signify his willingness to shed his blood for the sake of Christ's Church. When Paul III expressed support for the imprisoned bishop by creating him a cardinal, his action appears to have hastened Fisher's martyrdom on 22 June 1535. More's execution followed fourteen days later. The manner of his death easily distinguishes John Fisher from all the other English cardinals, but so too has his afterlife, for he was beatified in 1886 and canonised along with More on 19 May 1935. In view of the dominance of the English-speaking world in the twentieth century, an English-speaking saint was considered desirable by the Vatican and a non-clerical one all the more so. Thomas More fitted this bill very neatly indeed. It is interesting to speculate on Bishop Fisher's chances of canonisation had his death not coincided so closely in cause and in date with that of More.

Martyrs and their cults form one of the enduring legacies of the Reformation. Related to that is the confessionalism, both Protestant and Catholic, which has so severely distorted appreciation of sixteenth-century European history. A third, less obvious legacy is an idealisation of the pre-Reformation period as a time when men of letters enjoyed a freedom of movement and even freedom of thought which they were soon to lose. Wandering scholars were indeed free to study theology at Paris, law at Bologna or medicine at Montpellier or Padua; the reputation of the Aldine press could draw them to Venice or the patronage of Ferdinand and Isabella attract them to newly unified Spain. Many Englishmen were prominent citizens of this republic of letters, flocking to the universities of northern Italy and imbibing the humanist curriculum of Guarino da

Verona at Ferrara much as their predecessors had refined their scholastic knowledge in the Parisian Schools. For all his encouragement of learning and hospitality towards Erasmus, John Fisher's insularity set him apart from the first rank of Europe's pre-Reformation humanist scholars. The real inheritor of that integrated pan-European culture was England's next cardinal, Reginald Pole (1500–58), who spent the majority of his adult life in exile, first as a nobleman-scholar and then as an attainted opponent of Henry VIII's breach with Rome.[36] Pole's life is worthy of consideration, not merely for the light it sheds on popes, princes and poets, but also because it is a powerful reminder that sixteenth-century theology was not as clear-cut and conveniently black and white as some later martyrologists and eulogists might have one believe.

Reginald Pole's mother, Margaret, was the daughter of George, duke of Clarence, and therefore granddaughter of both Richard, duke of York, and of the 'kingmaker' Richard Neville. From 1513 she was countess of Salisbury in her own right. Although Reginald, his brothers Henry and Geoffrey and sister Ursula, were no more than the fairly distant cousins of kings, their lineage was sufficiently impressive to be regarded as a threat by the numerically limited Tudor dynasty. Royal kinship determined Reginald Pole's career and presumably also his character, making high office all the easier to accept with dignity and a sense of duty. A character trait which contemporaries admired or even found perplexing was Pole's reluctance to express strong emotion: 'a good man but very lukewarm' was the count of Feria's judgement in 1558.[37] Thus it was that he combined a dignified bearing with a reputation for holiness and integrity. His early formation was with the Carthusians at Sheen, before being admitted to Magdalen College, Oxford, in around 1512 and completing his bachelor's course of study in 1515. As his Oxford tutors included the Italian-educated William Latimer, it should not be surprising either that Pole's interests were those of the Christian humanists or that he chose to further his education at the University of Padua. From about 1520, living at the king's expense but with a small number of minor benefices in England, though he was not yet in holy orders, Pole's

Paduan household was a haven of culture and erudition for Englishmen and Italians alike.

The royal divorce was as much of a crisis for Pole as it was for Wolsey and Fisher. After returning to England and, more particularly, to the Charterhouse at Sheen in 1527, Pole's support was so assiduously sought by the king that he was offered either the archbishopric of York or the bishopric of Winchester after Wolsey's death in 1530. High birth and high principles made him a reasonably credible candidate, but contributed even more convincingly to his ability to resist such temptation. Pole's family was close to Queen Catherine and his mother was Princess Mary's governess, predisposing him to favour the queen's cause quite apart from his Christian humanist commitment to unity among Christians. When Henry sent him to solicit the opinions of scholars and divines at the University of Paris, Pole was able to feign impartiality, but even this sat uneasily on his conscience and matters came to a head in the early summer of 1531 when Pole could prevaricate no longer and bluntly told Henry of his complete opposition to the divorce. Permission to continue his studies abroad was finally granted and eagerly accepted in January 1532. Exile was a light sentence compared with the sacrifices made by More, Fisher and even Wolsey, but it was not the only price that Reginald Pole was forced to pay for his opposition to the divorce and the schism which issued from it. Whether he willed it or no, his social standing made him a figurehead for Englishmen who chose to remain loyal to Rome, accounting for the persistent rumour that a marriage was planned between himself and Princess Mary, with a view to them overthrowing Henry and restoring England's obedience to Rome. It also made him Paul III's choice as the leader of an anti-schismatic reaction, for he was made a cardinal on 22 December 1536, an honour which Pole accepted with the greatest reluctance, realising that it made his family all the more vulnerable in England. When the northern counties rebelled against Thomas Cromwell's dissolution of the monasteries in 1536, this Pilgrimage of Grace suggested to Rome that the time was ripe for decisive action against England, so in February 1537 the reluctant English cardinal was sent towards his homeland armed with legatine powers. He travelled slowly, but the nearer he came to England the greater was the danger in which he found himself; plots to kidnap or assassinate him were all too real. Even easier prey were the cardinal's mother and brothers. Geoffrey Pole was arrested in the summer of 1538; Henry Pole and his young son soon afterwards. In April 1539 Parliament attainted both the cardinal and the countess of Salisbury, who was claimed to be the key Margaret Beaufort-like player in the marriage plans, branding them as traitors. When she was finally executed after two years of imprisonment, the cardinal recognised that he was the intended victim, suffered accordingly and claimed it was a sign of divine grace that he should be the son of a martyr.[38] By that stage Pole was living in the papal territory of Carpentras, near Avignon, because Henry's assassins had pursued him as far as northern Italy.

In spite of his reputation as a scholar Pole was under no economic pressure to be an author, let alone a prolific one, but in 1536 he penned a hard-hitting treatise addressed to his schismatic kinsman Henry, *Pro ecclesiasticae unitatis defensione*. However, those seeking his thoughts on the pressing issues of those turbulent times are more likely to turn to Thomas Starkey's *Dialogue between Pole and Lupset*, which dates from the early 1530s. Starkey was Pole's chaplain in Padua and Thomas Lupset, another member of the household, was a very promising young humanist who died in 1530. Pole's opposition to Henry's anti-papal policies might well lead one to expect him to be a theological conservative, but this was far from being the case. Starkey's Pole clearly rejects heresy, but is, nevertheless, determined to seek out truth and, therefore, offers a balanced reaction to Martin Luther:

I wyl not folow the steppes of Luther, whose jugement I estyme veray lytyl; and yet he and hys dyscypullys be not so wykyd and folysch that in al thyngys they erre. Heretykes be not in al thyngys heretykes. Wherfor I wyl not so abhorre theyr heresye that for the hate thereof I wyl fly from the truth.[39]

These simple statements conceal complex theological debate and reflect the thinking current in the Paduan intellectual circles, to which Pole acted as a patron and, more particularly, reflect the thought of the Venetian patrician and Paduan graduate Gasparo Contarini.[40] Contarini was an active politician, diplomat and man of letters when, in 1511, he experienced a spiritual crisis which led him not into the eremitical life recently chosen by his closest friends, but rather to question the means by which a Christian soul is saved, to weigh the contribution which human virtues, actions or 'works' can make, and to conclude that this is miniscule in comparison to faith in Christ as Saviour. Luther, his contemporary, reached a similar conclusion, differentiated by the insistence that salvation comes from faith alone, *ex sola fide*. Precisely because justification by faith alone was so central to Lutheran belief, any variation on the theme, even if entirely non-Lutheran in origin, came to be regarded with extreme suspicion in Italy and to risk the charge of heresy. A convenient summary of Pole's thought on the relationship between faith and works was articulated by the Roman noblewoman, poet and friend of Michelangelo, Vittoria Colonna, who claimed that Pole advised her 'to believe as if . . . salvation depended upon faith alone, and to act, on the other hand, as if it depended upon good works'.[41]

Contarini's 'third way' formed the basis for discussions between humanistically minded Catholic and Protestant delegations held at Regensburg (Ratisbon) in 1541, the last serious attempt to find a negotiated solution to their differences. The talks collapsed and Contarini, who had been a cardinal since 1535, died the following year. The other cause which he championed was that of reform within the Church. This put him firmly in a Venetian tradition, which included his friends the Camaldolese hermits Paolo Giustiniani and Vincenzo Querini, whose *Libellus ad Leonem X* presented a programme of reform to the Fifth Lateran Council. In July 1536 Paul III appointed Contarini as the head of an important reform commission, the members of which included Girolamo Aleandro, Gregorio Cortese, Jacopo Sadoleto, Gian Pietro Carafa – a founder member of the Theatine Order – Gian Matteo Giberti, bishop of Verona and Reginald Pole. Sadoleto, Pole and Carafa were all made cardinals that year and Pole ordained deacon; Cortese followed them into the Sacred College at a later date, as did Pietro Bembo, the famous Venetian poet and a friend of Pole since the latter's early days in Padua. This was an exceptionally able group of individuals, yet their views varied considerably, ranging from those who were enthusiastic about discussion with Protestants through to the hardliner Carafa, to whom any such compromise was anathema. Pole was again identified as a reformer when the first session of the Council of Trent opened in 1542. Paul III was represented there by Cardinals Marcello Cervini, Giovanni Maria del Monte and Pole. The Englishman had high hopes of the council as the means by which the scandalous divisions within Christendom might be healed, but no business was transacted until December 1545. By June 1546 Pole was staying at the house of his friend Alvise Priuli in Padua, recovering from a bout of ill health: he took no further part in the council's many sessions. As the delegates were then discussing the nature of salvation, on which subject Pole found himself in a minority, the suspicion remains that his was something of a diplomatic retreat. He was dispensed from the office of legate in October that year. This apparent reverse notwithstanding, when Pope Paul died in November 1549, Pole was the favoured candidate of the imperial party, obtaining twenty-four votes in the second scrutiny, four short of the required two-thirds majority. Word came that four more French cardinals would arrive in Rome shortly. The imperialists feared that their candidate would not come so close to victory after their arrival and endeavoured to make Pole pope by acclamation, a legitimate procedure, but an offer which Pole rejected. His name was also mentioned in the first conclave of 1555, but he lacked imperial backing that time and the victor was the former legate Cervini, who became Pope Marcellus II. His three-week pontificate was naturally followed by yet another conclave. With no imperial candidate at all, the cardinals elected Gian Pietro Carafa who, as refounder of the Roman Inquisition, was a scourge of heretics and, as a Neapolitan, resented Spanish possession of the Regno and was soon on a political collision course with Charles V.

Between 1541 and 1550 Pole was based at Viterbo in his capacity as legate to the Patrimony of St Peter, the region around Rome, and there acted as a magnet for intellectuals, reformers and theologians, who can broadly be defined as being in the tradition of Erasmus and Contarini. They were known as *spirituali* and were the Italian counterparts of the French evangelicals or the Spanish *alumbrados*, combining the scriptural emphasis of the former with the mystical spirituality of the latter. Either way they can be regarded as the heirs of Erasmus. Among those attracted to Viterbo were the poets Vittoria Colonna and Marcantonio Flaminio. Elsewhere, Juan de Valdes inspired *spirituali* in Naples, while the like-minded general of the Capuchin order, Bernardino Ochino, gained great popularity as a preacher and other highly placed sympathisers included Gian Matteo Giberti, bishop of Verona, and Cardinal Giovanni Morone. However, following Carafa's refounding of the Roman Inquisition in 1540, the *spirituali* were in crisis. Valdés died in 1541, Contarini in 1542. In August 1542 Ochino and Pietro Martire Vermigli, abbot of S. Frediano in Lucca, dealt Italian evangelism its greatest blow by fleeing to Switzerland and declaring themselves Protestants. The Viterbo circle was increasingly vulnerable.[42]

The differences between Pole and Carafa became ever more marked as the initiatives collectively known as the Counter- or Catholic-Reformation grew in strength. When, his attainder reversed by parliament, Pole finally arrived in England as legate in November 1554, he absolved the kingdom from its corporate act of disobedience and formally reconciled it to the papacy after a breach of two decades: 'I cum to reconcyle, not to condemne. I cum not to compel but to call agayne. I am not cum to call anything in question already done, but my commission is of grace and clemency to such as will receive it.'[43] Such magnanimity was not Carafa's style. The education of priests and people was at the heart of both the Tridentine debates and of Pole's initiatives in England. One source of inspiration was Giberti's diocesan reforms in Verona in the 1530s; this example he sought to translate to the parishes and dioceses of England between 1555 and 1558, for he remained convinced that the English Reformation was a political process imposed on the people from above and that all the laity needed was sound teaching from well-educated parish priests and leadership from well-born bishops who could resist threats from the secular government. For a vision of how Pole's work might have developed, had time been on his side, one might look to the social and educational mission of Carlo Borromeo in his archdiocese of Milan, for he too was inspired by Giberti. By founding one of the new religious orders which so characterised the counter-reforming movement, Carafa embodied the more militant wing of the Catholic Reformation. The most notable and, ultimately, the most controversial of those new orders was the Society of Jesus, founded by Ignatius of Loyola and approved by Paul III in 1540. Although Pole was perfectly sympathetic to these orders in Italy and to the Jesuits in particular, when he returned to England he rejected Ignatius's offer of 'shock troops' to make up for the paucity of English priests. The Jesuits were simply too un-English. Not only were the Jesuits too foreign and, specifically, too Spanish, they were also adept at religious controversy and avoided emphasis on the externals of religion. Pole reckoned that what the English people needed was the comforting 'beauty of holiness', albeit in a suitably restrained manner: the Marian reaction did not even include revival of pilgrimage to Walsingham.[44] He put his faith in the older religious orders, refounding the Benedictine community at Westminster, the Bridgettines at Syon and the Observant Franciscans at Greenwich. It was to Greenwich that William Peto returned in the last years of his life and there also that Pole was ordained priest in 1556, three months after the papal sentence against Cranmer created a vacancy at Canterbury and the very day before Cranmer was burned at the stake in Oxford.

As Paul IV, Carafa naturally took a hard line against all enemies of the Church, among whom he counted the *spirituali*. Spaniards and imperialists also incurred papal wrath. Relations deteriorated so far that Spanish troops crossed from Naples into the Papal States. In spite of Mary's marriage to Philip of Spain, England declared herself neutral. Paul was not convinced and on 10 April 1557 recalled all legates in Hapsburg lands, naming Pole in particular. Cardinal

Morone, England's cardinal protector, was arrested on a heresy charge on 31 May, making Pole's intended fate all too apparent. His legateship was withdrawn and the last year of his life was spent lamenting the political gulf which remained between England and the papacy. The queen and the cardinal died within hours of each other on 17 November 1558, conveniently leaving England without an ecclesiastical prince on the eve of the Elizabethan Settlement and the creation of the Church of England.[45]

# FOUR

## *Exiles*

Rome remained a small city throughout the period from the Council of Trent in the sixteenth century to the time of Napoleon at the beginning of the nineteenth century; the population doubled between 1550 and 1700 from about 80,000 to as many as 176,000, but by the early 1800s it had fallen back to about 135,000. By this time London and Paris each boasted nearer to a million inhabitants. Nevertheless, with its splendid collection of ancient ruins (so vividly captured in the engravings of Giovanni Battista Piranesi (1720–78), one of the greatest artists in the history of etching and the *vedute* genre) and its great Renaissance redevelopment, it remained one of the most magnetic of European cities, attracting increasing numbers of pilgrims and tourists. The restoration of the aqueducts, celebrated in the provision of a wonderful array of fountains, made Rome a less unhealthy place than it had been hitherto, though the drainage of the malarial marshes was far from complete.

The Catholic Reformation transformed the papacy and gave it the central place it has since occupied in the Catholic Church. The Council of Trent, stemming from conciliar pressures and from the onslaughts of the Protestant Reformation, reactivated papal power. It was above all a papal council and during its proceedings, which lasted from 1545 to 1563, the papacy strengthened its prestige and the uniformity of the Roman Communion. A catechism of Church

85

doctrine and a standard liturgy reflected a unity centred on the papacy. In the second half of the sixteenth century the institutions of an absolutist Church-reformed curia, centralised religious orders, censorship and control of appointments were firmly put in place. There was much focusing of priorities and the broad, Renaissance-inspired Catholicism of the pre-Trent (or Tridentine) period was no more; all Erasmus's writings were placed on the Roman Index of Prohibited Books which first appeared in 1557. Nevertheless, papal Rome became a centre of genuine learning as well as a centre of government. The Gregorian University, established in 1572, and various national colleges enhanced *romanità* and encouraged unity. It was a unity increasingly based on strength rather than desperation. Papal authority could act as an engine of reform in the heartland of Christendom. More importantly, as in the crusades, the papacy emerged as the coordinator of the European powers in their missionary drive to the New World, Asia and the broken remnants of Protestantised Europe, including England. Increasing use was made of diplomacy through the appointment of nuncios, papal agents whose influence grew at the expense of the previously all-powerful papal legates, who progressively took on a ceremonial function.

The papacy expressed this new-found confidence in the rebuilding of Rome, which gave the city a new magnificence that obliterated or obscured so much of the medieval city. The new Rome was to be *Roma Sancta* and the Jubilee of 1575 began the series of magnificent celebrations of pilgrimage and papal primacy which punctuated the period. The beauty of holiness was accomplished, in equal measure, by fervent religious reform and strident triumphalism. Filippo Neri's Roman Oratory attempted to win the hearts as well as the minds of the Roman people. Ignatius of Loyola's Society of Jesus, approved in 1540, provided an élite clerical force armed with a powerful spirituality. The popes themselves were the usual combination of saints and sinners, but with more of the first and fewer of the latter. Pius V (1566–72), canonised for his sanctity, was responsible in the bull *Regnans in excelsis* (1570) for the excommunication of Elizabeth I of England and the reassertion of the papal claim to depose princes. Sixtus V (1585–90), perhaps the most influential of all the Counter-Reformation popes, not only completed the dome of St Peter's, but constructed a series of great new roads to improve access to the pilgrimage centres, improved the amenities of the city (making it possible to accommodate up to 500,000 pilgrims in a jubilee year) and maintained it as the artistic capital of the world. In 1582 Gregory XIII (1572–85) presided over the reform of the calendar, which meant that for much of the world time was Roman time; England did not accept the Gregorian Calendar until 1752. Speculations over the structure of the universe could lead to papal persecution. In 1600 the Dominican Giordano Bruno, later used as a symbol for anti-Catholic movements, was burnt for heresy; in 1584 he had published in London his *Cena de le ceneri* (*Ash Wednesday Supper*) which proposed a new cosmology based on Nicholas Copernicus's criticism of geocentricity. In 1632, even more famously, Galileo's Copernican astronomy was condemned by Urban VIII (1623–44) and he was put under house arrest.

The new St Peter's symbolised the power and privilege of the papacy and throughout this period Rome was undoubtedly the papal capital, its republican and imperial legacies being firmly eclipsed. All the popes of the period were Italian, as were most of their cardinals. Of the 147 cardinals created by the seven popes who ruled between 1566 and 1605, 106 (72 per cent) were Italian, eighteen (12 per cent) French and thirteen (9 per cent) Spanish. There was only one Englishman. During the half century from 1605 to 1655 another seven popes named 185 cardinals, of whom 152 (82 per cent) were Italians. Together with twelve (7 per cent) from France and thirteen (7 per cent) from Spain these three regions received 96 per cent of the red hats. The Papal States and the city of Rome itself continued to furnish the great majority of the Italian cardinals. Of the 498 cardinals created between 1655 and 1799, 80 per cent (393) were Italians and 170 of these were drawn from the Papal States. In his constitution *Postquam verus* (1586) Sixtus V decreed that cardinals should come from all parts of the Christian world, but an examination suggests that in the sixteenth, seventeenth and eighteenth centuries, with some exceptions, non-Italian cardinals were only created on the demands or even the threats of Catholic rulers. For some, like the Frenchman Richelieu, the cardinalate was seen as a way of furthering a political career. Political sensitivity was reflected in the practice of appointing cardinals *in petto* or *in pectore*, a custom which began in the fifteenth century, but was not used frequently until the pontificate of Urban VIII when fourteen were so named. Between 1644 and 1799 it was used about seventy-five times. In the decades up to 1846 ninety-seven cases are known. After 1846 it became unusual; only thirteen instances are recorded between 1847 and 1903.[1]

In such a cardinalatial world the English were, perforce, poorly represented. The English Catholic community was a small minority concentrated in London and Lancashire, with illegal priests and hidden chapels. A small core of families who remained faithful to the Roman connection provided chapels and patronage. These included the Howards of Norfolk and Sussex and the Petres of Essex. Only during the Stuart period, at least up to 1688 (and interrupted by the Civil War) was there any sign of 'public' Catholic worship outside foreign embassy chapels in London, although some 6,000 Catholic priests were ordained to work in England between 1558 and 1800, all of them educated abroad.[2] During the reign of Elizabeth I the English Catholics became known as recusants, from the Latin *recusare*, to refuse, because they would not attend the worship of the Established Church, an obligation enforced by the Act of Uniformity of 1559. Recusants were deprived of most civil and legal rights. After 1688 the failure of the Stuart cause, linked with Catholic fortunes, led to new penal legislation which was not repealed in full until the two Catholic Relief Acts of 1778 and 1791. Catholic Emancipation in 1829 gave wider freedoms to Catholics, but was influenced chiefly by Irish considerations. Formal legislation was given bite by the intensity of anti-Catholic feeling in England, which identified Catholics with unpatriotic disloyalty. This anti-Catholic tradition was to linger long after Emancipation and led to the feeling in the popular mind, fed by the historical myth of the ruling élite, that there was something both foreign and sinister about the Church of Rome. This was enshrined in the *Book of Common*

*Prayer*, after 1605, in which 'the Gunpowder Treason' was remembered as an 'unnatural conspiracy' by which the English people were delivered from 'popish tyranny and arbitrary power'.

During the years from 1558 to 1800 (and indeed to 1850) there was no formal Catholic hierarchy in England and Wales. An archpriest was appointed in 1598, but his jurisdiction was contested. The English Catholic clergy were also much disturbed by the controversies which raged between the secular clergy and the Jesuits, the latter as highly favoured by James II, in particular, as they had been shunned by Cardinal Pole in the previous century. In 1623 Pope Gregory XV (1621–3), who had established the missionary body Propaganda Fide, appointed a vicar apostolic for England, a prelate in episcopal orders, but not a diocesan bishop, directly answerable to Propaganda Fide in Rome. Cardinal protectors, for the most part Italians, also kept an eye on English Church affairs. The experiment of a single vicar apostolic did not last long and in 1688 Innocent XI revived the idea of the vicars apostolic for four districts – London, the Midlands, the North and the West – a division which survived until 1840. Whether in spite of or because of this reorganisation, the English Catholics experienced a growth in numbers and confidence by the beginning of the nineteenth century.[3] The French Revolution and the wars to which it gave rise changed the political map of Europe; from this turmoil Rome was not immune. Pope Pius VI (1775–99) had been a member of the coalition against France and in 1797 the French forced the treaty of Tolentino which robbed Rome of many of its treasures. Pius VII (1800–23) began to reassert his temporal power, only for the French presence to be restored by Napoleon until 1814. While Britain emerged as a dominant political and economic force, the *inglesi* were nevertheless viewed in Rome as a predominantly Protestant nation whose chief claim to fame was to provide a host of 'grand tourists' for the city's service industries.[4] English cardinals were, not surprisingly, few and far between in the years between Pole's death and the restoration of the English Catholic hierarchy in 1850, but they included three of the most politically important of the English princes of the Church: Allen, Philip Howard and Stuart.

William Allen's career was moulded by the failure of the Marian restoration, for he spent most of his life in exile, an exile which allowed him to become one of the chief architects of the English Roman Catholic Church-in-waiting.[5] Allen was less a link with the pre-Reformation Church than a bridge between Marian Catholicism and the new English Catholicism of Elizabeth's reign, exemplified by the missionary priests trained in the continental colleges. He was born in 1532 at Rossall in the Fylde, Lancashire, an area which retained its Catholic identity long after the Reformation had made itself felt in other parts of the country. He came from a gentry family and he was educated at home until his fifteenth year when he entered Oriel College, Oxford, graduating BA in 1550, proceeding MA in 1554, already a fellow. His career at the university, reflecting his strong Catholic views, flowered during Mary's reign and in 1556 he became principal of St Mary's Hall. It was a period of excitement and hope for one of his views. His exposure to the theology of the Marian university, with its newly installed Spanish Regius Professor of divinity, Juan de Villa Garcia, reinforced his convictions that a Catholic Christian future for England needed a European and what would now be called a Counter-Reformation perspective. He wanted renewal not with a Protestant face, but with a frankly Roman Catholic character. To Allen Marian Oxford was not backwards-looking, but rather a model for a new Church. It remained his inspiration.[6]

The Oxford Allen loved collapsed with the accession of Elizabeth in 1558 and the resurgence of Protestantism. In 1560 he resigned his university posts and in 1561 made his first visit to the Spanish Netherlands, where a body of like-minded thinkers was assembling, but then retreated to his native county. Lancashire was being assailed from central government and its Catholic soul undermined, at least in Allen's opinion. It was in 1565 that he left England, never to return. The Spanish Netherlands provided Allen with a platform and it was there that he made his reputation. Spain was the key political player in the expansion of papal authority and the sworn enemy of England. These Catholic provinces, with their strategic and economic importance and their great cultural tradition, had intellectual centres in the university towns of Louvain and Douai, the latter with its university newly chartered in 1559. Ordained priest at Malines, probably in 1566, Allen became well known for his ability as a controversialist and pamphleteer. His works were marked by an elegant and pithy style which, in the spirit of their age, specialised in the crushing put-down. Black and white were the most obvious colours; there were no grey areas. Those who died for the Protestant cause he declared 'can be no martyrs but damnable murderers of themselves' for 'to be shorte, Truth is the Church's dearlinge'.[7]

Allen's lasting memorial in the Low Countries was not his publications but his college, the English College at Douai, established as early as 1568. Sometimes seen as a model Tridentine seminary, its development and persona was in reality far more complex. In the beginning Allen may have seen his foundation as a place of temporary accommodation, awaiting a return to England, but it evolved into something far more permanent as the nature of the Elizabethan Religious Settlement became clearer. In 1568 Allen saw the foundation both as a continuation of Catholic Oxford and, in a totally non-nostalgic and forward-looking way, as a dynamic centre of Catholic theology and learning which would be an antidote to Protestantism; an All Souls of belligerent well-informed Catholic theologians and writers. Its eventual central role as a college for missionary priests and as a seminary became apparent only gradually as numbers of students increased. By the end of the 1570s the college had, on average, 100 students with as many as twenty ordinations a year; by 1580 about 100 priests had been sent from Douai to England. In the 1570s, too, an English College in Rome, on the site of the old English pilgrims' hospice, was established under Allen's influence.

Two exiles in Rome, both Welshmen, had as much claim as Allen to be founders of the Roman college. Morys Clynnog, who had been an Oxford doctor of theology, a student of law at Bologna and elsewhere, had been nominated to the see of Bangor under Mary and had come to Rome about 1563. Owen Lewis, formerly fellow of New College, Oxford and professor of canon law at Douai, came to

Rome in 1574 on legal business for the diocese of Cambrai. He ended his days as bishop of Cassano in the Spanish-ruled kingdom of Naples. These two men, hoping for an invasion of England, had the support of the pope and wanted Allen, summoned to Rome in 1576, to advise them. Allen floated a scheme to turn the pilgrim hospice into a college, both to provide accommodation for the overflowing college in Douai and a place less likely to be affected by the war between England and Spain. The first students arrived in Rome in 1577 and a bill of foundation dated 1 May 1579 inaugurated the Venerable College of St Thomas *de urbe* (Thomas of Canterbury). The first known reference to the college as *Venerabile Collegio degli Inglesi* is in a 1580 papal document granting indulgences to those visiting the college church and praying for the conversion of England to the Catholic faith. The Venerable English College went on to have a chequered history, not least because of the Italian Jesuit superiors imposed on it in its early days. In time, though, it produced not only a stream of martyrs (as did its sister college at Douai), but also proved itself to be a nursery of cardinals, a fact later celebrated in the 'cardinals corridor' at the college with its portraits, mainly undistinguished and indistinguishable, of all the English cardinals. Allen was aware from the beginning of the importance of having an English College at Rome itself:

> It pertaineth exceedingly to the general good and honour of our nation, that we may perpetually have a number of the most pregnant units brought up in the principal seat, place and foundation of our Christianity whatsoever is learned, wise, virtuous, of all the most famous universities, monasteries, societies and colleges through the world is reconciled . . . as to a continual mast of all kinds of doctrine and prudence.[8]

Further English colleges were founded in various Catholic havens, mainly under Spanish protection, but Allen's two colleges evolved a distinct style and spirituality in response to the English mission. *romanità* was special to the Venerabile but there were many shared characteristics. A great emphasis was placed on the study of

Scripture and Allen backed the publication of an English Catholic vernacular translation of the Bible, the *Douai-Rheims* version, often known as the *Douai Bible*, which remained the standard English text for Catholics until the middle of the twentieth century. Allen's colleges paid full attention to the insights of the then prevailing Jesuit piety and had a strong sacramental focus in their spirituality, centring on the Mass and Confession. Allen's aim, in line with Tridentine thinking, was to make his secular clergy an élite corps, professional pastors and effective opponents of Protestantism, something much more polished than the common sort of curate in 'old tyme'.

Allen regarded the continental colleges as crucial in his strategy for the conversion of England. He anticipated there would be those who died for their beliefs, martyrs for Christ and his Church. Like so many of the cardinals who came after him, Allen saw himself and his colleagues as true Englishmen and thought it inconceivable (as so many of his fellow countrymen did) that these seminary priests could be considered traitors. The first four Douai priests were ordained in 1573 and by the end of the 1570s over twenty were being ordained each year. In 1581 forty-three were ordained; of these fifteen were subsequently martyred. In 1583 ten out of twenty-nine were martyred. By 1596 there were over 300 seminary priests in England and that year the catalogue of martyrs already numbered 101 secular priests and four Jesuits. Allen's life was animated by a vision of a revived Catholic England and to this end he was prepared to follow any expedient. He was deeply embroiled in politics and maintained throughout his life in exile a largely pro-Spanish stance. Elizabeth's excommunication in 1570 was a defining moment for Allen, who could see no moral problem with involving himself in plots against the 'deposed monarch'. The xenophobic world of Elizabethan England reflected popular anti-Catholicism and rejoiced in the conspiracy which lingered in every Catholic corner. The atmosphere of plot and counterplot is brilliantly evoked by John Bossy in his *Giordano Bruno and the Embassy Affair* (London, 1991). In 1588, with the first Armada pending, he made a study of Pole's legatine mission to England. It is easy to speculate that if the Spanish invasion had succeeded, Allen would have been the man to reconstruct the Catholic Church in England and, like Pole, he would have been its archbishop of Canterbury. This was not to be, but his European reputation as England's leading Catholic was recognised on 7 August 1587 by Sixtus V appointing him as 'Cardinal of England' and cardinal priest of S. Martino dei Monti. In December 1586 the constitution of Sixtus V, *Postquam verus*, alluded to already, had fixed seventy as the maximum number of cardinals, a total not exceeded until John XXIII in the twentieth century. He also remodelled the curia, creating fifteen permanent congregations of cardinals, six to oversee secular matters, the rest spiritual. This reduced the power of the consistory, to such an extent that one Venetian ambassador declared: 'the only use of cardinals these days is to act as a grandiose crown for the Pope'.[9] The *Tempelstaat*, a religious state with a ruler who is both spiritual pastor and secular king, had become the model for the papacy.

Allen had to content himself with being the English cardinal in Rome and although he had neither the means nor the inclination to live a life of pomp or luxury, he played a full part in the life of the Roman Church and of the pontifical court. He retained an influence on the papacy in matters English and held an open house for English-speaking guests in his residence adjoining the English College and also took a particular interest in the German Church and its developing reformation. He worked on the revision of the Vulgate text of the Bible and on the maintenance of the Index of Prohibited Books and was appointed apostolic librarian by Gregory XIV, a post held more than three centuries later by another English cardinal, Gasquet. Attempts made by Philip II to have Allen appointed archbishop of Malines came to nothing. He died on 16 October 1594 and was buried in the church of the English College; however, his tomb did not survive the French occupation of the city.

Allen has been variously assessed: a remote and ineffectual don, a devious traitor, a leading player in the demonology of anti-Catholicism, a great and holy priest. There is no doubt of his central role in both the survival and character of English Catholicism. His foundations at Rome and Douai were to be the seed-bed of Catholic continuity and renewal; according to the cardinal, his college at Douai was 'next to God', 'the beginning and ground of all the good and salvation which is wrought in England'. He was one of the moving spirits behind the English-language Catholic version of the Bible and was an unusually strong focus for unity and peace in the English Catholic community which, after his death, became fragmented. 'Because of him', Eamon Duffy asserts, 'English Catholicism was given a life-line to the larger world of Christendom, and a surer clearer sense of its own identity: because of him it survived. Elizabethan England produced some really great men, fewer really good ones, and almost none who could be called great Europeans. William Allen was all three.'[10]

Continuing persecution, combined with a lack of organisation among the missionary priests, led to a period of struggle and uncertainty among the English Catholics in the early seventeenth century. This was perhaps symptomatic of an altogether confused political climate in which parliament men became regicides, but a sense of crisis, caused by economic instability and manifested in dynastic and civil conflicts, blighted many regions of western and central Europe in that period. In England the Stuarts' flirtation with Catholicism and their succession of Catholic wives, whether French, Portuguese or Italian, contributed to the monarchs' alienation from their fiercely anti-Catholic subjects. In the heady ecclesiastical world of the reign of Charles I, schemes for reunion were in the air and in 1633 an unknown agent is supposed to have offered a red hat to the leading Anglican William Laud, who declined the offer.[11] It was also during the period of Charles I's 'personal rule' that a rather elusive Scotsman called George Con (d. 1640), served as papal agent in London. Con was a member of the Roman household of the powerful papal *nipote* Francesco Barberini, cardinal protector of England and Scotland. Rumours that he was to be made a cardinal were frequent, but there is no evidence for his creation even *in petto*.[12] Con's tomb, complete with portrait bust, is in the Roman church of S. Lorenzo in Damaso, but the epitaph makes no allusion to a secret cardinalate.

No doubt surrounds the cardinalatial dignity of Philip Howard, who was born at Arundel House, London, on 21 September 1629, the third son of Henry Frederick Howard, afterwards 3rd earl of Arundel. His mother was Elizabeth, eldest daughter of Esmé Stuart, afterwards 3rd duke of Lennox.[13] His ancestry was distinguished both religiously and socially. His great-grandfather, Philip Howard, who died in 1595, was named after his godfather Philip of Spain, but as a committed Catholic and a correspondent of Cardinal Allen, he inevitably came to grief under Elizabeth and spent his last ten years in the Tower of London, dying there of dysentery. His body was taken to Arundel where it is now enshrined in the Catholic cathedral. He was canonised by Pope Paul VI in 1970. Thomas, earl of Arundel, St Philip Howard's only son and the cardinal's grandfather, was the greatest English private collector and patron of his generation and a connoisseur of European status. He not only restored the family fortunes (later dissipated by his extravagance), but set out to celebrate his family's pedigree and standing. What he achieved, however, was made possible by conforming to the Established Church in 1616. His son, Henry Frederick, had been brought up a Catholic and educated in Italy. However, despite the Howards' Catholic tradition, young Philip's background was officially as a member of the Established Church, although 'Church Papist' might be a better way of describing it. In 1640 Philip Howard briefly attended St John's College, Cambridge, and then accompanied his grandfather to the continent in 1641. He surprised everyone by deciding to become a Dominican, under, it seems, the persuasive influence of John Baptist Hackett. Hackett was a friar of exceptional talent, an Irishman who had entered the Dominicans at Cashel in Ireland around 1622. He studied in Spain and was ordained deacon and priest at Barcelona in 1630. Later he was a distinguished lecturer at the Dominican *Studia generalia* of Milan, Naples and Rome. He advised several cardinals on theological matters and one of them, Emilio Altieri, became Pope Clement X (1670–6), the pontiff who made Hackett's protégé Howard a cardinal and appointed him as his personal theologian.[14]

An intriguing insight into the relationship between Howard and his mentor is provided by a letter written by John Burbury in Howard's service and addressed to the young man's grandmother. It is dated 17 August 1645.

In the last Holy Week, Mr Philip was very inquisitive after some confessor against Easter Day, and having made choice of me to wait on him for that purpose to the Zoccolanti (Franciscans), where it was said that there was an Irish father, who being then out of town and we demanding if there were no other, they answered yes, and sent us to the Dominicans, where we lighted upon Father John Hacquett, who at the very first sight of Mr Philip was in love with him.

On Easter Day, after that Mr Philip had communicated, he carried us into his chamber and Mr Philip eggs wine and biscuit, and truly did strive very much to make Mr Philip welcome. Afterwards he gave Mr Philip a book of the description of Italy and other parts, and gave him medals and other things, and was very desirous to give him a diamond ring, which Mr Philip refused.

While also my lord stayed in Milan, Father John Hacquett carried Mr Philip into the castle and he being the governor's confessor we had free entrance and saw what was there. He carried Mr Philip likewise to other places, as churches which deserve to be seen, and in all his discourses did seek to draw Mr Philip to their order, telling how many brave saints had been of it, and how many cardinals and such like things. He told Mr Philip likewise that he had been professor of divinity at Padua, and should have three crowns a year of the Venetians, two of which he would give Mr Philip and have such a particular care of him that he would teach himself, and that if Mr Philip should desire to go to Rome, he would get leave to go live there for his sake, or at Antwerp, or at any other place which Mr Philip should like. He told Mr Philip also that he hoped to see him a cardinal, and said to him: you being the third brother, what can you expect? Which sayings Father John Hacquett also thought,

Mr Philip did only let in and out his ears, so I could not but be much amazed when I read in father Rector's letter that Mr Philip had taken the habit of Saint Dominic in the convent of Cremona.[15]

Howard was clothed as a Dominican on 28 June 1645 and took the religious name Thomas, after Aquinas. Like his saintly patron, Howard met with enormous family opposition and despite the fact that it became increasingly clear that Howard's vocation was genuine, the family sought a legal decision in Rome. John Martin Robinson suggests that the opposition may have been as much political as religious. The joining of a religious order, legal death in England, may have been seen by his family as a signal of disloyalty to them at a time when efforts were being made to regain confiscated estates.[16] Nevertheless, interviewed by Pope Innocent X (1644–55), who was impressed by his sincerity, Howard completed his novitiate with the Oratorians in Rome, made his Solemn Profession at S. Clemente, Rome, in 1646 and was ordained priest in 1652 at Rennes in Brittany.

Howard's first dream and greatest practical achievement was the revival of the English Dominicans. The Benedictine tradition had been renewed by the English Catholics in the first quarter of the seventeenth century, but it took longer for the friars to re-establish themselves. By the end of the recusant period the English Carmelites, Franciscans and Dominicans had been successfully restored on the continent and in English missions, if always on a small scale. Howard moved to Flanders, raised £1,600 and acquired a property at Bornhem, four miles north-west of Malines, which became the first English Dominican priory since the Reformation; in 1658 he was elected its first prior. A college was founded attached to the priory, which meant that the Dominicans now had a school for English pupils, run on similar lines to those already established by the seculars, Benedictines and Jesuits. Howard's claustral life proved to be a short one. In Brussels he came into contact with Charles II's English court in exile and as early as 1658 was engaged on a diplomatic mission to England. In 1660 he was involved in the marriage negotiations between Charles and Catherine of Braganza.

He was the only English witness at the royal wedding, which was blessed by his uncle, Lord Aubigny. Resident in London from the Restoration of the monarchy in 1660, Howard succeeded Aubigny as Queen Catherine's grand almoner in 1665. Not yet a cardinal, he lived in princely state in an apartment at Whitehall, with an annual stipend of £500 and a further £500 for domestic expenses. He dressed, out of discretion, not as a Dominican but as a French *abbé*, but was, nevertheless, the only Catholic priest in England allowed to appear in clericals in public. He presided over the services at the queen's chapel in St James's Palace, designed by Inigo Jones and still extant. His family and ecclesiastical contacts made him an indispensable diplomatic go-between and he took on the unofficial and potentially dangerous role of the chief representative of the Catholic party at court. This made his position highly controversial and in 1674, finding himself increasingly unpopular, he was forced to leave on the subterfuge that his 1669 book, *The Method of Saying the Rosary . . . as it is said in Her Majesty's Chapel at St James*, included a copy of an illegal papal bull. In 1672 he had been appointed – unknown to him – as vicar apostolic of England, an appointment regarded as inopportune and held in abeyance. He also played a decisive role in the marriage of James, duke of York (afterwards James II) to Mary of Modena. After the court's princely distractions, he was allowed a year at Bornhem before being made a cardinal by Pope Clement X on 9 June 1675. Howard progressed to Rome, where his first titular church was S. Cecilia and his second S. Maria sopra Minerva. Henceforth he assumed the name of Cardinal of Norfolk, his elder brother having become duke of Norfolk at the Restoration.

Philip Thomas Howard became a very energetic prince of the Church and could as well have been called the Cardinal of England as the Cardinal of Norfolk. He was the first Englishman to be appointed cardinal protector of his native country; the next was Cardinal Weld in the nineteenth century. This involved him granting faculties to priests on the English Mission, dealing with English correspondence (always considerable in Stuart times) and supervising the various English colleges. He was pleased to have extended the feast of the English king Edward the Confessor to the universal calendar, not least since the Confessor is supposed to have predicted a break with Rome and an eventual return to unity.

Howard favoured the simple life of a friar and resided most frequently at the Dominican headquarters at S. Sabina on the Aventine. His usual dress was a Dominican habit worn with a scarlet skullcap. His chief physical memorial is his rebuilding of the Venerable English College, completed in 1685. The design of the new building, adjoining the existing English College and intended for Howard's public life as cardinal, exhibited the grandeur characteristic of the age and may have suggested a triumphalism inappropriate to a humble friar. He took an active interest not only in the college buildings, but also in the students and, in particular, was concerned about the poor quality of English spoken in the continental colleges and abolished the custom of speaking Latin in college 'because these youths were beginning to forget their mother tongue'.[17]

Many visitors, not infrequently English Protestants, came to Howard's *salone* and were struck by his geniality. The ever-informative Bishop Burnet, for example, recorded his very favourable impressions. In 1685 Gilbert Burnet, not yet bishop of Salisbury, was on a visit to Rome. Calling on the cardinal one day, he found him giving some relics to two French gentlemen. Burnet whispered to him that it was odd that a priest of the Church of England should be 'helping them off with the wares of Babylon'. Howard was so pleased with this that he repeated it to the others in French, saying that they should tell their countrymen how bold the heretics, and how mild the cardinals, were at Rome'. Cardinal Howard, Burnet wrote elsewhere,

is too well known in England to need any character from me. The Elevation of his present condition hath not the least changed him, he hath all the sweetness and gentleness of Temper that we saw in him in England & he retains the unaffected simplicity & humility of a friar amidst all the dignity of the Purple, and as he sheweth all the generous care and concern of his countrymen that they can expect from him; so I met with so much of it in so many obliging marks of his goodness for myself, as went far beyond a common civility, that I cannot enough acknowledge it.[18]

In English Church matters Howard was more pragmatic than James II. He was in favour of the division of England into four districts under vicars apostolic which, from 30 June 1688 and for over 150 years thereafter, provided the administrative structure of the English Catholic Church. June 1688 also saw Cardinal Howard host a great feast to celebrate the birth of James Francis Edward, prince of Wales (later the Old Pretender) at which an ox roasted whole and stuffed with lambs and fowl was consumed. The year 1688 was one of ill portent for the Stuart and Catholic cause with the exile from England of James II and the arrival of William III. James II's tactless approach to matters Catholic is revealed in his attempt in 1685 to have his Jesuit adviser and privy councillor, Edward Petre, made a cardinal. Petre has a sinister reputation in much of the historiography of the period and is presented as a fanatical influence on the king but, despite James's support, he had very little chance of receiving the red hat. The Jesuits were out of favour in Rome and James and, by extension, Petre were regarded there as being too pro-French. 'If', as a contemporary put it, 'the Apostles were to come again by way of France they would not here be believed.'[19]

Howard lived long enough to take part in three conclaves, those which elected Innocent XI (1676), Alexander VIII (1689) and Innocent XII (1691), but, at heart, his priorities were first the Dominicans and second the English Mission. The re-establishment of the English Province of the Dominicans and the foundations of the communities at Bornhem and SS. Giovanni e Paolo in Rome, as well as a house for Dominican nuns at Vilvonde in Flanders, were tangible monuments to his work. Cardinal Howard died on 17 June 1694 and was buried in S. Maria sopra Minerva, his titular church, where a simple memorial inscription remains. His Benedictine secretary, Bishop Philip Ellis (1652–1726) was commended by him to the pope shortly before Howard's death, but never attained the red hat.[20] Ellis, a convert to Catholicism, became a monk at St Gregory's, Douai and in 1688 became first vicar apostolic of the Western District. He was prominent in the Stuart court and exiled in 1688. In 1705 he resigned his vicariate and became bishop of Segni, near Rome. Almost fifty years passed before another Englishman was admitted to the Sacred College. The strident baroque Rome of the seventeenth century came to terms in the eighteenth century with the gentler inclinations of enlightenment. Benedict XIV (1740–58) was a lawyer possessed of a subtle mind who saw that his papal world was no longer able to dictate to the states which composed Catholic Europe. Concordats were negotiated and careful arrangements made. It was becoming, however, a dangerous world for the popes. Catholic monarchs sponsored theological positions which minimised papal authority and extolled local anatomy. In France Gallicanism, a proclamation of the Frenchness of the French Church, epitomised this, although the Germans had their own version in Febronianism. Perhaps the Stuarts, so influenced by French exile, might have developed their own Anglo-Gallicanism or Cisalpinism.

Henry, Cardinal York, was the most princely of all the English cardinals by blood and by *de iure* title. The generously named Henry Benedict Thomas Edward Maria Clement Francis Xavier Stuart was born on 6 March 1725 in the Palazzo Muti, hard by the church of SS. Apostoli in Rome. Cannon fire from Castel Sant'Angelo heralded the event. His father was James Francis Edward Stuart (1688–1766), son of King James II, *de iure* James III, known as the Old Pretender or the Chevalier of St George; his mother was Maria Clementina Sobieska, granddaughter of King Jan Sobieski of Poland, the famous vanquisher of the Turks at the gates of Vienna. Their elder son was Charles Edward (1720–88), the Young Pretender, 'Bonnie Prince Charlie', and putative King Charles III. Prince Henry, as he was known until he became a cardinal, was baptised by Pope Benedict XIII and made duke of York by his father. He emerged as a somewhat precious youth whose love of music was his principal interest and, by the age of seventeen, he had become pious and solemn. He spoke English, French and Italian, but regarded himself as English, his Scottish ancestry being given short shrift. In 1745–6 he moved to the north of France to await his brother's call to England, but with the crushing defeat at Culloden he returned to Italy, where he was to spend the rest of his life.

On 3 July 1747 Pope Benedict XIV matched the young man's princely birth by making him a prince of the Church, though he was only twenty-two years old and not yet in Holy Orders. In his titular church, S. Maria in Campitelli, previously known as S. Maria in Portico, daily prayers were said for the conversion of England. It may be noted that Pope Benedict was a man of wide sympathies, described by Horace Walpole as 'a priest without insolence or interest, a prince without favourites, a Pope without nephews'.[21] Benedict XIV, nevertheless, found the young Henry a little tiresome: 'If all the Stuarts were as boring as him', he is reported to have said, 'no wonder the English drove them out.' The young royal cardinal's rise in the ecclesiastical firmament was steady and high. Ordained priest on 1 September 1748, after a crash course in theology, he was consecrated archbishop of Corinth *in partibus* on 19 November 1758. In 1751 he was appointed archpriest of St Peter's Basilica and in 1758 *camerlengo* (chamberlain) of the Roman Church, administering papal property and revenues. In 1763 he became vice chancellor of the Church and in 1803 dean of the Sacred College. In the same year he became cardinal bishop of Ostia and Velletri, but was allowed to continue residing at Frascati (Tusculum) where he had been bishop since 1761.

High among the extinct volcanoes of the Colli Albani, south of Rome, Frascati was the cardinal's favoured residence for most of his life and the town preserves many mementoes of its royal bishop, including his seminary, reorganised in 1770, where he collected 12,000 volumes known as the York Library. His residence, La Rocca, now has a somewhat gloomy aspect, but Henry himself had a sense of style which showed itself in his liking for dressing up; he was particularly proud of his magnificent cross of Sobieski diamonds. In appearance he was slim and elegant, with what James Boswell called 'the face of an angel'. His partiality for the company of handsome young clerics prompted contemporaries to hint that the cardinal might be homosexual, but the evidence suggests that, heedless of the customs that curtsy to kings and the example of his Stuart forebears in particular, he remained chaste.

On the death of Prince Charles Edward, who had frequently lapsed from his Catholicism, the Cardinal of York, as he was invariably known, presided at his funeral and burial at Frascati. The cardinal immediately asserted his hereditary right to the crown of Great Britain. A medal was struck bearing the inscription: 'Henry IX, King of Great Britain, France and Ireland, Defender of the Faith, Cardinal Bishop of Tusculum.' On the reverse a symbolic figure of religion looks at the royal crown and the cardinal's hat lying on the ground with the words 'Not by the Wish of Men, but by the Will of God' inscribed on it. The cardinal showed his royal dignity by touching for the king's evil, the last British 'sovereign' to do so. It is said that among those who came to be touched was George III's brother, the duke of Gloucester. Cardinal York always referred to George III as 'the Elector of Hanover' and, in his armorial bearings, had the royal crown blazoned under his cardinal's hat. To distinguish himself from the ranks of his brother cardinals, he preferred to be known as 'Altezza' rather than 'Eminenza'. It was all rather a sham, but, as James Lees-Milne has suggested, he was a man born to be king: 'of all the pretenders he was the one best qualified for it'.[22] The Cardinal King was the least conspiratorial of the Stuart pretenders. He liked to proclaim his constitutional right to be king, but was not politically aware and did not take an active part in international politics. No rebellion in England attempted to impose him on the English throne. At Frascati he held semi-royal state with courtiers in plenty and servants in livery. Unlike his brother Charles, he enjoyed being the royal patrician, but his personal tastes were generally frugal and, like so many royal personages, rather comfortless. When the comtesse de Boigne was taken to see him in 1792 she found him in his *salotto* with a hood on his head and two overcoats covering him. His hands were in a muff and his feet on a charcoal pan. Yet, he had his extravagances. He had a stable of sixty horses and his coach-and-six was famous for its speed and for its retinue of scarlet-liveried, running footmen.

The disruption of the French Revolutionary wars, arguably the papacy's lowest ebb, uprooted this most regal of cardinals from life in Rome and the Campagna. To many it might have seemed that the papacy was joining the House of Stuart in the dustbin of history. Its re-emergence in the nineteenth century and acquisition of an enhanced spiritual authority was one of the great surprises of the modern era. Cardinal York fled to Naples in 1798, to Sicily and to Venice, where he was much involved in the conclave which elected Pius VII at S. Giorgio Maggiore. His last years were, however, spent in Frascati, the poverty created by the French depredations alleviated by a pension from the British government. Following his death on 13 July 1807, his funeral was held in the church of S. Andrea della Valle in Rome, presided over by Pius VII, accompanied by twenty-seven cardinals. He was buried at St Peter's where a splendid monument to the three exiled Stuart 'kings', James III, Charles III and Henry IX, was erected to the design of Canova in 1819; only James III is referred to by his royal title.

Two of Cardinal York's protégés have small, but historically interesting parts to play in the story of England's cardinals. Charles Erskine was born in Rome on 13 February 1739, the eldest son of a Jacobite exile, Colin Erskine, himself the seventh son of Sir Alexander Erskine of Cambo and of his Italian wife, Agata Gigli.[23] He was educated from 1748 to 1753 at the Scots College, Rome, under Cardinal York's influence, but pursued a legal rather than an ecclesiastical career, becoming a doctor of law in 1770. He had a successful life in the papal service becoming a *monsignore*, a canon of St Peter's and, in 1782, dean of the College of Consistorial Advocates. On 28 August 1783 he was ordained deacon by Cardinal York, beyond which order he did not proceed. He spent a long period, from 1793 to 1801, in London as a semi-official papal agent and was responsible for arranging a requiem Mass for Pope Pius VI at St Patrick's Chapel, Soho. At this event, as at so many in the 1790s, there were many French clergy present; about 7,000 had been exiled to England following the French Civil Constitution of the clergy.[24] One of these, Jean Lefèbvre de Cheverus later became (in 1810) the first bishop of Boston, USA, then bishop of

Montauban in France (1823). In 1826 he became archbishop of Bordeaux and in 1836, shortly before his death, was created cardinal by Pope Leo XII.[25] On 23 February 1801 thirteen cardinals were appointed *in petto* and Erskine was among them. For his last few months in London Erskine was the first cardinal resident in England since Pole. In 1802 he became cardinal deacon of S. Maria in Campitelli, once Cardinal York's titular church, and in 1804 was made protector of Scotland. He died in Paris on 20 March 1811, after a generation of largely frustrated diplomatic work in papal service, under the shadow of the French Revolution and Napoleon, and was buried at the church of Ste Geneviève in Paris.

The second footnote to the history of the Stuart cardinal is provided by Ercole Consalvi, a student of Cardinal York's college at Frascati for five and a half years and whose ecclesiastical career owed much to the Cardinal King's patronage.[26] A skilled lawyer and a man of great charm, by 1792 he was an auditor of the Rota, the principal papal law court. In 1794 he witnessed Cardinal York's meeting with Prince Augustus, duke of Sussex and reported it to Sir John Coxe Hippisley, the British minister in Italy, who (with Consalvi) played a leading part in persuading George III to grant a pension for the would-be Henry IX. In 1799, with the reconquest of Rome from the French, the Union Flag flew briefly on the Roman Capitol for the only time in history. In the same year Pius VI died after a pontificate of twenty-six years, the longest to that date, bringing Consalvi to prominence as the secretary of the Venice conclave. On 11 August 1800 Consalvi was made cardinal deacon of S. Maria ad Martyres, the ancient Pantheon, and appointed secretary of state. As a diplomat he proved himself to have few equals and in the congresses and discussions which followed the defeat of Napoleon it was he who was largely responsible for saving the temporal power of the papacy. In June 1814 he appeared in London in full cardinalatial dress, aiming both to impress and persuade; he managed to do both. Pius VII sent him a note reminding him of the gravity of his mission: 'You are not only charged with a great diplomatic mission, you are at the same time the Representative of the Vicar of Jesus Christ on earth.' Expressing ignorance of the precedent set by Erskine, the pope continued with a plea for the English and Irish Catholics 'who for centuries and from generation to generation have suffered in their goods, their liberty and their rights in order to remain faithful to the ancient faith of their ancestors. You are the first Cardinal, since the reign of Elizabeth, who has obtained permission to set foot on British soil. This privilege obliges us not to close our ears to the cry of the persecuted.'[27]

Consalvi's London visit, which lasted twenty-six days, included several interviews with the foreign secretary, Castlereagh, and one with the Prince Regent, with whom he spoke in French. The Regent was not unaware of the historical significance of their encounter: 'Hush, hush, Cardinal Tempter, when listening to you I seem to see Henry VIII and his daughter Elizabeth following me as avenging spirits.' He also found time for sightseeing and for music and a ball was held at Burlington House in his honour. He remained a devoted anglophile and his friendship with Elizabeth, the widowed duchess of Devonshire, had one important consequence. It was through her good offices that the Stuart Papers, once in the possession of Cardinal York, came into Consalvi's hands and were given to the Prince Regent in thanks for the Regent's service to the Holy See. The handsome portrait of Consalvi in the Waterloo Chamber at Windsor Castle by Sir Thomas Lawrence is a lasting memorial to an Italian cardinal who loved England.

The peace congresses which followed the defeat of Napoleon in 1815, redrew the map of Europe, substituting Austrian for French hegemony in Italy. However, they could not deal with the anomaly of papal temporal power in an increasingly secular world. Backed by wealth from its expanding imperial possessions, Britain emerged as a significant force on the European scene and was recognised as such by papal diplomatists. For its part, the British Government softened its attitude towards Catholics, whether the Irish or Highland Scots it required for military service, or the French monarchists in flight from the Revolution, and consequently softened its attitude towards the papacy. From the 1770s onwards efforts were made towards lightening Catholic disabilities and the creation of an English cardinal as a symbol of reconciliation was an attractive notion, although it would have to be a cardinal resident in Rome rather than in England. Governmental and popular opinion would not tolerate an English Consalvi.

Peter Augustine Baines (1787–1843), born in Lancashire and educated at the English Benedictine monastery at Lamspringe in Germany, became a monk of Ampleforth in 1803 and was ordained priest in 1810. He made his name as a sparkling and controversial preacher at Bath, where he served the Benedictine mission from 1817. He was consecrated as titular Bishop of Siga in 1823 and appointed coadjutor to the vicar apostolic of the Western District, Bishop Peter Bernardine Collingridge, whom he succeeded in 1829. He was often in conflict with his fellow monks and vicars apostolic. He favoured a strong episcopal style and made the headquarters, Prior Park College in Bath, which he founded in 1830, a vision of what an English Roman Catholic centre could be like. In 1826 Baines travelled to Rome on a private visit and, according to Nicholas Wiseman, was favoured by Leo XII (1823–9) for the cardinalate. 'It is evident', Wiseman maintained, suggesting that Leo, a protégé of the Benedictine Pius VII, was seeking a black monk candidate for the purple, 'that Dr Baines would have been made a Cardinal, not on national grounds, but as a Benedictine.'[28] As Cardinal Annibale Della Genga, Leo had been a rival of Consalvi. In spite of his desire for a spiritual rather than political pontificate, this unpopular pontiff was much preoccupied with the Emancipation debate in England. In the event, Baines was not elevated. Nor was John Lingard.

John Lingard (1771–1851), born in Winchester, educated at Douai before and during the French Revolution, was one of the founding fathers of Ushaw College (the northern descendant of the English College, Douai) and for forty years, from 1811 to 1851, the resident Catholic priest at Hornby in Lancashire. Here, refusing high office, he became one of the central figures in the English Catholic 'Enlightenment' and the author of a *History of England*, which was a model of scholarly erudition in his day. Lingard's neglected status as a historian has been pointed out recently by two revisionist scholars, Norman Davies and Edwin Jones, who rate him very highly, especially as a counterweight to what they see as a superficial and still prevalent anglocentricity.[29] His sympathies were somewhat cisalpine, as the English preferred to call Gallicanism, but in 1821, rejecting the title and dignity of *monsignore* as too 'foreign', he was appointed a doctor of divinity, civil and canon law by Pius VII. Five years later there were rumours of a higher honour. In October 1826 Leo XII named his nuncios at Paris, Madrid, Lisbon and Moscow as cardinals, together with several others *reservati in petto*, one of whom was known only as a man of great talents, a most accomplished scholar whose writings had rendered great service to religion. Many, including Lingard himself, much to his discomfort, thought he was about to be elevated. Nicholas Wiseman, on the other hand, considered that the French theologian F. de Lamennais was the secret cardinal. Whatever the true identity, Lingard remained in his Lancastrian fastness. 'Whatever I might have done twenty years ago', he wrote on 27 January 1829 to John Bradley, a priest at Ushaw, 'I should now feel extremely unwilling to go to Rome, and there have to undergo all the fuss and parade, and ceremony of a cardinal's life.'[30]

The man who emerged as the desired symbol of reconciliation was arguably a much less likely candidate than either Baines or Lingard. Thomas Weld (1773–1837) was born at Lulworth in Dorset, the eldest son of another Thomas Weld, a wealthy landowner and one of the great benefactors of the English Catholic community; among other things the elder Thomas presented Stonyhurst to the Jesuits. The younger Thomas was educated privately at home, probably spent a year under Jesuit tutelage at Liège and in 1796 married Lucy Clifford of Tixall, Staffordshire, niece of the 5th Lord Clifford. Along with Manning, he is only one of two English cardinals to have been married and the only one known to have fathered a child in wedlock, a daughter, Mary Lucy. A grandson, William Clifford (1823–93), became bishop of Clifton and played a leading role in the First Vatican Council. Until his father's death the younger Thomas lived the pleasant life of a gentleman at York Place in Clifton and then took on the responsibility for the family estates.

His wife's death in 1815 transformed his life; he decided to take Holy Orders.[31] Weld's life as a Catholic gentleman was typical of his age. The Catholic gentleman, who represented by the beginning of the nineteenth century perhaps one in a hundred of his class, pursued a life similar to those of his contemporaries and was distinguished most clearly by his absence from public life. The Welds were among the largest landowners in Dorset, but remained aloof from political life even if favoured, as they were, by four personal visits from King George III, including one in 1789 when the king visited their recently completed Catholic chapel.

Weld pursued theological studies in Paris under the care of the Abbé Guy Carron, who had spent many years of exile in London during the French Revolution and had a reputation for great personal holiness. Weld was ordained priest in 1821 and went to London as an assistant priest to another French exiled priest, Voyaux de Franous, at the Catholic chapel in Chelsea, now St Mary's, Cadogan Street, built in part for the use of Catholic soldiers in Chelsea. In 1826 Weld was consecrated as Bishop of Amycla and appointed coadjutor to the Vicar Apostolic of Lower Canada, but remained resident in London, the appointment of Catholic bishops in the colonies was a delicate issue in a decade when Catholic Emancipation, achieved in 1829, still remained one of the hottest items on the political agenda. In 1828 Bishop Weld made the Lulworth estate over to his brother Joseph and waited for the call to Canada. Instead there came a call to Rome. On 15 March 1830, perhaps as a token of thanks and recognition for the granting of Emancipation, Thomas Weld was made cardinal priest of S. Marcello. He moved to the city and lived first in the Palazzo Odescalchi. Weld was created cardinal by Pope Pius VIII (1829–30), whose pontificate was one of the shortest of the modern period. Within months there was a papal election. The conclave of 1831 elected Gregory XVI (1831–46), but a possible candidate was Cardinal Giacomo Giustiniani, who had English ancestry; his grandmother was a member of the Clifford family of Chudleigh in Devon, the in-laws of the new Cardinal Weld.[32] A group portrait kept at Ugbrooke, the Clifford house in Devon, depicts the cardinal and his family.

Weld lived in princely state and after the death of his daughter, Mary Lucy, in 1831, he was often seen in the company of one of his six grandchildren. He was, not without cause, known as 'the cardinal of the seven sacraments'. He played as much a part as he could, given his lack of both Italian and theological training, in the life of the Church and was the centre of the English-speaking life of the city. Nicholas Wiseman, rector of the English College during Weld's cardinalate, recalled him fondly:

As his share, the Cardinal brought into his council, sterling good sense and businesslike habits, thorough uprightness and sincere humility; and soon acquired considerable influence in the congregations or departments of ecclesiastical affairs to which he was attached. At the same time he was genuinely courteous, hospitable and obliging. His apartments in the Odescalchi Palace were splendidly furnished and periodically filled with the aristocracy of Rome, native and foreign, and with multitudes of his countrymen, all of whom found him always ready to render them any service. Indeed if he has a fault, it was the excessiveness of his kindness, too often undiscriminating in to objects, and liable to be imposed on by the designing or the unworthy. But surely if one must look back at life's close upon some past frailty, it would not be this defect that would beget most remorse. . . . Seldom has a stranger been more deeply and feelingly regretted by the inhabitants of a city, than was this holy man by the poor of Rome.[33]

At his death, of chronic bronchitis aggravated by an unusually severe fever, he was buried beside his daughter and son-in-law in the church of S. Marcello in Rome.

The last of the exiled cardinals was Charles Januarius Acton, the son of Sir John Francis Acton, sixth baronet of Aldenham Hall, Bridgnorth, Shropshire. If that county connection suggests unsophisticated gentility of the sort typified by Thomas Weld, it would be highly misleading, for the Actons were nothing if not cosmopolitan. The natal and marital genealogies of the cardinal's nephew, the great Liberal historian Lord Acton, most vividly reveal the extent to which they were enmeshed in a pan-European Catholic noble élite. Sir John was a man of considerable ability, which his Catholic allegiance made unavailable to the British Crown. Instead he served as chief minister of the crown of Naples, attracting the allegation that his hold on power was due to being the queen's lover. The future cardinal was born in Naples on 6 March 1806, the second son to be born after the sixty-four-year-old Sir John contracted a marriage with his seventeen-year-old niece.[34] On Sir John's death in 1811, Charles was sent to England alongside his elder brother to be educated at the Abbé Quequet's school at Parsons Green and to another school in Isleworth, both in the western suburbs of London, then with an Anglican clergyman in Kent. In 1819 he proceeded to Cambridge where he was a member of Magdalene College, completing his education but not (being a Catholic) his degree in 1823. As an undergraduate he discovered that discipline was light and that lectures were not compulsory and were poorly attended.[35] Owen Chadwick has remarked that in the conclave following the death of Gregory XVI in 1846 Acton became 'the first and so far only student at Magdalene College, Cambridge to receive a vote in a papal election'.[36] He was the first and last Cambridge-educated English cardinal since Philip Howard.

Charles Acton went from Cambridge to Rome, where he conducted his studies for the priesthood at the Accademia dei Nobili Ecclesiastici and from which he proceeded to the papal court as a chamberlain. He was appointed secretary to Monsignor (afterwards Cardinal) Lambruschini, the papal nuncio at Paris; in 1828 he was nominated vice-legate or governor of Bologna. Rome-based offices followed, including that of secretary to the Disciplina Regolare, the Congregation in charge of religious orders. Gregory XVI, a Camaldolese monk and former abbot of S. Gregorio Magno in Rome, who expressed his hostility to the modern age by banning railways in the Papal States, created Acton a cardinal in 1842. He did not enjoy that dignity for long, for he was a victim of consumption and died in the Jesuit house in Naples on 23 June 1847, after years of failing health. Naples remained his family home and there were requests for him to return there as archbishop; these were resisted and his short life as a cardinal was spent at the curia, 'a meek, unsmiling prelate nurtured in an ecclesiastical conservatism of a Metternichian tinge.[37] His homeland was Italy, but he made several journeys to England in later life, mainly on family business. He was cardinal protector of the Venerabile from 1843 until his death and took a central role in the division of England into eight vicariates in 1840, a prelude, as it happened, to the restoration of the hierarchy in 1850, proposals for which Acton regarded as inopportune. Acton's sphere of operation remained European and Roman. In 1845, for example, he was the interpreter, presumably from French to Italian, for a private meeting between Tsar Nicholas of Russia and the pope. He was the only witness of this meeting and kept his counsel as to its content. By contrast, the later nineteenth-century English cardinals, with the exception of the second Cardinal Howard, were to live their lives on a predominantly English stage.

# FIVE

## *Eminent Victorians*

The Catholic Church in the nineteenth century stood increasingly against the modern world. The forces of enlightenment and, especially, of nationalism threatened the pope's temporal power and pushed the Church towards an increasingly high view of its destiny, unrelated to the world outside it. The key period was the long reign of Pius IX (1846–78). Pio Nono began his pontificate as a political and social liberal but, following the revolutions of 1848, when he was forced into exile at Gaeta in Neapolitan territory while Rome itself became (briefly) a republic, he withdrew into an increasing hostility to change and died as 'the Prisoner of the Vatican', left with only a vestige of territory. The Papal States were crucial, he argued, to the Church: 'the Patrimony of Peter was "the seamless robe of Jesus Christ", committed to each pope as a sacred trust, as the guarantee and defence of the Pope's universal spiritual ministry'.[1] Its protection and a perceived threat to the very future of Christianity led to apocalyptic language and actions. In 1870, at the First Vatican Council, papal infallibility was defined and proclaimed. Pius IX's struggle for the Papal States was seen in microcosm as 'the last heroic stand of Christian civilisation against the forces of atheism and rebellion against God', the temporal power being, in Cardinal Manning's words 'the sign of the freedom, the independence, the sovereignty of the kingdom of God on earth'.[2] 'The Roman question' was one of the great questions of the day: what would be the future of the city and the pope's part in it. The response in many parts of the Church to the threatened status of the pope was an ultramontanism, which exalted the papal mystique and looked to him as the sole source of authority in the Church.

Ultramontanism became associated, too, with a flamboyant and popular piety which expressed itself in the increased devotion to the Sacred Heart and in a rich Marian spirituality which reached its apogee in the apparitions at Lourdes and in the declaration of the doctrine of the Immaculate Conception in 1854. The person of the pope, celebrated in the newspapers and portrayed in cheap prints, became known to all the faithful; Catholicism in Europe and beyond experienced a popular revival, which contrasted sharply with the continuing attacks on Christian credibility. Under Leo XIII (1878–1903) ultramontanism took on a more liberal tone politically and his great encyclical *Rerum novarum* (1891) identified the Church once and for all not with the governing classes alone as a force of social cohesion, but with the poor and dispossessed as a power of revival and justice.

The experience of the English Catholic community reflected the turbulence in Rome. Catholic Emancipation in 1829 was followed in 1850 by a restoration of the Catholic hierarchy. Meanwhile, the Church of England, struggling to rediscover its historic roots, experienced a movement of Catholic revival centred in Oxford which attempted to lessen the reliance of the Church on the secular state. A great debate on the rational basis of the Christian faith and the historicity of the Bible was engendered by the writings of Charles Darwin. The Victorian period was full of dominating personalities and in three of its cardinals, Wiseman, Manning and Newman, the English Catholics experienced the influence of very remarkable and strongly contrasted men.

Nicholas Patrick Wiseman was born in Seville on 2 August 1802. Seville, a city in decline by the time of Wiseman's birth, had a huge ecclesiastical establishment and a sizeable community of Irish exiles, many of them 'hard-headed entrepreneurs who were quick to exploit the opportunities in Atlantic trade which their Spanish counterparts neglected or disdained'.[3] The Wisemans had come

**Cardinal Langham's tomb, Westminster Abbey**
The lavish tomb in St Benedict's Chapel has an alabaster effigy with inlays of blue glass. The medieval grille survives, though the canopy has disappeared. Langham (d. 1376) wears a mitre, rather than a cardinal's hat.
(*Conway Library, Courtauld Institute of Art*)

**Statue of Cardinal Beaufort, St Cross Hospital, Winchester**
Henry of Blois, bishop of Winchester, founded the hospital in 1136, but the present buildings appear to date from Beaufort's refoundation of *c.* 1445. This stone statue is set in a niche on the gatehouse tower, beside two other niches which are now empty, but which may have contained figures of Christ and Henry of Blois. (*John Crook*)

**Cardinal Morton's tomb, Canterbury Cathedral**

Morton (d. 1500) was buried at his own request in a simple grave in the crypt of Canterbury Cathedral. This cenotaph, also situated in the crypt, is decorated with Tudor roses: in death, as in life, the cardinal is associated with the dynasty he served so loyally. (*University of Warwick, History of Art Photograph Collection. Reproduced by kind permission of the Dean and Chapter of Canterbury Cathedral.*)

GUILIELMUS ALANUS, S.R.E. CARDINALIS, S.T.D
*Duac. Archiēpus Mechlin. designatus; obiit Romæ*
*Aº. MDXCIV.*

**Cardinal Allen**

The exiled cardinal is here identified as archbishop-designate of Malines, a see he never actually held. (*Reproduced from B. Ward,* History of St Edmund's College, Old Hall)

Philip Cardinal Howard.
Son of Henry E. of Arundel.

**Cardinal Philip Thomas Howard**

The 'Cardinal of Norfolk', the first of the two Howard cardinals, from the portrait at Arundel Castle (Italian School). (*Photographic Survey, Courtauld Institute of Art. Reproduced by permission of His Grace the Duke of Norfolk.*)

HENRICVS TIT: S.  MARIÆ IN PORTICV
S.R.E.PRESB:CARD:  DVX EBORACENSIS
SACROSANCTÆ BASIL:  VATIC: ARCHIPRESB:

**Cardinal Henry Stuart**
The 'Cardinal King's' portrait appears above a combination of the royal arms and a cardinal's hat, the latter having a modest number of *fiocchi*. (*Drambuie Collection*)

**Cardinal Thomas Weld admitted to the Sacred College**

The painting, by G. Jones R.A., depicts the presentation of the red hat to Weld in the presence not only of the papal court, but of the cardinal's daughter and her family, discreetly positioned behind a curtain. (*Vincent Murphy. Reproduced by permission of Lord Clifford of Chudleigh.*)

**'Mr. Newboy holding up Mr. Wiseboy's tail'**
Newman and Wiseman portrayed in a *Punch* cartoon of 1850, one of the magazine's many visual responses to the restoration of the hierarchy. (Punch, *1850*)

**Cardinal Gasquet**
With Edward, Prince of Wales, at Downside School, Somerset, 1923: the cardinal as patriot. (*Downside Abbey*)

originally from Waterford and the brothers James and Patrick, by the end of the eighteenth century, had become involved in many business activities, including banking and a liquorice factory set up with an English entrepreneur, Nathan Wetherell. The large family house survives in a road now named *Fabiola* in honour of James Wiseman's cardinal son, the author of a historical novel of that title. James Wiseman was married twice, first to Mariana Dunphy, the mother of four daughters, then, after her death, to Xaviera Strange of Aylwardstown Castle, County Kildare, Ireland. The second marriage took place on 18 April 1800 in the suitably mercantile setting of the Catholic chapel on Commercial Road in London's docklands. Nicholas was the second son of the three children of this union. His father's death in 1804 led to his mother's return to Ireland and the family's departure from Spain. In 1810 Nicholas and his brother James were taken to Ushaw in County Durham to begin their education in earnest. Ushaw, dedicated to St Cuthbert, and Old Hall Green, near Ware, in Hertfordshire, dedicated to St Edmund, were the northern and southern heirs to the English College, Douai, which had perished with the French Revolution. He was at Ushaw for almost nine years and although early on he had received the care and patronage of Lingard, who left the college in 1811, he was a shy and awkward student, even if a diligent and dedicated one who had decided to offer himself for the priesthood.

In 1818, at the beginning of the academic year, Wiseman and nine other students entered the Venerabile, the first students there since the French ransacked the college in 1798. He proved himself a brilliant scholar in Rome, especially as an orientalist, publishing his *Horae Syriacae* in 1827, two years after his priestly ordination on 10 March 1825 at the age of twenty-two. In 1827 he was appointed vice rector of the Venerabile and special preacher to the many English visitors to Rome. In 1828 Wiseman became rector of the Venerabile with George Errington, another gifted young man as vice rector. Cardinal Gasquet saw the twelve years of Wiseman's rectorship as 'the golden age of the English College'. His European reputation as a scholar was now being augmented by a growing network of contacts in England, much assisted by his role as agent for the English vicars apostolic. Among those was the ebullient Bishop Baines whose cause he was to foster strenuously; Baines's vision of a renewed Church in England had much in common with his own and in 1834 there was a scheme to bring Wiseman to Prior Park to activate Baines's proposed university.

In 1835, at the height of the Oxford Movement, which was to give two of its members to Rome as cardinals, Wiseman came for a prolonged visit to England; John Henry Newman had visited Wiseman at the Venerabile in 1833. Wiseman's tour of the English Church in 1835–6 exposed him both to the Catholics' immature organisation and to the burgeoning religious energy especially shown by talented converts. 'I cannot tell you', he wrote to his sister in April 1839, 'how anxious I am to quit Rome.' England, he added, 'is in the most interesting condition, and calls for all the exertions of those that wish her well.'[4]

In 1840, as part of the scheme to reinvigorate the vicars apostolic by increasing the number of vicariates from four to eight, Wiseman was appointed coadjutor to be vicar apostolic of the Midland District with the titular see of Melipotamus, and rector of Oscott College in the outskirts of Birmingham, a Catholic college with the potential to be a central force in the English Catholic community. At Oscott, where magnificent Gothic buildings were already in place, Wiseman encouraged university converts and following his change of Church allegiance in 1845, Newman was offered a refuge in the Old Oscott College buildings at what became known as Maryvale. The historian Lord Acton, at Oscott in the 1840s under Wiseman, saw the future cardinal as unconcerned with routine administration (George Errington had been brought in as a prefect of studies and provided the necessary balance), but 'looking far afield, and these other things were what characterised him. We used to see him with Lord Shrewsbury, with O'Connell, with Father Mathew, with a Mesopotamian patriarch, with Newman, with Pugin and we had a feeling that Oscott, next to Pekin, was a centre of the world. I think that this was stimulating and encouraging, and certainly made for his authority.'[5]

In 1847 Wiseman was part of a delegation to Rome to reopen negotiations for the restoration of a Catholic hierarchy in England

and Wales. Cardinal Acton, whose early death in 1847 coincided with the initiative, had been much opposed to any such scheme on the grounds that it would not necessarily benefit the English Catholics to alienate the English Establishment by such an act. Others felt, too, that while the English Mission, with its growing number of educated converts, was crying out for a proper organisation, the English clergy could not furnish enough suitable candidates for the episcopate. In September 1847 on his return to England (he had been appointed pro-vicar apostolic of London while in Rome), Wiseman urged his fellow bishops to sign a petition requesting a hierarchy. By 1848 plans for a hierarchy were in their final stages in Rome and Wiseman found himself as coadjutor to Thomas Walsh, translated to London from the Midlands as vicar apostolic and destined to be archbishop of Westminster; Wiseman was to have right of succession. Walsh's death in 1849 brought Wiseman to the centre of Catholic ecclesiastical power. He was summoned to Rome where Monsignor George Talbot, Pius IX's English confidant and chamberlain, who was never to be elevated to the purple and was to die insane, had been canvassing information on how the English would receive a cardinal. 'I should think English people (*some* Catholics excepted)', Talbot mused, 'would hardly leave their company to receive him at the door and have a red carpet spread for him as in the case of royalty.'[6]

On 29 September 1850 apostolic letters re-established the English hierarchy and named Wiseman as the first archbishop of Westminster. On 30 September, at a consistory, he was created cardinal priest of S. Pudenziana. Three days of celebration followed with receptions arranged by Lord Shrewsbury's daughter, the Princess Doria; all the diplomatic corps in Rome were presented to the new cardinal. In England, there was less celebration and much more open hostility as the contents of Wiseman's pastoral letter, *From without the Flaminian Gate*, dated 7 October 1850, inflamed public opinion and prompted Queen Victoria to ask, 'Am I Queen of England or am I not?'[7] For Wiseman 'Catholic England had been restored to its orbit in the ecclesiastical firmament, from which its light had long vanished, and begins now anew its course of regularly adjusted action round the centre of unity, the source of jurisdiction, of light and of vigour.'[8] To the Prime Minister, Lord John Russell, the act of restoration was the 'aggression of the Pope upon our Protestantism',[9] and he reflected wide-ranging public opinion; on 7 February 1851 the Ecclesiastical Titles Act made it an offence to assume any title outside the Church of England. The duke of Norfolk became an Anglican.

Wiseman, installed as England's only Catholic archbishop and the first cardinal fully resident in England since Pole, was full of grand plans and ambitious proposals. Like all his successors at Westminster, he was metropolitan, but never primate in the way that the pre-Reformation archbishops of Canterbury had been. He loved display and travelled about London in a carriage decked with gorgeous trappings. Robert Browning the poet depicted, in his Bishop Blougram, a caricature of the first cardinal archbishop of Westminster. The waspish Lytton Strachey, reserving his venom for Manning, the first of his *Eminent Victorians*, was kinder to Wiseman:

A man of vast physique – 'your immense', an Irish servant used respectfully to call him – of sanguine temperament, of genial disposition, of versatile capacity, he seemed to have engraved upon the robustness of his English nature the facile, child-like, and expansive qualities of the South. So far from being a Bishop Blougram (as the rumour went) he was, in fact, the very antithesis of that subtle and worldly wise ecclesiastic. He had innocently looked forward all his life to the reunion of England to the See of St Peter, and eventually had come to believe that, in God's hand, he was the instrument destined to bring about the miraculous consummation. . . . He devoted much time and attention to the ceremonial details of his princely office. . . . His leisure hours he spent in the writing of edifying novels, the composition of acrostics in Latin verse, and in playing battledore and shuttlecock with his little nieces. There is, indeed, only one point in which he resembled Bishop Blougram – his love of a good table. Some of Newman's disciples were astounded and grieved to find that he sat

120

down to four courses of fish during Lent. 'I am sorry to say', remarked one of them afterwards, 'that there is a lobster salad side to the cardinal.'[10]

Wiseman's period in office as archbishop, destined to last until 1865, was distinguished by an episcopal style which was both pompous and detached; he never learnt the art of listening and his high-handedness alienated many friends, including George Errington, whose time as Wiseman's coadjutor in Westminster was cut short by the rising influence of Henry Manning. Yet, Wiseman had vision and saw an episcopally led and well-focused Catholic community as an antidote to 'the spirit of the age' and an instrument of transformation which would facilitate the conversion of England. He held a series of provincial synods, beginning in July 1852 at Oscott, which attempted to construct a 'normal' Church. Best remembered for Newman's sermon on 'The Second Spring', preached at the synod and later used as a title to describe the expansive quality of Victorian Catholicism, the meeting also grappled with the problem of Church education and the status of parish clergy. Further provincial synods were held in 1855 and 1859. All revealed the tensions as well as the hopes of a Church which had emerged from its recusant shadows, but was still attempting to find an identity and a united voice. The enthusiasms of 1850 were giving way to a rather dark fatalism, as far as Wiseman was concerned. Endless controversy had dogged attempts to reform ecclesiastical education. His fellow bishops were hardly talking to him. The financial plight of his diocese and of the whole Catholic Church in England remained deeply problematic.

It would give a false impression, however, to dismiss the latter years of the first of the Victorian cardinals as a coda to a life of great promise. His diocese grew in numbers of priests and in confidence. Wiseman encouraged many religious orders of both men and women to his diocese and seems to have been intuitive in recommending the Oratorians to Newman and the Oblates to Manning. He visited Ireland in 1858 and made a triumphal progress; in many senses he had the claim to be the first Irish cardinal. In his declining years he gave active support to the young Herbert Vaughan's plan for a college in London to provide missionaries for the British Empire. He continued to address public meetings; in 1863 he addressed the Royal Institution in London on 'The Point of Contact between Science and Art' and later in the same year he was the principal speaker at the Catholic Congress at Malines. However, his speech on the progress of English Catholicism was overshadowed by the speech of the leading liberal Montalembert on the always vexed question of the pope's temporal power. Wiseman had suffered from diabetes and a weak heart for many years and he died on 15 February 1865. His requiem was in his pro-cathedral of St Mary, Moorfields, on the edge of the City of London and the sermon was preached by Manning, provost of the Westminster Cathedral Chapter. He was buried at Kensal Green and his funeral was compared by *The Times*, so hostile to him in 1850, to the state funeral of the duke of Wellington. The public and the press realised that there was something special about him. He changed the face of the English Catholic community. 'He found them a persecuted sect', wrote Wilfrid Ward, 'he left them a church.' Posterity has allowed Wiseman to become overshadowed by Manning and Newman but, as a prince of the Church, he was their equal. His ideas were a curious blend of the English and the Roman. Derek Holmes assessed him as follows:

Wiseman was a man of wide vision and optimism who did more than anyone else to create the modern English Roman Catholic Church and to avoid the dangers of a native insularity. But he must accept a large part of responsibility for the ultimate success of the Romanizing or Ultramontane policy which did not have entirely happy results. Wiseman and Manning apparently became convinced that when English Catholicism was 'assimilated to the . . . spirit of Rome', it would be better able to influence and share the life of the English people, or at least these two questions were associated in some way. But although English Catholics might gain support and a sense of confidence from the strength of Catholicism abroad, it is difficult to see how they could expect to identify themselves with England and things English by imitating Roman practices and adopting a foreign emphasis which in the event simply alienated Protestant Englishmen.[11]

Wiseman's ultramontanism, reflecting Pius IX's increasing rigidity, was also an antidote to the Cisalpine ecclesiology of the recusant families. Wiseman's flock, swollen by Irish immigration, was a different beast and his care for the poor was to be a feature of all the aspirations of the English cardinals. Indeed, as V.A. McClelland has suggested, 'it was the great achievement of the Roman Catholic Church in England and Wales between 1850 and the death of Manning in 1892, that it became manifestly as conscious of problems engendered by social deprivation outside its own confessional identity as it did of those within.'[12]

Wiseman's Irish background was suitable for an English Catholic community, which, from the 1840s onwards, was becoming increasingly dominated by Irish immigration. What began as a response to the potato famine in 1845–7 continued as a search for employment. In 1887 Wiseman's successor, Manning, reflected that 'I have spent my life in working for the Irish occupation of England'. The census of 1841 showed the number of Irish-born people living in Britain as 419,000, a figure rising to an estimated 714,000 in 1851 and 805,000 in 1861. The Irish congregated in the large cities, especially in the north of England (Liverpool, in particular, became a city with a huge Irish presence) and began to build new churches and schools. Catholicism and the Irish community became closely identified.

Sometimes, as the drive to Irish independence grew stronger and the Church inevitably got drawn into the conflicts, English Catholics of an Irish background could be portrayed as disloyal. In Ireland itself, the Church's leadership received Roman approval with the appointment in 1866 of the first Irish cardinal resident in Ireland – Paul Cullen (1803–78) who was archbishop of Dublin from 1852 to 1878; he was a firm constitutionalist, but a staunch defender of the rights of Irish tenant farmers. His nephew, Patrick Moran (1830–1911), began his episcopal career in Ireland, but in 1884 succeeded Bede Vaughan as archbishop of Sydney, becoming the first Australian cardinal; he was a great advocate of Australian identity and, like his contemporary, Cardinal Manning, a champion of spiritual care.

Henry Edward Manning, the youngest son of William Manning, a West India merchant of London, a Tory MP for almost forty years and governor of the Bank of England in 1812, and his second wife, Mary Hunter of Beech Hall, near Reading, was born at Copped Hall, Totteridge, Hertfordshire, on 15 July 1808. He was educated at Harrow, where he was an undistinguished scholar, but an excellent sportsman: he was in the Harrow Cricket XI for two years. In the Winchester–Harrow match at Lords in 1825 he was dismissed for a duck in the second innings, caught by Christopher Wordsworth, later bishop of Lincoln. Despite such pursuits he was a chronic asthmatic who 'cultivated a sort of arrogant aloofness, which earned him the nickname of 'the general' (which he preferred, it is interesting to note, to the other nickname which accompanied him from home – 'the parson').[13]

In 1827 he went up to Balliol College, Oxford, where he acquired a new seriousness and met up with William Ewart Gladstone, the future prime minister. He worked hard on his classical studies and taught himself Italian in his free time; this was later to be of great use to him. He became a star at the Oxford Union, then in its infancy, and ultimately its president. The glittering prizes of a public career seemed to be in his grasp, but with his father's bankruptcy in 1831 making impossible such a course, he turned to a career in the Church of England and was ordained deacon on 23 December 1832, having been elected a fellow of Merton in April 1832. In 1833 (having been ordained priest) he became rector of Lavington in Sussex and married Caroline Sargent, daughter of John Sargent, an evangelical clergyman with good connections. Manning's was a rapid courtship and a love match, despite W.G. Ward's acid comment that his proposal took the form of the seven words: 'Caroline, I have spoken to your mother.' The death of his wife in 1837, a personal tragedy to him, left him free to pursue with great energy his ecclesiastical interests, which were now developing far beyond his small rectory. In particular, at that time a confidant of Newman, he was moving towards a vision of the English Church which was apostolic and anti-Erastian and, at the same time, encouraging the development of popular education, an abiding interest. Manning's growing status was marked in 1840 by his appointment as archdeacon of Chichester.

Manning's 1840s witnessed the strengthening of his interests and the clarification of his ideas. He evolved a strong social conscience with a real sense of the dignity of the working man and the poor. He preached on the unity and catholicity of the Church and remained, even after Newman's conversion in 1845, an advocate of Anglicanism. Yet, he was increasingly strained in his health and his loyalties and began to show the symptoms of the tuberculosis which had killed his wife; in 1847, he went abroad for the sake of his health. He visited Rome and had a private audience with Pius IX on 11 May 1848, at the very moment the liberal pope was becoming something quite different. In Milan he visited the tomb of S. Carlo Borromeo. There he felt a call from the saint: 'If only I could know that St Charles who represents the Council of Trent was right and we wrong.'[14] His decision to move over to Rome became inevitable when the so-called Gorham Judgment of 1850 showed the Anglican Church, in Manning's eyes, to be at the mercy of state influence. G.C. Gorham, a vicar in the Exeter diocese, had been examined by his bishop, who found him to be unsound on the doctrine of baptismal regeneration. Gorham appealed to the Judicial Committee of the Privy Council which upheld his appointment. The Privy Council had overruled a bishop on a point of theology. The restoration of the Catholic hierarchy in 1850 and its attendant anti-Catholic demonstrations proved to be the last straw. On 6 April 1851 Manning was received into the Roman Communion at the Jesuit church in Farm Street, Mayfair and, with great haste, was ordained priest by Cardinal Wiseman on 14 June 1852. He never looked back.

Manning spent much of the next three years in Rome studying Catholic ways and was attached to the Accademia dei Nobili Ecclesiastici. He was at ease with Pius IX who granted him free access, but found the Accademia unhelpful. In the holidays he returned to England to preach, proselytise and speak, gaining a growing reputation as an apostle for Rome. His intimacy with Wiseman developed and it was the first archbishop of Westminster who found in Manning a priest of kindred spirit if of marked physical contrast (Manning was as lean as Wiseman was fat) who shared his care for the London poor and had the energy in his Oblates of St Charles to put into action Wiseman's dreams. The quick and easy way in which Manning was inserted into the Catholic hierarchy – spectacularly revealed by Pius IX's personal appointment of Manning as the provost of the Westminster Cathedral Chapter in 1857 – made him as many enemies as friends.

The increasingly testy relationship between Manning and Newman was given edge by their increasingly divergent emphasis on the question of the temporal power of the papacy, vital to Manning, who saw the papacy as a bulwark against infidelity, but far less important to Newman, and on their very different approaches to the place of Catholicism in the ancient English universities, especially Oxford, where Newman wished to develop an Oratory. The personal difficulties between the two men were to take on a greater importance when, on the death of Wiseman, Manning became the second archbishop of Westminster. He was consecrated at the Moorfields pro-cathedral on 8 June 1865, with Bishop Bernard Ullathorne of Birmingham as the presiding prelate.

Archbishop Manning attended the First Vatican Council (1869–70) and saw the doctrine of papal infallibility secured and his ultramontane wishes fulfilled. It was the glory of the Catholic Church and the pope which underpinned Manning's exceptionally active episcopate, although it was not until 1865 that he was elevated to the 'sublime dignity of cardinal' and appointed on 29 March titular of the church of S. Gregorio Magno on the Caelian Hill, from which Augustine of Canterbury had been dispatched to England in 596.

Manning displayed a deep care for the poor and to the Irish immigrants who had flooded into England. This paternalistic concern was based on a determination to improve both social conditions and education. He had an acute awareness of the importance of the rise of Irish nationalism. In 1865 Manning's first pastoral letter called for a greater commitment among his co-religionists to the education of the London poor Catholics and a year later he set up a fund to finance schools and orphanages. He was, from the beginning, working alongside (and sometimes in opposition to) the emerging State education system, given substance in the 1870 Education Act. Manning, in his twenty-seven years as archbishop, became a skilled political lobbyist and attempted to plead both for the Catholic voluntary causes and the Irish cause to various governments of very different political views. Education, especially at university level (he established a short-lived Catholic university in Kensington), and a proper training for the parish clergy, who Manning regarded as the key to any real conversion of England, remained his preoccupations, although it was his 'Christian Socialism' and his mediation in the Dock Strike of 1889 which probably remain his most distinctive characteristics; no other English cardinal was so identified with the working class.

In 1880 his Lenten pastoral letter dealt with the growing contrast between poverty and wealth in England: 'not poverty alone, which is an honourable state, when it is honest and inevitable, but also pauperism, which is the corruption of poverty and the debasement of the poor'. In 1884 he became a member of the Royal Commission on the Housing of the Working Classes, on which the prince of Wales, later King Edward VII, also served. During 1887–8, a time of great distress in London, he defended what was called 'Manning's right to thieving', a simple statement that the destitute have a right to claim on the wider community for support. He became an international figure in labour welfare. In 1887 Cardinal Gibbons of Baltimore called on him to appeal against the papal ban on the Knights of Labor, a North American movement of unskilled labourers. Manning's authority helped to reverse the decision. *Rerum novarum* reflected the Church's full approbation of Manning's stance. Cardinals were now able to be champions of the poor as well as of courtiers.

At least two future non-English cardinals were resident for a time in Manning's England. One was the Irishman Joseph MacRory (1861–1945), who taught moral theology and scripture at the St Bernard's Seminary at Olton in the Birmingham diocese from 1887 to 1889 and who eventually, in 1928, became archbishop of Armagh and a cardinal in 1929. The other was Alexis Lépicier (1863–1936) who entered the Servite Order in London in 1878 and was, in 1890, their novice master at Bognor Regis. A noted spiritual writer and teacher, in 1912 he was apostolic visitor to Scotland. Prior general of the Servites from 1913 to 1920, he became a cardinal in 1927 and worked in the Roman curia as prefect of the Congregation for Religious.

Manning's activity was conducted on an energetic level to his very last days. He never took a holiday or a drop of alcohol (his temperance was of an evangelical intensity) and lived in a comfortless barrack-like building in Carlisle Place, Victoria, where his increasingly austere presence presided over what could not be described as convivial gatherings; yet his character was magnetic and his reputation, by the time of his death on 14 January 1892, so great that it meant that his funeral was the most spectacular in London since the duke of Wellington's forty years earlier, outdoing even Wiseman's. In the 1880s the young G.K. Chesterton had seen the venerable cardinal approaching his pro-cathedral in Kensington High Street and described the vision in vivid terms as:

> . . . a ghost clad in flames. Nothing in the shilling paint box had ever spread such a conflagration of scarlet, such lakes of lace . . . with all the glowing draperies like a great crimson cloud of sunset, lifting long frail fingers over the crowd in blessing. And then I looked at his face and was startled with a contrast; for his face was dead pale like ivory and very wrinkled and old, fitted together out of naked nerve and bone and sinew; with hollow eyes in shadow; but not ugly; having in every line the ruin of a great beauty. The face was so extraordinary that for a moment I even forgot such perfectly scrumptious scarlet clothes.[15]

*The Tablet*, more soberly, celebrating his silver jubilee as archbishop concluded:

> To Cardinal Manning more than to any man is due that English Catholics had at last outgrown the narrow cramped life of their past of persecution, and stand in all things on a footing of equality with their fellow-countrymen. . . . An Englishman down to the marrow of his bones, he has always thrown himself into every movement which worked for the greatness and advancement of England. . . . No good cause, from Imperial Federation to Express Postage, ever appealed to him in vain.[16]

Manning's posthumous reputation was immediately damaged by the journalist E.S. Purcell's biography, published in 1896, which presented the cardinal as a schemer fueled by ambition and as a *politique*, themes exploited by Lytton Strachey in his *Eminent Victorians* (1918), which portrayed Manning in the most unfavourable light; Purcell was Strachey's source and inspiration.[17] Rehabilitation has been slow and began in earnest only with Shane Leslie's *Henry Edward Manning* (1921) and V.A. McClelland's *Cardinal Manning: His Public Life and Influence* (1962) and it has been given impetus by James Pereira whose *Cardinal Manning: An Intellectual Biography* (1998) puts Manning's thinking in context and extends his contribution to the world of ideas beyond his most influential published work, *The Eternal Priesthood* (1883). Priesthood was crucial to Manning, whose strategy as a bishop was focused on the raising of the aspiration of the secular clergy, 'Our Lord's own order', by encouraging as great a love for their diocese and bishops as religious orders had for their own institutes and superiors. Robert Gray's popular biography, published in 1985 presents a rounded portrait of the man and David Newsome's *The Convert Cardinals* (1993) illustrates the contrasts and similarities between Newman and Manning. It is the conflict between these two that has concealed Manning's true stature. Manning, whose butler was called Newman, has become all too easy to lampoon since Strachey and the biographical treatment of the two cardinals has encouraged the notion, as Shane Leslie put it, that every good Catholic, at some stage or another, has to pose himself the first question of the Anglican Catechism – 'What is your name? Answer "N or M".'[18]

On 12 May 1879 John Henry Newman was created cardinal deacon of S. Giorgio in Velabro by Pope Leo XIII. His elevation owed much to his English lay friends and in particular to the Howards. It was a recognition of the enormous contribution that Newman, never a bishop, had made to the intellectual and spiritual life of the Church. Already aged seventy-eight, the cardinalate came to Newman late, but it gave him a status within his adopted Church which expressed approval for a life which developed as a constant search for God.

Newman was born on 21 February 1801 in the City of London, the eldest of six children. His father, a banker, was of Dutch ancestry; his mother, Jemima Foundrinier, came from a Huguenot family. He was educated at a private school in Ealing and was admitted to Trinity College, Oxford, in 1816. A sensitive and intelligent child, with a love of music (and especially of playing the violin) he had undergone a deep, personal, evangelical conversion experience before Oxford which made him a convinced Calvinist; to him the elect were always to be a select band. Nervous in disposition, he failed to take a good degree in 1820, but in 1822 he secured a prize fellowship at Oriel College. Oxford was to be his home for the next twenty years and it was with the Oxford Movement that his name was to be intimately linked.

Oriel had a distinguished fellowship and its influence on the Anglican Church of its age was formative. There the Oxford Movement found its heart. What Newman and his associates wanted was a revival of a true Church of England based on Catholic principles, the authority of Church Fathers (in which Newman became deeply read) and free from the State in spiritual matters. John Keble was the poet of the movement, Edward Pusey its most faithful apologist, John Henry Newman its most eloquent proponent. At Oriel Blanco White, whose background resembled Wiseman's, was also a fellow and brought Newman his first contact with a real Catholic priest, even if no longer an active one. Appointed vicar of St Mary the Virgin, the University church, in 1828, its pulpit became Newman's platform. His sermons were beautifully composed and delivered. 'Who can forget the charm of that spiritual apparition, gliding through the dim afternoon light of St Mary's', Matthew Arnold asked, 'rising into the pulpit, and then breaking the silence with a spiritual music, subtle, sweet, mournful?' He published, in collaboration with his friends, a series of pamphlets, known as *Tracts for the Times* which argued for the Catholicity of the Church of England; Newman's party were soon to be known as Tractarians. *Tract 90* in 1841 met with a stormy reception and was seen by many to reveal incipient Romanism.

After 1841 Newman was in personal spiritual turmoil and withdrew to Littlemore, outside Oxford, where he lived quietly with a group of his friends and wrote his book on *The Development of Christian Doctrine*, published in 1845. As with so many of his later writings, this work, with its reflections on tradition and change, was hugely influential. Newman was an instinctive Anglican, but he was becoming convinced that it was only in the Roman fold that he could find catholicity and, crucially for him, apostolicity. He was received into the Catholic Church at Littlemore on 9 October 1845 by Dominic Barberi, an Italian Passionist. His move was a body blow to all his supporters in the Church of England and a surprise to his new co-religionists. In 1846 he spent some months with Wiseman at Oscott; Newman had already come across the future archbishop of Westminster through his writings which, with their learned observations on the apostolicity of the Roman Church, had much impressed the young Oxford don. In the same year he went to Rome, was ordained a priest in the College of Propaganda Fide on 1 June 1847 and made a doctor of divinity by Pius IX. He soon discovered S. Filippo Neri and his Oratory, a Counter-Reformation congregation which had a community life without monastic vows. It was as an Oratorian he returned to England in 1847.

Newman's Oratory in Birmingham was to be his home until his death, with an excursus in Ireland, where he became rector of the Catholic University in Dublin and delivered again the lectures which were to become *The Idea of a University* (1873). The lectures were first delivered in London in 1852. Much of his life was spent in writing, thinking and praying. His poem *The Dream of Gerontius* (1874) was set to music by Elgar and first performed a decade after the cardinal's death. He was engaged in endless controversy. His 1851 *Lectures on the Present Position of Catholics* included a denunciation of a former Catholic priest, G.G. Achilli, who had become a Protestant propagandist and led Newman into a libel trial and a heavy fine. His editorship of the theological periodical *The Rambler* led to intense hostility from some Catholics, who even suggested that Newman was going to return to the Church of England. An attack on him by Charles Kingsley, calling into question Newman's integrity, evinced Newman's most famous work, the *Apologia pro vita sua* (1873), which is a masterpiece of spiritual precision and English prose. In *A Grammar of Assent* (1870) Newman also answered those who regarded infidelity or nationalism as the prevailing nineteenth-century religion. Throughout his writing and his life he retained a strong, personal faith, in which the heart was very important; Newman's cardinalatial motto, *cor ad cor loquitur*, 'heart speaks to heart', summarised his personal philosophy. Over 20,000 letters that Newman wrote survive and are gradually being edited; his contacts were with every corner of the wide Victorian intellectual world.

Newman died on 11 August 1890 and after a requiem in the church of the Birmingham Oratory he was buried at the Oratorian plot at nearby Rednal, in the same grave as Ambrose St John, a fellow Oratorian and one of his closest friends. On his memorial tablet, at his own request, were the words *ex umbris et imaginibus in veritatem*, 'from the shadows and the reflections into the truth'. Newman has had many biographers including two recent studies by Ian Ker[19] and Sheridan Gilley[20] and continues to attract attention and interest. The Catholic Church opened the cause for his beatification in 1958 and it is possible he may become both the second English cardinal to be canonised and the first to be a doctor of the Church. On 22 January 1991 Pope John Paul II signed the document acknowledging his heroic virtue and he was declared

Venerable. Very much a man of his age, a Victorian in outlook and education, his thought transcends not only his time, but many other barriers: he has been claimed as the father of modern Catholic theology and the deepest influence on the Second Vatican Council; he has been presented as a traditionalist Catholic and as a prophet of ecumenism; he has been celebrated both by the Anglican and Roman Catholic Churches. A man for all seasons, Newman is probably the most important of all the English cardinals in his enduring impact and reputation.

Alongside the famous Victorian cardinals, another Englishman, Edward Henry Howard, was elevated to the cardinalate in 1877. The second member of the Howard family to be so honoured, he was born at Nottingham, the eldest son of Edward Gyles Howard, of the Glossop line of the family, and Frances Heneage. He was educated at Oscott, where he was a contemporary of the future Monsignor Talbot and received a commission in the 2nd Life Guards. He was chosen to command the Life Guards, who led the military procession at the funeral of the duke of Wellington in 1852. However, he abandoned his military career in favour of the Church and attended the Accademia dei Nobili Ecclesiastici at the same time as Manning and Herbert Vaughan. He was ordained priest by Cardinal Wiseman at the Venerabile on 8 December 1854, the day on which Pius IX defined the dogma of the Immaculate Conception. Like Vaughan, Howard was dedicated to the foreign missions and acquired proficiency in several oriental languages; he was sent by the pope to Goa to negotiate between the Portuguese and British authorities.

The bulk of his career was not in the East, however, but in Rome, where he continued his interests in mission and in the eastern Churches. He became a confidant of Pius IX and in 1872, was consecrated as Archbishop of Neocaesaria *in partibus*. His rise was rapid. In 1881 he was made archpriest and prefect of St Peter's, having been created cardinal priest of SS. Giovanni e Paolo on the Caelian Hill, on 12 March 1877. He served as protector of the English College in Rome and in 1884 became cardinal bishop of Frascati, the honour previously held by the Cardinal King. He was an aristocratic cardinal of noble appearance and fine bearing, his character caught by Mark Bence-Jones:

As a Prince of the Church, Teddy Howard was still very much the Guards officer, with his great height and powerful build he was the best looking ecclesiastic in Rome. He departed from precedent by going about Rome on foot, in red and gold hat, red-trimmed overcoat and silver-buckled shoes, followed by a liveried footman carrying his prayer books. He was a jovial host at the Villa Vegroni where he lived in some state, entertaining guests of all nationalities and conversing with them in a dozen languages. After luncheon he always took his guests to see his black carriage horses of which he was inordinately proud, bringing an apple with him to give to his favourite. Some people thought him vain; when he stayed with the Denbighs at Newnham the family noticed he would stroke his red stocking and they called it 'the Adoration of the Golden Calf'. But he practised the private austerity of having only one meal a day.[21]

In 1887 he became seriously ill and suffered a breakdown in his mental health. According to Isaacson, 'he lived in strict seclusion' in Brighton and died on 16 September 1892 at Hatch Beauchamp, a villa on the edge of the town.[22] He was given a grand family funeral at the Fitzalan Chapel at Arundel where he was buried. 'The small congregation included the Duke of Norfolk and Lord Edmund Talbot (representing the family), Mgr the Duc de Stacpool and Mgr Lord Petre (representing the Pope) and two privates and a subaltern of the 2nd Life Guards (representing his regiment).'[23] Howard was the English gentleman as cardinal. The worldwide status of the British Empire was shown by the fact that, for a brief time, there were three English cardinals in the Sacred College.

Herbert Alfred Vaughan, the last of the Victorian cardinals and the first child of John and Louisa Elizabeth Vaughan, was born on 15 April 1832 at the appropriately cardinalatial address of Beaufort Buildings in Gloucester. One of his godfathers was Joseph Weld, a great-uncle, brother of Cardinal Weld. The Vaughan family, a recusant tribe, were settled at Courtfield in Monmouthshire. He has some claim to be the first Welsh cardinal. Vaughan's mother, always known as Eliza, came from a Protestant, evangelical background; her maiden name was Rolls. She became a Catholic on her marriage in 1830. Eliza was deeply religious and of her fourteen children eleven entered the religious life: Herbert, the cardinal; Roger Bede (1834– 83), a Benedictine and second archbishop of Sydney; Kenelm (1840–1909), a priest; Joseph (1841–96), a Benedictine; Bernard (1847– 1922), a Jesuit; Bishop John Vaughan (1853–1925); Gwladys (1837–80), a Visitation nun; Helen (1839–61), a Sister of Charity and Clare (1843–62), a Poor Clare.

Herbert Vaughan followed his father to Stonyhurst College, the Jesuit school in Lancashire, but remained there only four years (1841–5) before going to another Jesuit school at Brugelette, near Ath, in Belgium. His thoughts turned to the priesthood, much to his mother's pleasure, but not to his father's, who thought he should have a career as a soldier followed by succession to the Courtfield estate.[25] Herbert wished to learn Welsh to minister to the people of his native country, but this did not happen. Instead, in 1850, he went to Downside, where three of his brothers were to follow him and two to enter the monastery. He was a 'parlour boarder', attending lectures with the monks and also taking part in the school, where he established a debating society. He was handsome and athletic in appearance but suffered from a weak heart. His ecclesiastical studies begun at Downside continued in Rome where he resided for several years at the Accademia dei Nobili Ecclesiastici where, after a difficult start, he became friendly with Manning. He was ordained at Lucca on 28 October 1854 and appointed almost immediately as vice president of St Edmund's College. He had no formal academic qualifications, but prepared for his task by visiting many European seminaries.

St Edmund's was at the centre of Wiseman's plans for romanising the English Catholics and the centre, too, of much controversy. The role of the prominent ultramontane convert and layman W.G. Ward as a professor of theology in the middle 1850s gave rise to much dispute. Even more steam was released by the decision of Vaughan and two other members of the St Edmund's staff to join Wiseman's new group of Oblates of St Charles, under Manning's leadership; a group of secular priests dedicated to the ideals of Wiseman and living as a community. While at Old Hall he worked in various local missions, including Hertford, where a church dedicated in honour of the Immaculate Conception and St Joseph was opened in 1858. It was 'the mission' which increasingly inspired him, as the disputes about jurisdiction and the place of the seminary in the Church led to the removal of Vaughan and the other oblates in 1861.

Vaughan's growing interest in the foreign mission field, a Catholic reflection of the great growth of Protestant missions in the Victorian period, was undaunted by the internal problems of the English Catholics and inspired by the work of Catholic missionaries from other European countries, especially France. In 1860 he visited All Hallows College in Dublin, which trained missionaries for the Irish diaspora, and colleges in France and Italy. In 1863, suffering from ill health and depression, he stayed some time in Seville, residing with the Zuluetas, friends of Wiseman and kinsmen of the future Cardinal Merry del Val. His contacts with the Jesuits in Spain strengthened him in his resolve to pursue his missionary ideal. 'He decided to begin a journey to the Americas in search of funds needed to support the training of priests for the foreign missions. He was inspired by Seville, its cathedral and historic connections with the exploration and evangelisation of the Western hemisphere.'[26]

Embarking from Southampton in December 1863 Vaughan began a great journey which lasted until July 1865. It took him to many countries in South America as well as to the United States and made him the only English cardinal with a wide knowledge of the 'New World'. It also provided him with funds (£11,000 and more) for a new foreign missionary college. Wilfrid Ward commented that Pius IX had advised Vaughan that his trip would achieve nothing in the way of financial reward. Vaughan, on his return, wrote to a friend of the pope: 'Tell his holiness that his blessing was worth more than his prophecy.'[27] A property was acquired in the northern outskirts of London at Mill Hill. At this time he also received the patronage of Mary Elizabeth Herbert (1822–1911), widow of Sydney Herbert,

Lord Herbert of Lea. The Herberts, of Wilton House, near Salisbury, were related to the Vaughans and Lady Herbert was a Catholic convert. She supported all his activities which, despite his always precarious health, multiplied in the 1860s. St Joseph's Missionary College was his chief concern and in June 1869 the foundation stone of a spacious new college was laid. He also founded the Catholic Truth Society in 1868 and took an active part in running *The Tablet*, a Catholic magazine founded in 1840, of which he became proprietor in 1868. Visits to America and Rome were conducted, in search of an appropriate mission field for his missionaries, and recognition for what was to become a new religious congregation, the St Joseph's Missionary Society or Mill Hill Missionaries, with an independent American branch, the Josephites.

Catholic initiatives in overseas missions had been given impetus by Gregory XVI in his *Neminem profecto* (1845), which advocated both local hierarchies and the encouragement of a local clergy. The Catholic Church in Australia, at first manned episcopally by the English Benedictines, had its hierarchical structure in place before England and Wales and, to some extent, provided a model for the 1850 restoration. Colonisation in Africa provided new opportunities for English Protestant and Catholic missionaries, especially after 1885 when the treaty of Berlin divided Africa into different spheres of influence. This made boundaries clearer, but much work had already been done, most noticeably under the inspiration of the Frenchman Cardinal Charles-Martial Lavigerie (1825–92) who, in 1868, had founded his own African missionaries, the White Fathers, but believed that all true missionary activity was best done by natives.

In 1872 Vaughan was given his own personal mission: he was made Bishop of Salford in industrial Lancashire with the pastoral charge of the great city of Manchester. He was consecrated by Manning on 28 October 1872 and the sermon was preached by Bishop Ullathorne of Birmingham, a prelate closely associated with the birth of the Catholic Church in Australia and the doyen of the English hierarchy. Vaughan was bishop of Salford for some twenty years and unaccustomed as he was to the north, he became a much-respected pastor. He engaged in a controversy with the

Jesuits over education in Manchester, which led to a decisive document *Romanos pontifices* (1881) on the religious orders and their place in the structure of the Church. In 1875 he founded St Bede's College, a commercial school, one of the first of its kind, aimed at preparing students of the middle classes destined for business or the professions. In the 1880s Vaughan made the cause of poor Catholic children lost to the Church a very personal one and founded what he called the 'Rescue Society'. Throughout all his diocesan activity he remained superior of his growing missionary congregation.

In March 1892 Vaughan was appointed archbishop of Westminster in succession to Manning, an appointment which came in spite of his own reluctance contained in a letter to Leo XIII:

> The See of Westminster ought to be occupied by a bishop distinguished for some gift of superior learning or by remarkable sanctity, for he ought to be commended to the Church and to the people of England (for whose conversion he may be able to do more than anyone else) by some manifest superiority or excellence. Holy Father, it is no mock modesty or fashion of speech which makes the confession that I have no qualification of learning for such a post. I do not excel as a preacher, an author, a theologian, a philosopher, or even as a classical scholar. Whatever I may be in these matters, in none am I above a poor mediocrity. It will be very easy in such a position as the See of Westminster to compromise the interests of religion in England by errors of judgement – and the very quality of a certain tenacity and determination would make these errors still more serious.[28]

Vaughan was enthroned at the pro-cathedral of Our Lady of Victories in Kensington on 8 May 1892 and received the pallium at the church of the London Oratory on 16 August. Abbot Gasquet preached and Archbishop Edmund Stonor, an English prelate resident in Rome, brought the pallium from the pope. On 16 January 1893 he was created a cardinal by Pope Leo XIII with the title of S. Gregorio, Manning's titular.

In Westminster Vaughan cut a majestic figure, although he could be awkward and dull. He set to work with his usual efficiency and determination. In 1895 the laying of the foundation stone of the new Westminster Cathedral marked the project which would take his whole period in office to complete and was to be a symbol of Catholic resurgence. Some questioned such expenditure on a building, but Vaughan was determined and found in his architect, John Francis Bentley, a man who understood his ideals. He desired a great congregational space and the style chosen, Byzantine, was something new to London. He also wanted a community of monks (either from Downside or the French community at Solesmes) to sing the divine office. He hoped that his cathedral would not only be a showpiece, but a place of prayer and a heart for the diocese.[29]

Vaughan's activities in the direction of relations with other Christian Churches in England were fraught with difficulty. An undoubted triumphalist, he was one with Merry del Val and Gasquet in the rejection of the validity of Anglican Orders in the papal bull *Apostolicae curae* (13 September 1896). He became associated, however, with the beginnings of an official Catholic involvement in the universities of Oxford and Cambridge, so distrusted by Manning, but he was a reluctant moderate whose vision was always inspired by the cause and aggrandisement of Rome. According to Wilfrid Ward, to many Englishmen his red biretta was a 'red rag to the bull'; like Wiseman's it was an embodiment of papal aggression.[30] Vaughan's declining years were darkened by depression and by 1903 'the burden of existence was a terrible trial' for him as 'he moved from place to place seeking somewhere to die in seclusion and repose'. He died, at St Joseph's, Mill Hill, on 19 June 1903. His body was taken to the still incomplete Westminster Cathedral where, at his requiem on 25 June, the eulogy was given by the Benedictine Bishop Cuthbert Hedley of Newport and the final absolution by the Irish primate, Cardinal Logue. His body was then taken on 26 June to Mill Hill where, following another Mass (at which his brother Bernard the Jesuit preached), Vaughan's body was interred in a simple grave on Calvary, as it was called, a site to the north of St Joseph's College. His memorial at Westminster Cathedral is a cenotaph.

Vaughan is a difficult man to assess. His most recent biographer, Robert O'Neil, ends his survey by quoting Vaughan's words over the entrance of St Joseph's College library: 'It doesn't matter who does the work as long as the work gets done.' 'The work', according to O'Neil, 'was to be done, in spite of every obstacle, by apostles in God's service. . . . His words can often chill with their impersonal severity and spirit of self-sacrifice . . . the accomplishments they led to, and their legacy, cannot be denied.'[31] 'If', Derek Holmes concludes, 'Vaughan was not a great man, and he does not appear so at least in comparison with his predecessors, he showed some remarkable qualities as a devoted pastor and able administrator . . . a pattern for later English bishops . . . an Ultramontane descendent of an old Catholic family, who had been a devoted and successful, if uncomplicated, pastor of the Irish in Lancashire.'[32]

The English cardinals of the Victorian Age had formidable opponents – secularism, the cult of reason and poverty among them – but by the end of the nineteenth century the English Catholics were more secure and more settled than they had been for more than three centuries and, for the first time, the cardinals, however ultramontane in their mentality, were thoroughly English, reflecting the self-confidence of the time. The twentieth century, which was to bring greater prosperity and numbers to the English Catholic community, was also to bring new challenges. Cardinal Vaughan marked the end of an era. He had died 'with lucid mind and great fortitude, impressed by the frailty of human faith, tired in spirit and yet attaining an ultimate serenity' on the feast of the Sacred Heart.[33]

# SIX

## Twentieth Century

In the first decade of the twentieth century two English writers, erstwhile friends and collaborators, created fictional English popes: *Hadrian VII*, the semi-autobiographical novel by the would-be cleric Frederick Rolfe, alias Baron Corvo, was published in 1904, followed in 1907 by Robert Hugh Benson's *The Lord of the World*. Beyond the high camp, which led eventually to Peter Luke's adaptation of *Hadrian VII* (1968) for the theatre and witnessed an unprecedented explosion of ecclesiastical scarlet on the London stage, both novels had an apocalyptic ring about them. Rolfe's Hadrian is assassinated by an Irish Republican and Benson's Pope Silvester presides over a dispossessed Church besieged by the Antichrist in the last days of the world.

These books reflect the hostile world of the twentieth century which, especially as far as Europe was concerned, was probably the most tumultuous in history. World wars, the rise and fall of communism, the hydrogen bomb, the genocide of Hitler and Stalin, all cast their shadows across an era which was also marked by a series of technological revolutions which, as the contemporary cliché put it, made the world a smaller, if no less dangerous place. In 1840 Macaulay, the archetypal Whig historian, in a celebrated review of Ranke's history of the popes, had suggested that the papacy, despite the Age of Reason and the Protestant Reformation, had an extraordinary durability: 'and she may still exist in undiminished

141

vigour when some traveller from New Zealand shall, in the midst of a vast solitude, taken his stand on a broken arch of London Bridge to sketch the ruins of St Pauls';[1] and even the twentieth century proved him right.

At one level the popes were confined to the Vatican but, from Paul VI onwards, they were far more mobile than ever before. Nevertheless, they still had the same priorities as in previous centuries: maintaining the integrity of the Church and the territorial independence of the Holy See. The first was reflected in the papacy of Pius X by a renewal of liturgy and church music and a restriction of theological modernism, which bred an atmosphere of suspicion and censure. It was also a factor in John XXIII calling of the Second Vatican Council by, the council which attempted to present the Catholic Church to the modern world. The second priority led in 1929 to the Lateran concordant, which made an accommodation between the papacy and the secular Italian State, in the person of Benito Mussolini, and guaranteed the independence of the Vatican City. It led, too, to an increasing role for Vatican diplomacy in the troubled international affairs of the century, to the peace proposals of Benedict XV in the First World War, to the controversial silence of Pius XII in the Second World War, and to the remorseless energy of John Paul II, who was to play so prominent a part in the collapse of communism.

Tentative diplomatic links between the Holy See and Great Britain, as we have seen, were made during the period of the French Revolution and Napoleon, but it was only in the twentieth century that such relations were made formal. In 1917 a British delegation to the Holy See was established and in 1938 an apostolic delegation was opened in London, becoming a pro-nunciature in 1982 and a nunciature in 1985. By this time the British Government had its own embassy to the Holy See. Growing *rapprochement* was shown in royal visits to Rome and the unprecedented visit of Pope John Paul II to England in 1978. Improved communication between the Church of England and the Catholic Church reflected a growing mood of public cooperation. While the leaders of the English Churches gradually grew together, the English cardinals of the twentieth century, from Vaughan onwards, began to identify themselves more closely with the English people as a whole, a process which reached its apogee with Cardinal Basil Hume.

The vacancy at Westminster caused by Vaughan's death in 1903 led the Westminster Chapter to select a *terna*, a list of three candidates, which, in the event, had two future cardinals on it, but no archbishop of Westminster. The three names were Rafael Merry del Val, Aidan Gasquet and Cuthbert Hedley. Merry del Val and Gasquet were both to receive the red hat. Rome chose Francis Bourne for Westminster on the grounds that Merry del Val was not English enough and that the other two were Benedictines. Bourne's appointment owed much to the influence of the octogenarian, Irish-born archbishop of Sydney, Cardinal Patrick Moran, who had succeeded the English Benedictine Bede Vaughan, brother of Herbert, as archbishop and had an aversion to both Englishmen and Benedictines.[2]

Merry del Val saw himself as 'English to all intents and purposes', but it was a tenuous Englishness, rather similar to that of Wiseman. Rafael Merry del Val was born in London on 11 October 1865, the son of a diplomat. The Merry family traced their descent from the O'Hollichans of Hy-Main in Connaught who adopted the name Merry. One branch of the family, previously established in Waterford, settled in Seville, where they were merchants. The future cardinal's great-grandfather, Pedro Juan de Zulueta, was an émigré in London and his grandfather, Pedro José de Zulueta, joined the Church of England. Through his grandmother Merry del Val also had Scottish and Dutch ancestry. Rafael's background had its surprises, but his own career was typical of a well-born cleric of his time, although its conclusion was particularly successful. Educated in England and Belgium, he studied as a seminarian at Ushaw College and then transferred, in 1885, to the Scots College in Rome, from which he was removed to the Accademia dei Nobili Ecclesiastici, where he was ordained priest (for the archdiocese of Westminster) on 30 December 1888. He was never to serve in England. His whole career was that of a consummate politician in the papal diplomatic service. He was appointed on missions to

London, Berlin and Vienna and in 1897 he was apostolic delegate to Canada. In 1899 he became rector of the Accademia dei Nobili Ecclesiastici and in 1900 titular archbishop of Nicaea. He was secretary of the conclave in 1903 which elected Cardinal Sarto, as Pius X. Guiseppe Melchiore Sarto (1835–1914), who had been patriarch of Venice since 1893, was of humble origins, but was a man of high religious principles; his motto was an uncompromising 'to restore all things in Christ' (Eph. 1:10). Merry del Val was to be his right-hand man. He became both secretary of state and cardinal within a few months of the conclave. He served his master well both in foreign affairs and in his assiduous work in maintaining Church order.

Merry del Val abandoned any attempt at 'accommodation in Europe, North and South America, and the East'. Instead, with Pius X's blessing, he refocused the Church's attention on the conscience of the faithful.

In concert with the infallibility and jurisdiction definitions of the First Vatican Council, Merry del Val and Pius strove to substitute control over what its members believed for direct influence on the legislation and administration of countries now outside its power. 'Foreign' policy under Merry del Val became an anti-Modernist campaign to protect the substance of faith. Under his secretariat, the collapse of the Church State in 1870, a product of the previous seventy years, became no longer an interlude but an accepted state of affairs. For the sake of an anti-Modernist programme that had been under preparation for half a century, if not longer, Merry del Val went to war over a Modernist 'crisis' of which he was at least one of the authors, if not the chief motivator.[4]

Relations with Republican France were particularly poor and on 30 July 1904 there was a formal diplomatic break between the Holy See and France, where the ministry of Émile Combes (1902–5) was fiercely anticlerical and anti-Catholic. Pius X and Merry del Val did not wish to reach any compromises and their stand undermined the finances, if not the integrity, of the French Church. They were staunch opponents of the separation of Church and State in Portugal (1911) and advocates of the minority rights of the Poles and the Irish. Only in Italy was there a significant move in the direction of conciliation with the post-Risorgimento State. No ground was given on the 'Roman Question', but on 11 June 1905 Pius X relaxed his predecessor's ban on Catholic participation in elections.

No relaxation was experienced in the world of theology and open Catholic thinking. As patriarch of Venice Pius X had looked with suspicion on any liberating tendencies and, as pope, ably supported by Merry del Val, rigorous methods were applied to keep modernism under control. In the decree *Lamentabili* (3 July 1907) 'modernism' was branded as a 'synthesis of all heresies' and the encyclical *Pascendi* (8 September 1907) became the blueprint of a new orthodoxy. The *motu proprio* (papal letter) *Sacrorum antistitum* (1 September 1910) imposed an anti-modernist oath on all Catholic clergy. There was a strong anti-intellectual current in the Church and a witch-hunt ensued: in England the principal victim was the Jesuit George Tyrell. In 1907, when the English bishops sent a joint letter of submission to the Holy See following *Pascendi*, Merry del Val could still find fault with 'one sentence which does not come very opportunely now. I mean where it is said that there is little or nothing of modernism among Roman Catholics – there are not many English Modernists, there is quite a sufficient number of them.'[5]

Merry del Val, who had (and has) a following among many 'traditionalist' Catholics (the opening of his cause for beatification began as early as 1953) as the exemplar of a pure, integral Catholicism, had no time for overtures to English Protestants. *Rapprochement* between the Church of England and the Roman Catholic Church centred on the place of the Anglican clergy and their Orders and some proto-ecumenists, including the French Abbé Portal and the English Lord Halifax, looked hopefully to Rome for a favourable judgement. A decision on the validity of Anglican Orders was made in 1896 in the bull *Apostolicae curae*, drafted by Merry del Val and much influenced by Cardinals Gasquet and Vaughan, following a much less decisive commission: Anglican Orders were declared 'absolutely null and utterly void'. With the death of Pius X in August 1914, Merry del Val's influence was on the wane and Benedict XV (1914) appointed Merry del Val's rival Pietro Gasparri as secretary of state. Under him, a more moderating policy prevailed. Merry del Val lived on until 1930, dutifully carrying out his responsibilities as archpriest of St Peter's and his many other activities. He was buried in the grotto of St Peter's Basilica at the foot of Pius X's tomb. He had combined the grandeur of a prince of the Church with a simple, traditional piety. He also exhibited an impeccable loyalty to the pope and an unbending attitude to what he conceived as the eternal deposit of faith.

Truth was perhaps more of a problem for Aidan Gasquet, made a cardinal in 1914 as a reward in part for his celebrity as a historian. Gasquet, unlike Merry del Val, played the English gentleman cardinal to the manner born; English visitors to Rome were reassured that his study was 'quite like an English room', and the formidable Eugénie Strong, of the British School at Rome, recommended always kissing the ring of Merry del Val but never Gasquet's: he was 'too English and preferred to shake hands'.[6]

Francis Neil Gasquet (always known to his friends as Frank; Aidan was his name in religion) was born on 5 October 1846 in Somers Town, north London, the third son among six children of Raymond Gasquet, whose father had been a refugee from the French Revolution. His mother, Mary Apollonia Kay, was of Yorkshire origin. Gasquet's home parish had been established by the Abbé Carron, who had been charged with the ecclesiastical education of Cardinal Weld. After his father's death in 1856 Gasquet's family became parishioners of Henry Edward Manning at Bayswater, where the young Frank acted as server to Manning and as train-bearer to Cardinal Wiseman, whose master of ceremonies, Monsignor Edmund Stonor, 'directed ceremonies as they were wont to be in Rome'.

Gasquet was educated by the Benedictines at Downside in Somerset, a community much associated at the time of his arrival (1862) with the Australian Church and the erection of its hierarchy. It was Archbishop Bede Vaughan who inspired his vocation to the

Benedictine life and led, in 1866, to his admission as a novice. His education for the priesthood was entirely with the monks, at Downside itself and at Belmont, the Benedictine house of studies near Hereford. Many of the Downside monks lived and worked on 'the mission', in parishes, and the younger members of the community were charged with the house's administration. Gasquet, having served as prefect of studies, or headmaster, of the school and as 'professor' of theology in the monastery, was elected as prior, or religious superior, in 1878. Gasquet's term of office, which ended in 1885, coincided with the 1880 celebration of the fourteenth centenary of St Benedict's birth and was part of the Benedictine reform movement which was Europe-wide and, as far as England was concerned, had its heart at Downside. This reform looked to a rediscovered sense of monastic identity and a proper understanding of the Benedictine charism. It was, in part, a response to secularism; monasticism offering an antidote to contemporary values and a radical alternative. Its character could best be discerned by a renewed look at monastic history.

The study of the past had long been part of Benedictine activity, but Pope Leo XIII's call for monastic historians in the brief *Saepenumero* (18 August 1883) led to the foundation of a house of historical studies in London under the patronage of Cardinal Manning and the duke of Norfolk. Gasquet was assigned to this work; he had already dabbled in historical writing and it was now to be his principal occupation. His mentor was Edmund Bishop, the pioneering liturgical scholar long associated with the Downside community. His intentions were ambitious and were reflected in extended research visits to the British Museum and the Public Record Office, together with a fully researched, fully documented historiography. Publications proliferated and honours followed. In 1891 he was awarded a Roman DD by Leo XIII. On being admitted to the degree by Manning the only available biretta was the cardinal's own: 'The colour does not matter', said the cardinal putting it on Gasquet's head, 'and perhaps some day you will get one like it.'

All, however, was not well with Gasquet's scholarship. New sources had indeed been exploited and a solid narrative style presented findings with suitable panache, but the works were undermined by numerous small errors and, some of his critics felt, falsehoods introduced to represent the Church in the best possible light. The Cambridge medievalist, G.G. Coulton (1858–1947) conducted a crusade against Gasquet's scholarship and Dom David Knowles, another Downside monk and the greatest of twentieth-century English monastic historians, in a celebrated lecture, regarded Gasquet's capacity for carelessness as amounting almost to genius. Nevertheless, as even Knowles admitted, 'If it is perilous to accept Gasquet uncritically, it is foolish utterly to neglect or despise him.'

He was, for example, the first historian of the dissolution of the monasteries to explore methodically the pages of Thomas Cromwell and the Court of Augmentations, as well as the pension lists of Cardinal Pole. He was probably also the first to appreciate the value of using medieval books as evidence of the tastes and interests of their scribes and to use medieval sermon notes. He was the first, too, to stress the importance of the Black Death in the medieval world and to reveal the particular strength of its English documentation.[7]

Whatever his subsequent reputation, Rome thought highly of him and he played a central role in the commission on Anglican Orders in 1896. In his capacity as abbot president of the English Benedictines, from 1900 to 1914, he was charged with implementing the reformed constitutions of 1899, which restored the abbatial system of government to the English monasteries. In 1907 he was appointed chairman of the Vulgate commission by Pius X and in 1917 prefect of the archives of the Holy See; in 1919 he became librarian of the Holy Roman Church. Shortly before Pius X's death in 1914 Gasquet was made a cardinal.

Benedict XV's successor, Achille Ratti, who became pope in 1922, had also been a Vatican librarian but, elected in the fourteenth ballot, he was known as a difficult man prone to rages. It was an indication of Gasquet's personality that he once reflected to the pope: 'well, we are none of us infallible', a phrase he may also have said to Benedict XV. His wit, self-congratulatory and Johnsonian perhaps, had also been reflected in a contretemps with the archivist of the Inquisition who had refused Gasquet access to documents in his collection. A letter to the pope followed and a summons to an audience. 'Why do you write to me like that?' 'I had to', replied Gasquet, 'I thought your Holiness was master of the archive of the Inquisition. I was wrong.' The pope then ordered the relevant pages to be released. The former Cardinal Ratti was no stranger to English scholars and scholarship, having been admitted as a reader at the Bodleian Library in 1914.

As a cardinal *in curia* during the First World War Gasquet pursued a patriotic stance, defending English interests with vigour. This isolated him from the mainstream. Benedict XV was a man of peace and some accused him of being pro-German; his seven-point peace plan of August 1917 proposed a peace based on justice rather than military victory, but it came to nothing. It was clear, on the other hand, that Benedict, preoccupied with the Roman Question, was attracted by Germany's offer of a return of Rome to the papacy following an Italian defeat. Gasquet saw no attraction in that proposal. The only cardinal prepared to dine with Gasquet was Merry del Val. Cardinal Hartmann, archbishop of Cologne, reflected to Gasquet: 'Eminence, I will not insult you by talking of the war.' 'Eminence', replied Gasquet, 'I will not mock you by talking about peace.' When he took possession of his titular church, S. Maria in Campitelli, so long associated with English cardinals, Gasquet declared that 'we are fighting for the Might of Right not for the Right of Might'. Gasquet's unequal pursuit of the allied interest in Rome put him in a strong position to pursue improved relations with the British Government. He acted as a link with the English special envoy and plenipotentiary, Sir Henry Howard, who arrived in Rome in 1914, and played host to many receptions at his residence, the Palazzo S. Callisto. In 1923 the cardinal was prominent in the welcome given in Rome to King George V and Queen Mary. In his love of country Gasquet was to be in line with many other twentieth-century cardinals – Bourne, Hinsley and Hume in particular.

Gasquet identified himself with the English colleges in Rome, the Venerabile and the Beda, the latter established in the late nineteenth century for the training of convert Anglican clergymen. He played a crucial part in the visitation of the Venerabile in 1916 and the appointment of Arthur Hinsley as rector. He also acted as an intermediary between the Holy See and the English bishops and seemed to be on good terms with many of them. By his death in 1929 he had carved out for himself a highly influential role in the English Church. His exotic tomb at Downside, a 1930s confection by Sir Giles Gilbert Scott, is the most magnificent memorial to any modern cardinal. It reflects his flamboyant and dignified character and the great esteem he was held in at the time. However, he is now largely forgotten.

Francis Alphonsus Bourne, who succeeded Vaughan in 1903 as Archbishop of Westminster, was as dignified as Gasquet, and was said to have celebrated Mass with the greatest of unction (he was the first to have Westminster Cathedral at his disposal), but had a colourless personality, 'the quiet cardinal', whose two-volume biography by Ernest Oldmeadow reveals little of the inner man.[8] Bourne was a native of Clapham where he was born on 23 March 1861, the younger son of Henry Bourne, who worked for the Post Office, and of his wife Ellen, daughter of John Byrne of Dublin. His childhood and education made him the perfect ecclesiastic: he exuded a clericalism which represented the priestly ideals of the time. He was educated briefly at Ushaw, then at St Edmund's, Ware, to which he had a lifelong devotion, and at St Thomas's Seminary, Hammersmith. It was at Saint-Sulpice in Paris that he completed his training and was ordained deacon in 1883. The Sulpician style of devotion and liturgical exactitude set him apart from those who trained in Rome and his international outlook, completed by a few months at Louvain before his priestly ordination in 1884, had nothing of the Roman in it. As a bishop his non-Roman background came to the fore; he had no enthusiasm for the modernist persecution and, in consequence, his cardinal's hat was a long time in coming. The distinguished Jesuit Father Cyril Martindale reflected: 'He reminded me of great French ecclesiastics, with a period dignity linked to an exalted sense of his ecclesiastical position: not asking to be understood by men, and not always understanding them.'[9]

Bourne was not a brilliant student, writer or preacher but he had a great devotion to the education of the young and the encouragement of vocations. In 1891 he was appointed by Bishop John Butt to be the first rector of a new seminary for his diocese, Southwark, at Wonersh, near Guildford. Bourne was charged with the vital work of the building of a seminary, in partnership with his bishop, who soon nominated Bourne as his coadjutor with right of succession.[10] Rome agreed to Bourne's appointment and he was consecrated titular Bishop of Epiphania by Cardinal Vaughan in 1896. A year later, still in his mid-thirties, he succeeded Butt as bishop of Southwark and moved to Lambeth where his house adjoined St George's Cathedral. It was from here, in August 1903, that he was translated to Westminster.

In 1903 Westminster was seen as the key diocese, partly because it was in London, but also especially because it was not until 1911 that other metropolitan sees were created. The whole of Bourne's episcopate was overshadowed by the stand-off between the archbishop and his successor at Southwark, Peter Amigo, over Bourne's desire to make London one large diocese, eliminating Southwark.[11] Catholic politics remained an issue throughout his career and Amigo's friends in Rome probably delayed his appointment as a cardinal by Pope Pius X, to November 1911; his titular church, like Wiseman's, was S. Pudenziana. Bourne's promotion followed the great success of the Roman Catholic International Eucharistic Congress in London in 1908, a politically sensitive event, but a great public act of Catholic triumphalism. This congress, the nineteenth of its kind but the first in England, received huge coverage in the press on account of the proposed procession of the Blessed Sacrament around Westminster Cathedral. The incipient anti-Catholicism traditional in England since the Reformation received its last major outing. Bourne's words were not always helpful. Referring to Anglican churches as places of worship he declared:

Every one of our old churches, cold and empty as they now appear in our eyes, testifies by its forlorn condition to the worship

151

which once gave it life. Mass and Holy Communion gave meaning to these churches, as they meant spiritual life to those who worshipped within their beautiful walls.

Protestant extremists, royal disquiet from King Edward VII and public opinion led Herbert Asquith, the Prime Minister, to fear a serious disturbance precipitated by 'this gang of foreign cardinals taking advantage of our hospitality to parade their idolatries through the streets of London: a thing without precedent since the days of Bloody Mary'. The triumphalism of the procession was reduced, but it went ahead.[12] 1908 was, too, the year in which the papal constitution *Sapienti consilio* declared that England was no longer a mission territory directly answerable to Propaganda Fide.

Bourne's quiet persistence was of great importance in the education issue, maintaining and strengthening the Catholic voluntary school sector. He had a great commitment to Catholic secondary education and during his episcopate many Catholic grammar schools were established. He was the leading English advocate of the new Salesian teaching congregation of St John Bosco (1815–88), which he introduced to the Southwark diocese. He also attempted to make St Edmund's, his diocesan college, into a great school and a renewed seminary. Substantial buildings were erected, a great personal interest maintained and gifted teachers recruited. These included Ronald Knox, the convert son of the bishop of Manchester, who was one of the wittiest priests of his generation.[13]

Bourne's political stand for Catholic education was backed up, in the First World War and after, by a deep patriotism. He encouraged the officer training corps at St Edmund's and wrote a pamphlet for the Duty and Discipline Movement on the necessity and desirability of universal military training. Bourne attempted to emphasise Catholic loyalty in the First World War at a time when Benedict XV's neutrality and the wartime politics of Irish nationalism put it into doubt. In March 1917 he consecrated the armies of Britain, France and Italy to the Sacred Heart. As a Francophile and as an English Catholic nationalist he saw the Germans as neo-pagan, Protestant despoilers of Catholic Belgium, Poland and France. His wartime stand secured his French credentials and in May 1931 he acted as cardinal legate at Rouen for the celebrations surrounding the canonisation of Joan of Arc.

His attitude to Irish independence, an issue which came into sharp focus with the emergence of the Irish Free State, remained ambiguous: he was deeply committed to the idea of the British Empire. 'The protection of the Empire', he said, 'is as important for Ireland as for us: and it is as important for civilisation, I think, as for us both. Given *that*, I am for Irish self-government as far as the Irish people themselves desire it. I want England to trust Ireland and Ireland to trust England, for I love them both as I love justice and peace.'[14]

He believed in order and in 1926, at a Mass at Westminster Cathedral, he condemned the General Strike of that year in no uncertain terms:

There is no moral justification for a general strike of this character. It is a direct challenge to a lawfully constituted authority and inflicts, without adequate reason, immense discomfort and injury on millions of our fellow-countrymen. It is therefore a sin against the obedience which we owe to God, who is the source of that authority; and against the charity and brotherly love which are due to our brethren.[15]

Bourne was archbishop of Westminster for over thirty-one years, the longest tenure of any of the holders of the see. His public impact was relatively small, but the development of a Catholic infrastructure of parishes and schools in his diocese and beyond marked the major achievement of his quiet episcopate. He died on 1 January 1935. He was buried at St Edmund's College, Ware, in a simple tomb, and his heart was taken to Wonersh.

Bourne received an honorary doctorate from Oxford, but not from Cambridge, where Coulton and his supporters blocked such degrees for both Gasquet and Bourne. In contrast, Cardinal Hinsley, Bourne's successor at Westminster, was celebrated as 'the great Englishman' when he received his DCL from Oxford. Hinsley's public profile was high indeed.[16] His career was varied and had great highs and lows before his appointment to Westminster in

1935. Like Bourne, Hinsley had an Irish mother. He was born at Carlton, near Selby, in Yorkshire, on a Howard estate, the second son of a carpenter, Thomas Hinsley and his wife Bridget, daughter of John Ryan, a farmer from Cloonascragh, Tuam. He attended a local Catholic elementary school and then, aged eleven, he proceeded to Ushaw to study for the priesthood. In the last quarter of the nineteenth century a number of Catholic colleges affiliated themselves with the University of London and he took his BA degree in 1889. He was only one of three twentieth-century English cardinals to have a degree from an English university; the others, Heard and Hume, were Oxford graduates. After Ushaw he went to the Venerabile and graduated DD at Rome's Gregorian University. He was ordained priest on 23 December 1893 and taught at Ushaw until 1897. He was an assistant priest at Keighley, Yorkshire, from 1897 until 1899, when he became the first headmaster of St Bede's Grammar School in Bradford, a Catholic school. Following a disagreement with his bishop, he transferred to the diocese of Southwark in 1904 where he taught at Wonersh and administered parishes at Sutton Park (1904–11) and Sydenham (1911–17). He became close to Bishop Amigo and to Cardinal Gasquet, who admired his Yorkshire bluntness.

Hinsley was a great rector of the Venerabile from 1917 to 1927: 'the boss' to his students, the saviour of the college's buildings from Mussolini's scheme for a street market, the purchaser of the college's summer residence at Palazzola and, most important, the dispenser of *romanità* to a generation of future English bishops, including Cardinals Griffin and Heenan. It was said that to be a Catholic bishop in England you had to be male, celibate and a former student of the Venerabile; the first two can be dispensed, but not the third.[17] Hinsley's distinction was recognised by his consecration as titular bishop of Sebastapol by Cardinal Merry del Val in 1926, a prelude to his work in Africa in 1927 as visitor apostolic, and in 1930 as apostolic delegate, by which time he was based in Mombasa and held the title of archbishop of Sardis. His principal work was to bring the various missionary schools in line with the standards set by the British colonial officials. By 1934, when he was forced to leave Africa with an attack of paratyphoid, Hinsley had emerged as a gifted and diplomatic liaison between the Catholic Church and the British Government; it might have appeared as the end of a distinguished career, especially given his appointment to what could appear to be the sinecure of a canonry of St Peter's, Rome.

However, in 1935 he was appointed archbishop of Westminster by Pius XI and, in December 1937, was created cardinal priest of S. Susanna by the same pope. As archbishop he continued the work of Bourne in the pursuit of Catholic education, but he was prepared to use new methods. A stranger to the diocese, he developed a personal and direct style in dealing with his priests. He built up a small group of personal advisors, a kitchen cabinet, of men of talent who included David Mathew, historian and future archbishop, Val Elwes, later Catholic chaplain at Oxford, and the young John Heenan, who was to become his biographer. Indeed, writing to the historian Christopher Dawson in 1941, Hinsley reflected of the young John Heenan that 'he knows his theology and he knows my mind'.[18] As diocesan, following the quiet years of Bourne, he sought action and wide consultation. He encouraged 'Catholic Action', the movement to involve the laity in the invigorating of the Church's grass roots. He set up a diocesan council, a finance committee and a schools commission, on which laymen as well as clergy served.

It was not, however, Hinsley's vision and achievements as a bishop which made his reputation, but his interest in international affairs, given focus by the Second World War. He had great experience of dealing with the British Government from his time in Africa, but his activities were never narrowly patriotic or political. He became a noted wartime broadcaster and saw England as a bulwark against disorder, but he appreciated a bigger picture and saw the world of his day locked in a conflict between Christ and Antichrist. It could be a black and white vision and he had some perhaps unlikely heroes; a photograph of Franco, to him the defender of Christian Spain, remained on his desk until his death.[19] 'The Sword of the Spirit' movement, launched with the fall of France in 1940, stood for civilisation against disorder and the cardinal was pleased to be in concert with the archbishop of Canterbury in what were to be the first faltering steps in the direction of ecumenical dialogue.

Hinsley's celebrity, by the time of his death in 1943, was considerable. Churchill, looking for a new archbishop of Canterbury, is said to have mused that it was 'a pity we can't have the old man at Westminster'. A diarist of the time and Conservative MP, Cuthbert Headlam (1876–1964) put it well:

*Tuesday 23 March*   I have just been listening to the BBC recording of the Requiem Mass for Cardinal Hinsley. . . . Hinsley is a real national loss – a big man – a patriot and a great churchman. It is amazing how quickly he made himself felt here – one read his speeches and pronouncements with such admiration and respect because one seemed to feel his absolute sincerity and complete disinterestedness – there is nothing of the politician about the man – one could regard him as a leader and a real exponent of Christian tradition and principle.[20]

Bernard William Griffin, born in Birmingham on 21 February 1899, was the twin son of William Griffin, a cycle manufacturer's manager, and his wife Helen Swadkins.[21] He was one of five children. He entered the junior seminary at Cotton College in 1913 soon after his twin, Walter, had begun his education at Douai Abbey, where he eventually became a Benedictine monk. Between 1917 and 1919 the future cardinal served in the Royal Naval Air Service and the Royal Air Force before continuing his studies at the Venerabile, where Hinsley was then rector. Ordained priest in 1924 and graduating as a doctor in both divinity and canon law, he returned to Birmingham where he pursued a career as an ecclesiastical administrator, serving as secretary to two archbishops of Birmingham. He was energetic and efficient, despite less than robust health, and it came as no surprise when, in 1938, he was appointed auxiliary bishop to Archbishop Thomas Williams; he was at the time of his consecration the youngest of the English bishops.

His appointment in December 1943, as successor to Hinsley, was unexpected and he lacked the forthright style of his bluff predecessor. He was perceptive in warnings about Soviet intentions in eastern Europe and was a staunch spokesman for Catholic Poland. Like Hinsley he was always a defender of Christian civilisation. He defended Catholic interests in the postwar debate on the Welfare State, but was never a national figure. In 1946 he was created a cardinal on his forty-seventh birthday by Pope Pius XII.

The breakdown in the cardinal's health in 1949, which left him partially paralysed and unable to speak clearly, led to a remarkable period in which the English Catholic community developed and grew with an auto-pilot in control. In that period resignation was not an option and such great events as the centenary of the Catholic hierarchy in 1950 were masterminded by his consummate secretary, Derek Worlock, never a cardinal himself, but the power behind the throne for more than a decade.[22] Griffin died, following a series of heart attacks, at Polzeath in Cornwall, on 20 August 1956 and was buried in the crypt of Westminster Cathedral.

The year 1950 had witnessed an unsurpassed celebration of the English Catholic community in the Hierarchy Centenary Congress. Publicity was organised by Monsignor Worlock and others and during the culminating week of events, from 25 September to 1 October, seven cardinals as well as numerous bishops and archbishops were present at one event or another. The ailing Griffin was papal legate *a latere* with the commission of Pope Pius XII to preside 'in Our name and at all public gatherings and sacred ceremonies, and enhance the splendour of them with the dignity of the Roman purple'.[23] In the broadest message which the pope gave during the High Mass at Wembley Stadium, to an estimated crowd of 85,000, he not only remembered Catholic suffering, but expressed his 'sentiments of profound esteem' for King George VI and Queen Elizabeth and wished them 'a long, prosperous and peaceful reign'.[24] The 1950s were perhaps the high-water mark not only of the Catholic community itself, but also of its integration into national life.

William Godfrey, born in Liverpool on 25 September 1889, the younger son of George and Maria Godfrey, was educated at Ushaw and the Venerabile, where he studied for his doctorates in divinity and philosophy. Ordained priest in 1916, he served for two years as a curate at St Michael's, Liverpool, from where he returned to Ushaw to teach first classics and later, from 1928, theology. He was a man of great personal piety and a rather tedious pedagogue with a solemn manner; his mimicry on the French horn, seen as a pleasing sign of humanity, was confined to his colleagues.[25]

In 1930 he succeeded Cardinal Hinsley as rector of the English College and it was there, perhaps, he found his truest *métier*. Many of his students went on to the episcopate and 'Uncle Bill' became a central figure in the English Catholic world. For example, in 1937 he began to play a diplomatic role, acting as counsellor in the papal mission for George VI's coronation, although his appointment as first apostolic delegate to Great Britain in 1938 was in some ways a curious one; an Englishman representing a foreign power. Perhaps this pinpointed the continuing ambiguity of a Catholic prelate's position in England, despite the great public relations work of Hinsley. Godfrey had a quiet war and avoided patriotic involvement; in 1953 the titular archbishop of Cius (as he had become in 1939) was translated to Liverpool as archbishop, where again he lived quietly, until December 1956 when he was appointed seventh archbishop of Westminster in succession to Cardinal Griffin. In 1957 he was also appointed apostolic exarch to the Byzantine-rite Ukranians in England and Wales. In 1958, at Pope John XXIII's first consistory, he was created cardinal priest of SS. Nereo e Achilleo.

For the Catholic community Godfrey's Westminster years were ones of great expansion. Thirty-seven new churches, numerous ordinations and an increase of 50,000 in population, brought a feeling of consolidation in the Westminster diocese. However, in the wider community, Godfrey made little impact; his distant paternalism made few enemies, but attracted few friends. In the 1920s he had published a couple of edifying books, but he wrote little later. His pastoral letters were pedestrian with one exception: the 'poodle' pastoral in which he suggested that pets as well as their owners should join family fast days. Like Griffin he relied heavily on the services of Derek Worlock. Clerical wits of the time were said to amuse themselves with such questions as 'why is this man Godfrey signing Monsignor Worlock's letters?'[26]

Godfrey's influence on the character of the English Catholics from 1939 until his death was to be crucial. Godfrey's years at Westminster may have been seen by many clergy of his diocese as 'the safe period', but the English episcopate had been transformed into what Adrian Hastings has called 'a Roman clique' by appointing only one sort of bishop: secular priests trained at the Venerabile under Hinsley and Godfrey.

The Venerabile spirit was that of a clerical élite, isolated by seven long years in Rome with little personal contact permitted outside the circle of fifty fellow students. It was a regime of strict rules punctuated by Christmas Theatricals and long summers playing cricket. It cultivated a polite disdain alike for Anglicans and for continental theology. Rome was adored but Italian was seldom learnt (Godfrey was an exception in this): insularity was as important as Ultramontanism.[27]

Godfrey's health was in terminal decline by the time of the first session of the Second Vatican Council in December 1962. He had been appointed a member of the Central Preparatory Commission for the Council in 1961 and had emerged as a deeply conservative defender of old Church values. His death, on 22 January 1963, at Westminster Hospital and his funeral (and burial) at Westminster Cathedral brought an end to a period in which Church growth was underpinned by unquestioned values and a deep Roman clericalism.

Cardinal Heard appears as a thorough Scot but, by education (in part) and by diocese (Southwark), he was English and his association with the English College, Rome, was a prolonged one.[28] William Theodore Heard was born in the lodge of Fettes College, Edinburgh, where his father, William Augustus Heard, was headmaster. His mother, Elizabeth Tamar Burt, was from Southport, Lancashire: she died when the future cardinal was four. He was educated at Fettes and at Balliol where he had an undistinguished academic career, but rowed in the Oxford boat against Cambridge in 1907; he remains to date the only Oxbridge blue to be made a cardinal. In 1910 he was admitted a solicitor and in the same year, on 9 August, was received into the Catholic Church at the Jesuit church in Farm Street. He had first come into contact with the Catholic Church through his work with the Downside monks' boys club in Bermondsey.

On 26 October 1913 Heard entered the Venerabile. He was older than the other students and one of his contemporaries quipped that 'Heard's breakfast always consisted of black coffee and a frown'. He was ordained priest on 30 March 1918 in the Lateran basilica and proceeded to obtain doctorates in divinity and canon law. He returned to England in 1921 and spent six years as a curate in the church of the Holy Trinity, Dockhead, Bermondsey.

In September 1926 he was appointed to the Sacred Roman Rota, as *auditore* (judge) and made a domestic prelate of the pope. He remained working for the Rota for forty-six years, only rarely returning to the United Kingdom for his holidays. He established a formidable reputation as an ecclesiastical judge, combining a great knowledge of the law with perfect equity in applying it. In 1958 he became dean of the Rota and the following year, at the age of seventy-five and in poor health, was made cardinal deacon of S. Teodoro on the Palatine Hill. In 1961 he became cardinal protector of the English College and on 5 April 1962 was consecrated archbishop of Ferardi Maggiore by John XXIII. He was a member of the Central Preparatory Commission for the Second Vatican Council and between 1962 and 1964 he took part in all four sessions of the Council and was part of a commission dedicated to the reform of the Roman curia, of which he was so much a part. In 1963 he was the only cardinal from the British Isles to enter the conclave which elected Pope Paul VI. In April 1969 he became senior cardinal deacon, the person who, in the event of a conclave, announces the name of the new pope. He resigned this post in May 1970 when he was appointed cardinal priest, retaining S. Teodoro as his church; it was raised *pro hac vice* to the rank of presbyterial church.

Cardinal Heard had a long decline marked by failing sight and hearing and he died on 16 September 1973 at the clinic of the Blue Sisters at S. Stefano Rotondo in Rome. His funeral was in St Peter's on 19 September, the feast of St Theodore of Canterbury, and his body was taken to the Campo Verano for interment in the vault of the

English College. Heard had been a possible candidate for Westminster following Bourne's death, but in 1963 he was too old and it was the dynamic Heenan, Hinsley's protégé, who received the appointment.

John Carmel Heenan was one of the three English cardinals of the twentieth century to become truly national figures, the others being Hinsley and Hume. His last years were overshadowed by ill health and the heady atmosphere of the post-Vatican II Church which, for all his energy and vision, he found difficult to accept. Heenan reflected many of the trends of the Church in England in the first half of the twentieth century.[29] He was born in suburban Essex, in Ilford, the youngest of a family of four; his father, James Carmel Heenan, was a civil servant at the Patent Office. His parents (his mother was born Anne Pilkington) were both Irish and the local church and its vigorous priest, Canon Palmer, was the centre of his life. His desire to be a priest came young and he proceeded from the Jesuit St Ignatius College in Stamford Hill, London, to Ushaw. In 1924 he passed, almost inevitably, to the Venerabile and obtained doctorates in philosophy and theology. Never an intellectual, he had proved himself an exceptionally hard worker with a flair for communication. Ordained in 1930 for the diocese of Brentwood, he served as an assistant priest in Barking from 1931 to 1937 and as parish priest at Manor Park from 1937 to 1947. His time as a parish priest was of exceptional length for a future cardinal and he always retained a great devotion to the pastoral ministry and an innate understanding of ordinary Catholic lay people.

He was, however, no ordinary parish priest. It was at Manor Park that his national life began. He owed much to the patronage and encouragement of Cardinal Hinsley, whose staff he joined on a part-time basis. In his unrevealing first volume of autobiography, the aptly named *Not the Whole Truth* (1973), much was made of his fact-finding visit to the Soviet Union in 1936, disguised as a lecturer in psychology. In due course he became an accomplished performer on both radio and television, always with a ready manner and a well-groomed *suavitas*, the nearest the English public got to Bishop Fulton Sheen, the popular Catholic American broadcaster. It was no surprise in 1947 that he was asked by the English Catholic bishops to head the re-established Catholic Missionary Society, with its house in Golders Green and a hand-picked team of diocesan priests charged with giving missions across the country. Heenan himself was an ebullient and gifted preacher whose talents were in great demand.

In 1951 Heenan became bishop of Leeds and earned the diocese the epithet, 'The Cruel See', reflecting a popular novel of the time, on account of the rapid redeployment of many of its senior clergy. He later admitted that he had perhaps pursued his ends with too much energy. In 1957 he was translated to Liverpool as its eighth archbishop and during his time there commissioned and almost completed the city's metropolitan cathedral. Lutyens's overwhelming cathedral church, designed on a scale to match and surpass the gigantic Anglican cathedral at the other end of Hope Street, had become prohibitively expensive to finish; only the crypt had been completed. Heenan jettisoned the plan and engaged Frederick Gibberd, an architect who worked in the contemporary style, to design a church for the 1960s, a Catholic answer to Basil Spence's Coventry. In Liverpool the Essex archbishop was much loved and, although sectarian hostility remained strong in the city (Heenan was even pelted with stones), he began the work of reconciliation in the city's Christian community, which was to be continued by his successor-but-one, Derek Worlock, and the latter's Anglican counterpart, David Sheppard.

In 1963, with the death of Godfrey, Heenan was translated to Westminster as eighth archbishop. Despite his Ushaw and Venerabile background, Heenan appeared to be a new broom and the removal of the all-powerful secretary, Worlock, first to an East End parish (to give him pastoral credibility) and then to the diocese of Portsmouth, left Heenan able to engage on a fresh start. In 1965 he was created cardinal priest of S. Silvestro in Capite, a Roman church closely associated with the English Catholics resident in Rome, whose church it became in the 1880s.

Attendance at the Second Vatican Council meant that Rome was the centre of Heenan's attention during the early years of his time at Westminster. He did not take a leading part, but was active in the preparatory work on the Council's decree on ecumenism and declaration on non-Christian religions. Hinsley had already broken the ice with the Church of England and it was in 1960 that Archbishop Geoffrey Fisher of Canterbury made his historic official visit to the pope, but it was in Heenan's period of office that a regular exchange of pulpits and good personal relations became the norm, even if the cardinal himself felt more at home in the sunny world of suburban triumphalism. Michael Ramsey (1904–88), archbishop of Canterbury from 1961 to 1974, enjoyed close contacts with Pope Paul VI and had several friends in the Sacred College, including Léon-Joseph Suenens (1904–96) of Malines, in Belgium, whose great affection for the Church of England was similar to that of his predecessor, Cardinal Mercier. Désiré-Joseph Mercier (1851–1926), archbishop of Malines from 1906 and cardinal from 1907, presided over the so-called Malines Conversations (1921–5) which looked at the possibilities of reunion between Catholics and Anglicans. Ramsey was also on good terms with Heenan, but there was little warmth in the relationship. Nevertheless, Heenan and Ramsey became personal friends on Christian name terms, Jack and Michael, the first such friendship since the archbishopric of Westminster was created in 1850.[30]

At the end of 1965 the Second Vatican Council was over and Heenan's remaining years were dominated by its implications. It was not so much the teachings of the Council, as its atmosphere which created turmoil. Heenan's attitude remained ambiguous. 'There is a story, *ben trovato*, no doubt', which Adrian Hastings recounts, 'that two groups of journalists each selected a football team from among the Council Fathers – one to represent the Conservatives, the other the Progressives. When they compared notes they found that each had selected Heenan to play centre forward.'[31] His genuine, if guarded, backing for reform, on his own terms perhaps, seemed to be undermined by events. The crucial year was 1966, witnessing as it did the great public reception by Pope Paul VI – an Anglophile, an admirer of Newman and openly ecumenical – of Archbishop Ramsey in Rome and the defection of one of England's leading Catholic theologians and a priest of Heenan's diocese, Charles

Davis. The attack on the institutional Church, of which Charles Davis became emblematic, reached its highest level in 1968 with the reaffirmation of the traditional teaching on contraception in the encyclical *Humanae vitae* (29 July 1968). Heenan's greatest fear was that the Church's unity would be destroyed. From 1968 until his death in 1975 he became increasingly pessimistic about the state of the Church of which he had been so notable a son. After his death at Westminster Hospital on 7 November 1975 he was buried beside the fourteenth of Eric Gill's Stations of the Cross in Westminster Cathedral, his great hat the last to be placed over the tomb of an English cardinal. 'It was his task', commented Cormac Murphy-O'Connor, then rector of the Venerabile and archbishop of Westminster-but-one, at a requiem Mass for Cardinal Heenan in Rome on 19 November 1975 'to lead the Church in England and Wales during the past exhilarating and challenging years, the uncertain time of bright promise and budding hopes and yet withal of keen blasts and sudden showers and storms'.[32]

Heenan's grasp of popular Catholicism and his gift of communication never left him, but he died an isolated figure, too liberal for the conservatives, too clerically ultramontane for the progressives. The long terminal illnesses of nearly all the twentieth-century archbishops of Westminster paralysed the Church repeatedly. With Heenan's death the succession was perhaps more crucial then ever. One name, which had also been canvassed in 1963, was the intellectually outstanding former abbot of Downside, Christopher Butler, who had been made an auxiliary Bishop of Westminster by Heenan in 1966 and whose contributions to the Second Vatican Council had been the most significant of any Anglophone participant, but in 1975 he was already in his seventies and perhaps suspect in Rome for his forthright comments in 1968 about *Humanae vitae*. Butler, as senior auxiliary, administered the diocese in the interim and in 1976 had the satisfaction of seeing a fellow Benedictine, Abbot Basil Hume, appointed to Westminster. Some had hoped that Butler's distinction might be recognised, like Newman's, by a red hat in old age, but he had to be content with being appointed an 'Assistant at the Pontifical Throne'. Butler's *romanità*, despite his deep classical learning, was subdued, and Hume, like Bourne, owed more to France and to French culture than to Roman traditions. The deep patriotism he showed to England had none of the reservations of Heenan's Irish-tinged ultramontanism and while Heenan was prepared to explain the Catholic position to the English people, Hume managed to suggest that Catholicism was part of English life. Catholic infiltration of the Establishment, especially the armed forces, had been a gradual process throughout the twentieth century, but it was only under Hume that the Catholic clerical élite was accepted, almost, as part of the Establishment: 'My cardinal', as Queen Elizabeth II is reported to have called him.

George Hume (Basil was his name in religion) was born on 2 March 1923 in Newcastle upon Tyne, the son of a Scottish Protestant, Sir William Elrington Hume, a prominent heart surgeon, and his wife Maria Elizabeth, née Tisseyre, always known as Mimi, a French Catholic, seventeen years his junior.[33] George had three sisters and a younger brother. He was educated for two years at Newcastle Preparatory School, then from 1933 at Gilling Castle (the Ampleforth prep school) and Ampleforth itself. Ampleforth College was then a large boys' boarding school, established in North Yorkshire in the early nineteenth century, attached to the English Benedictine Ampleforth Abbey. He captained the Ampleforth Rugby XV and in 1941 entered the monastery, making his vows in 1942 and being Solemnly Professed in 1945. He was ordained priest at Ampleforth on 23 July 1950, following a history degree at Oxford (as a member of St Benet's Hall, the Ampleforth house of studies) and four years at Fribourg in Switzerland.

He had the varied life which, perhaps surprisingly, seems characteristic of the English Benedictines. He coached the 1st XV, was head of modern languages in Ampleforth College, assistant priest in the village's Catholic church, a housemaster from 1955 to 1963, a teacher in theology in the monastery and *magister scholarum*, responsible for the academic training of student monks for the English Benedictine Congregation. On 17 April 1963, aged forty, he was elected fourth abbot of Ampleforth, an office he held until 1976 (English Benedictine abbots are elected for a term of eight years; Hume was re-elected in 1971).

Ampleforth weathered the post-Vatican II storm better than many monasteries and, as abbot, Hume introduced many initiatives into his community, especially in the areas of opening the monastery's resources to the wider world and encouraging ecumenical encounters. Ampleforth College enjoyed a great period of academic and sporting success under its headmaster, Patrick Barry. Abbot Hume became a trusted adviser of the abbot primate in Rome, Rembert Weakland, who went on to become archbishop of Milwaukee. But life was not easy for an abbot in the 1960s. The *Ampleforth Journal* noted the contrast between the portraits of Hume by Derek Clarke at Ampleforth and Michael Noakes at Westminster:

> Both reveal strong hands right over left. But in the profile the change is stark. The Westminster portrait shows firmness, strength, control and maturity, the face soft in texture and smooth lines. The Ampleforth one reveals a man tired with office, head slightly drooped to the left, melancholy, vulnerable and wounded (often words close to his heart), rather craggy in feature. Paradoxically it was being Abbot of Ampleforth for thirteen years at the most testing of times which wore him out; Westminster was almost a release, a new energy and different set of challenges, broader in range but less immediate, personal, yes, but with time to breathe and even have peace and quiet in his private chapel.[34]

Hume was a surprise choice as successor to Heenan, Worlock being the most obvious candidate (he was appointed to the vacant archbishopric of Liverpool) and Butler the most distinguished alternative. He was consecrated and installed at Westminster Cathedral on 25 March 1976 and created cardinal priest of S. Silvestro in Capite on 24 May 1976. He held many national Catholic and ecumenical positions and served as president of the European Council of Episcopal Conferences. The official record of his life, the *rogito*, traditional to a cardinal, that was buried with him, makes impressive reading. In his work as archbishop he developed five pastoral areas with their own bishops, he eliminated the debt of the Westminster diocese and saved the cathedral choir school from closure. He addressed the problem of homelessness with various initiatives and for the twenty years of his episcopate maintained excellent relations with the media, growing in power and influence throughout this time. On 30 November 1995, the centenary year of Westminster Cathedral, the cardinal welcomed Queen Elizabeth II to Vespers, the first time since the reign of James II that an English monarch had officially attended a Catholic service. On 2 June 1999, a fortnight before his death, he received the Order of Merit in person from the Queen at Buckingham Palace. He had written to the priests of his diocese on 16 April that he had terminal cancer and he died on 17 June.

The obituaries in the newspapers were united in his praise. 'An outstandingly popular Archbishop of Westminster,' the *Daily Telegraph* (18 June 1999) declared, 'whose sincerity and expertly judged public pronouncements strengthen both the reputation and the self-confidence of Roman Catholics in England and Wales.' William Rees-Mogg, writing in *The Times* (28 June 1999) after the televised funeral, concurred with the view that he was the most influential Catholic churchman in England since Newman and hoped 'that he, like Newman, will eventually be added to the relatively short list of English saints'. The only English cardinal to have been canonised to date is the martyred Fisher. *The Times* obituarist commented that 'few churchmen this century, inside or outside the Catholic Church, had died more deeply loved'. Paul Vallely, writing in the *Independent* (18 June 1999), declared that 'even in Rome he was numbered among those considered *papabile* although in contrast to those cardinals who were ready to go to Rome at the drop of a biretta, he would flee the place when his presence was not essential, once leaving on the eve of a consistory where more ambitious mortals would have stayed to network with other cardinals.'

Any assessment of Cardinal Hume's lasting place in the history of the English Church needs to wait a while, although Adrian Hastings has offered a 'provisional evaluation' of him. He concludes that it was not the great public success of his period in office, including the papal visit in 1982 during the Falklands War, but his 'witness' which counted. As the century ended the Catholic community was declining numerically and increasingly fenced in by a rising tide of secularism and active hostility, but Cardinal Hume continued, in general, to be held in affection and respect:

> In retrospect what matters most about Basil Hume was not the correctness of every opinion or policy but his spiritual integrity, recognition of which united Catholics of very differing theological opinions as well as the national community as a whole. He was a sound teacher but a superb witness through the gentle holiness of his behaviour and, as he said himself, 'Modern man listens more readily to witnesses than to teachers.'[35]

*Catholicism and History* happens to be the title of Owen Chadwick's volume of lectures on the opening of the Vatican archive to scholars in the nineteenth century, but it also draws attention to the central importance of tradition within Catholic Christianity. This was illustrated by the convert historian Christopher Dawson when he maintained that it is only by living as a Catholic that the scholar can appreciate the essence of medieval European civilisation. Modern English Catholics have certainly proved to be particularly sensitive to the history of their persecuted ancestors and co-religionists in the early modern period. At the beginning of the third millennium of the Christian era, religious tolerance may have replaced persecution in the experience of English Catholics, but the possibility remains that it could be a tolerance born of apathy in a society diverted by materialism. The challenge of providing Christian leadership at national and even supranational level has now fallen to Cormac Murphy-O'Connor, archbishop of Westminster from 2000, raised to the cardinalate in February 2001.

While the latest English cardinal must deal with the challenges of the present, his biography neatly reflects many of the distinguishing features of the English Catholic past. Although he himself was born in Reading in 1932, his family's Irish ancestry gives him much in common with a large percentage of Catholics in moden Britain. His education at Prior Park College, Bath, provides a connection with that period of optimism experienced by English Catholics in the early nineteenth century. That he trained for the priesthood at the Venerable English College in Rome and obtained his licentiates in theology and philosophy from the Gregorian University there provides innumerable links with English clerics of all periods covered by this book. Between 1971 and 1977 he returned to the Venerabile as its rector, his subsequent career providing an obvious parallel with those of Cardinals Hinsley and Godfrey. As bishop of Arundel and Brighton from 1977 to 2000 his sphere of activity overlapped with that of the Howard family, for so long prominent figures in the history of English Catholicism, but it was also during that period that he became particularly noted in ecumenical initiatives, as joint-chairman of ARCIC II (the Anglican-Roman Catholic International Commission) and as chairman of the Catholic Bishops' Committee for Christian Unity. The Howard connection resurfaces more subtly in the granting of S. Maria sopra Minerva to Cardinal Murphy-O'Connor as his titular church, for it was previously held by the seventeenth-century Dominican Cardinal Philip Thomas Howard.

In spite of all these connections between English cardinals of different periods, our theme throughout this volume has been that of a particular group of Englishmen operating not in the exclusively insular environment favoured and perhaps misleadingly created by generations of British historians, but rather as players on a pan-Eurpoean stage. Any future historian of the English cardinals will be required to appreciate the extra-European, global perspective as well, for the College to which Cardinal Murphy-O'Connor was admitted on 21 February 2001 contained, for the first time in the history of the Church, a majority of non-European cardinals.

# Table 1 The Princely Cardinals of Renaissance England

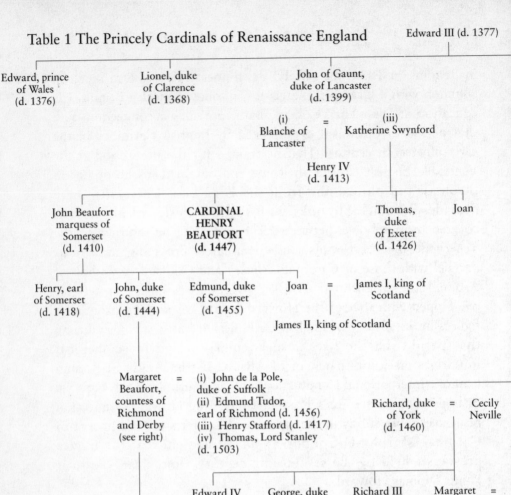

Edward III (d. 1377)

Edward, prince of Wales (d. 1376)

Lionel, duke of Clarence (d. 1368)

John of Gaunt, duke of Lancaster (d. 1399)

(i) Blanche of Lancaster = (iii) Katherine Swynford

Henry IV (d. 1413)

John Beaufort marquess of Somerset (d. 1410)

**CARDINAL HENRY BEAUFORT (d. 1447)**

Thomas, duke of Exeter (d. 1426)

Joan

Henry, earl of Somerset (d. 1418)

John, duke of Somerset (d. 1444)

Edmund, duke of Somerset (d. 1455)

Joan = James I, king of Scotland

James II, king of Scotland

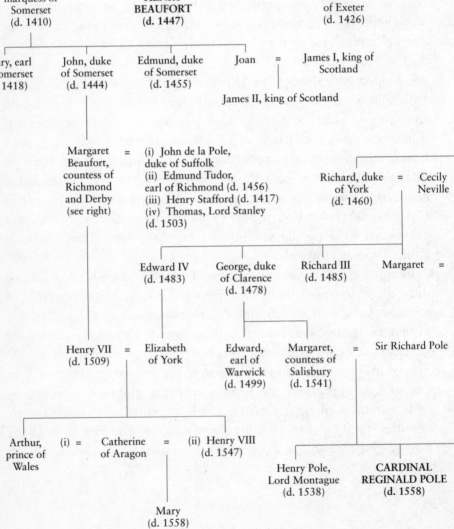

Margaret Beaufort, countess of Richmond and Derby (see right) = (i) John de la Pole, duke of Suffolk (ii) Edmund Tudor, earl of Richmond (d. 1456) (iii) Henry Stafford (d. 1417) (iv) Thomas, Lord Stanley (d. 1503)

Richard, duke of York (d. 1460) = Cecily Neville

Edward IV (d. 1483)

George, duke of Clarence (d. 1478)

Richard III (d. 1485)

Margaret =

Henry VII (d. 1509) = Elizabeth of York

Edward, earl of Warwick (d. 1499)

Margaret, countess of Salisbury (d. 1541) = Sir Richard Pole

Arthur, prince of Wales (i) = Catherine of Aragon = (ii) Henry VIII (d. 1547)

Henry Pole, Lord Montague (d. 1538)

**CARDINAL REGINALD POLE (d. 1558)**

Mary (d. 1558)

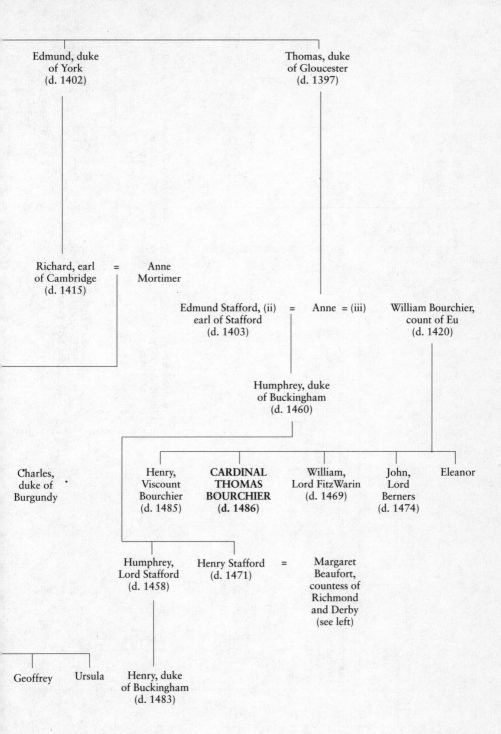

Edmund, duke
of York
(d. 1402)

Thomas, duke
of Gloucester
(d. 1397)

Richard, earl   =   Anne
of Cambridge      Mortimer
(d. 1415)

Edmund Stafford, (ii)   =   Anne   = (iii)   William Bourchier,
earl of Stafford                                count of Eu
(d. 1403)                                       (d. 1420)

Humphrey, duke
of Buckingham
(d. 1460)

Charles,
duke of
Burgundy

Henry,
Viscount
Bourchier
(d. 1485)

CARDINAL
THOMAS
BOURCHIER
(d. 1486)

William,
Lord FitzWarin
(d. 1469)

John,
Lord
Berners
(d. 1474)

Eleanor

Humphrey,
Lord Stafford
(d. 1458)

Henry Stafford
(d. 1471)

=

Margaret
Beaufort,
countess of
Richmond
and Derby
(see left)

Geoffrey    Ursula

Henry, duke
of Buckingham
(d. 1483)

171

# Table 2 The Howard Cardinals

Based on John Martin Robinson, *The Dukes of Norfolk: a Quincentennial History* (1982), Genealogical Table II

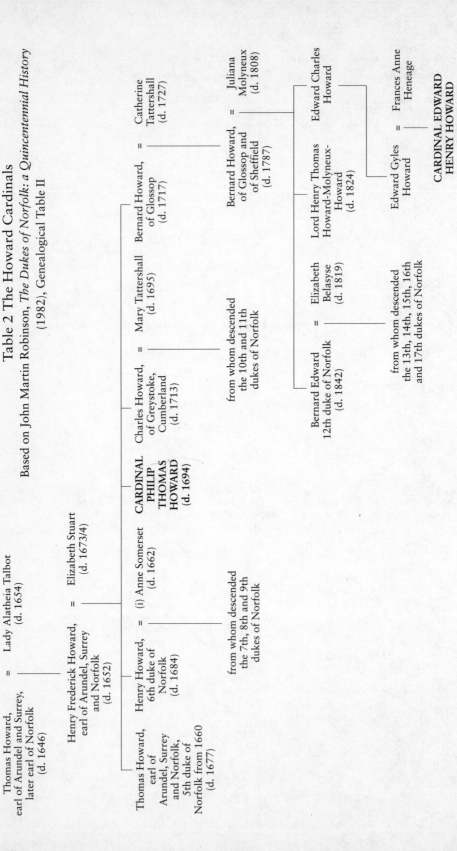

Thomas Howard, earl of Arundel and Surrey, later earl of Norfolk (d. 1646) = Lady Alatheia Talbot (d. 1654)

Henry Frederick Howard, earl of Arundel, Surrey and Norfolk (d. 1652) = Elizabeth Stuart (d. 1673/4)

Thomas Howard, earl of Arundel, Surrey and Norfolk, *5th duke of Norfolk from 1660* (d. 1677)

Henry Howard, 6th duke of Norfolk (d. 1684) = (i) Anne Somerset (d. 1662)

from whom descended the 7th, 8th and 9th dukes of Norfolk

**CARDINAL PHILIP THOMAS HOWARD** (d. 1694)

Charles Howard, of Greystoke, Cumberland (d. 1713) = Mary Tattershall (d. 1695)

Bernard Howard, of Glossop (d. 1717) = Catherine Tattershall (d. 1727)

from whom descended the 10th and 11th dukes of Norfolk

Bernard Howard, of Glossop and of Sheffield (d. 1787) = Juliana Molyneux (d. 1808)

Bernard Edward 12th duke of Norfolk (d. 1842) = Elizabeth Belasyse (d. 1819)

Lord Henry Thomas Howard-Molyneux-Howard (d. 1824)

Edward Charles Howard

from whom descended the 13th, 14th, 15th, 16th and 17th dukes of Norfolk

Edward Gyles Howard = Frances Anne Heneage

**CARDINAL EDWARD HENRY HOWARD** (d. 1892)

## Appendix I    English Cardinals at Home and in Rome

| Year created cardinal | Name of cardinal | Order | Bishoprics/archbishoprics (with dates)* | Promoted to Sacred College by | Titular church or suburbicarian bishopric (with dates) | Year of death | Where buried |
|---|---|---|---|---|---|---|---|
| c. 1144 | Robert Pullen | – | – | Lucius II | – | c. 1147 | – |
| pre-1150 | Nicholas Breakspear | Aug. canon | Pope Adrian IV (1154–9) | Eugenius III | Cardinal bishop of Albano (from 1146) | 1159 | St Peter's, Rome |
| 1205 | Stephen Langton | – | Canterbury (1207–28) | Innocent III | S. Crisogono (1205–28) | 1228 | Canterbury Cathedral |
| 1216 | Robert Curzon | – | – | Innocent III | S. Stefano in Monte Celio (1216–19) | 1219 | Damietta |
| 1239 | Robert Somercote | – | – | Gregory IX | S. Eustachio (1239–41) | 1241 | S. Crisogono, Rome |
| 1244 | John of Toledo | OCist. | – | Innocent IV | S. Lorenzo in Lucina (1244–61) Cardinal bishop of Porto and S. Rufina (1262–78) | 1275 | – |
| 1278 | Robert Kilwardby | OP | Canterbury (1272–8) | Nicholas III | Cardinal bishop of Porto and S. Rufina (1278–9) | 1279 | Dominican convent, Viterbo |
| 1281 | Hugh of Evesham | – | – | Martin IV | S. Lorenzo in Lucina (1281–7) | 1287 | S. Lorenzo in Lucina, Rome |
| 1303 | †William Macclesfield | OP | – | Benedict XI | S. Sabina (1303–4) | 1303/4 | – |

| Year created cardinal | Name of cardinal | Order | Bishoprics/archbishoprics (with dates)* | Promoted to Sacred College by | Titular church or suburbicarian bishopric (with dates) | Year of death | Where buried |
|---|---|---|---|---|---|---|---|
| 1304 | Walter Winterbourne | OP | – | Benedict XI | S. Sabina (1304–5) | 1305 | Genoa; reburied Blackfriars, London |
| 1305 | Thomas Jorz | OP | – | Clement V | S. Sabina (1305–10) | 1310 | – |
| 1368 | Simon Langham | OSB | Ely (1361–6) Canterbury (1366–8) | Urban V | S. Sisto (1368–73) Cardinal bishop of Palestrina (1373–6) | 1376 | Carthusian convent, Bonpas, near Avignon; reburied Westminster Abbey |
| 1378 | †William Courtenay | – | Hereford (1369–75) London (1375–81) Canterbury (1381–96) | Urban VI | – | 1396 | Canterbury Cathedral |
| 1381 | Adam Easton | OSB | – | Urban VI | S. Cecilia | 1398 | S. Cecilia, Rome |
| 1408 | †Philip Repyngdon | Aug. canon | Lincoln (1404–19/20) | Gregory XII | SS. Nereo e Achilleo (1408–34) | 1434 | Lincoln Cathedral |
| 1411 | †Thomas Langley | – | Durham (1406–37) | 'John XXIII' | – | 1437 | Durham Cathedral |
| 1411 | †Robert Hallum | – | York (1406–7) Salisbury (1407–17) | 'John XXIII' | – | 1417 | Constance Cathedral |

| Year created cardinal | Name of cardinal | Order | Bishoprics/archbishoprics (with dates)* | Promoted to Sacred College by | Titular church or suburbicarian bishopric (with dates) | Year of death | Where buried |
|---|---|---|---|---|---|---|---|
| 1426 | Henry Beaufort | – | Lincoln (1398–1404) Winchester (1404–47) | Martin V | S. Eusebio (1426–47) | 1447 | Winchester Cathedral |
| 1439 | John Kemp | – | Rochester (1419–21) Chichester (1421) London (1421–5) York (1425–52) Canterbury (1452–4) | Eugenius IV | S. Balbina (1439–42) Cardinal bishop of Porto and S. Rufina (1452–4) | 1454 | Canterbury Cathedral |
| 1467 | Thomas Bourchier | – | Worcester (1433–43) Ely (1443–54) Canterbury (1454–86) | Paul II | S. Ciriaco (1467–86) | 1486 | Canterbury Cathedral |
| 1493 | John Morton | – | Ely (1478–86) Canterbury (1486–1500) | Alexander VI | S. Anastasia (1493–1500) | 1500 | Canterbury Cathedral |
| 1511 | Christopher Bainbridge | – | Durham (1507–8) York (1508–14) | Julius II | SS. Marcellino e Pietro (1511) S. Prassede (1511–14) | 1514 | Venerable English College, Rome |

| Year created cardinal | Name of cardinal | Order | Bishoprics/archbishoprics (with dates)* | Promoted to Sacred College by | Titular church or suburbicarian bishopric (with dates) | Year of death | Where buried |
|---|---|---|---|---|---|---|---|
| 1515 | Thomas Wolsey | – | Lincoln (1514) York (1514–30) Bath and Wells (1518–23) Durham (1523–9) Winchester (1529–30) | Leo X | S. Cecilia (1515–30) | 1530 | Leicester Abbey |
| 1535 | John Fisher | – | Rochester (1504–35) | Paul III | S. Vitale (1535) | 1535 | All Hallows, Barking; reburied St Peter ad Vincula, Tower of London |
| 1536 | Reginald Pole | – | Canterbury (1555–8) | Paul III | SS. Nereo e Achilleo (1537–40) SS. Vito e Modesto (1540) S. Maria in Cosmedin (1540–58) | 1558 | Canterbury Cathedral |
| 1557 | William Peto | OFM Obs. | Salisbury (1543–58) | Paul IV | – | 1558 | Greenwich |
| 1587 | William Allen | – | – | Sixtus V | S. Martino ai Monti (1587–94) | 1594 | Venerable English College, Rome |
| 1675 | Philip Thomas Howard | OP | – | Clement X | S. Cecilia (1676–9) S. Maria sopra Minerva (1679–94) | 1675 | S. Maria sopra Minerva, Rome |

| Year created cardinal | Name of cardinal | Order | Bishoprics/archbishoprics (with dates)* | Promoted to Sacred College by | Titular church or suburbicarian bishopric (with dates) | Year of death | Where buried |
| --- | --- | --- | --- | --- | --- | --- | --- |
| 1747 | Henry Benedict Stuart, duke of York | – | – | Benedict XIV | S. Maria in Portico in Campitelli (1747–52); SS. Apostoli (1752–9); S. Maria in Trastevere (1759–61); Cardinal bishop of Tusculum/Frascati (1761–1803); S. Lorenzo in Damaso (1763–1803); Cardinal Bishop of Ostia and Velletri (1803–7) | 1807 | St Peter's, Rome |
| 1830 | Thomas Weld | – | – | Pius VIII | S. Marcello (1830–7) | 1837 | S. Marcello, Rome |
| 1842 | Charles Acton | – | – | Gregory XVI | S. Maria della Pace (1842–6); S. Marco (1846–7) | 1847 | Naples |
| 1850 | Nicholas Wiseman | – | Westminster (1850–65) | Pius IX | S. Pudenziana (1850–65) | 1865 | Kensal Green; reburied Westminster Cathedral |
| 1875 | Henry Edward Manning | – | Westminster (1865–92) | Pius IX | S. Gregorio Magno (1875–92) | 1892 | Kensal Green; reburied Westminster Cathedral |
| 1877 | Edward Henry Howard | – | – | Pius IX | SS. Giovanni e Paolo (1877–84); Cardinal bishop of Tusculum/Frascati (1884–92) | 1892 | Fitzalan Chapel, Arundel |

| Year created cardinal | Name of cardinal | Order | Bishoprics/archbishoprics (with dates)* | Promoted to Sacred College by | Titular church or suburbicarian bishopric (with dates) | Year of death | Where buried |
|---|---|---|---|---|---|---|---|
| 1879 | John Henry Newman | Cong. Orat. | – | Leo XIII | S. Giorgio in Velabro (1879–90) | 1890 | Rednal, Birmingham |
| 1893 | Herbert Vaughan | – | Westminster (1892–1903) | Leo XIII | S. Gregorio Magno (1893–1903) | 1903 | Mill Hill, London |
| 1903 | Rafael Merry del Val | – | – | Pius X | S. Prassede (1903–30) | 1930 | St Peter's, Rome |
| 1911 | Francis Bourne | – | Southwark (1897–1903) Westminster (1903–35) | Pius X | S. Pudenziana (1911–35) | 1935 | St Edmund's, Ware and Wonersh |
| 1914 | Francis Aidan Gasquet | OSB | – | Pius X | S. Giorgio in Velabro (1914–15) S. Maria in Portico in Campitelli (1915–29) | 1929 | Downside Abbey |
| 1937 | Arthur Hinsley | – | Westminster (1935–43) | Pius XI | S. Susanna (1937–43) | 1943 | Westminster Cathedral |
| 1946 | Bernard Griffin | – | Westminster (1943–56) | Pius XII | S. Gregorio Magno (1946–56) | 1956 | Westminster Cathedral |
| 1958 | William Godfrey | – | Liverpool (1953–6) Westminster (1956–63) | John XXIII | SS. Nereo e Achilleo (1958–63) | 1963 | Westminster Cathedral |

178

| Year created cardinal | Name of cardinal | Order | Bishoprics/ archbishoprics (with dates)* | Promoted to Sacred College by | Titular church or suburbicarian bishopric (with dates) | Year of death | Where buried |
|---|---|---|---|---|---|---|---|
| 1959 | William Heard | – | – | John XXIII | S. Teodoro (1959–73) | 1973 | Campo Verano, Rome |
| 1965 | John Carmel Heenan | – | Leeds (1951–7) Liverpool (1957–63) Westminster (1963–75) | Paul VI | S. Silvestro in Capite (1965–75) | 1975 | Westminster Cathedral |
| 1976 | George Basil Hume | OSB | Westminster (1976–99) | Paul VI | S. Silvestro in Capite (1976–99) | 1999 | Westminster Cathedral |
| 2001 | Cormac Murphy-O'Connor | – | Arundel and Brighton (1977–2000) Westminster (2000–) | John Paul II | S. Maria sopra Minerva (2001–) | | |

\* Titular sees *in partibus infidelium* are not included in this list.
† Promotion to Sacred College not accepted or acknowledged, or title not used in England

| | | |
|---|---|---|
| Aug. canon | Augustinian canon regular | |
| Cong. Orat. | Congregation of the Oratory | |
| OCist. | Cistercian | |
| OFM Obs. | Observant Franciscan | |
| OP | Order of Preachers/Dominican | |
| OSB | Order of St Benedict/Benedictine | |

179

# Appendix II    Scottish Cardinals

| Year created cardinal | Name of cardinal | Order | Bishoprics/ archbishoprics (with dates)* | Promoted to Sacred College by | Titular church or suburbicarian bishopric (with dates) | Year of death | Where buried |
|---|---|---|---|---|---|---|---|
| 1538 | David Beaton (or Bethune) | – | Mirepoix (1538) St Andrews (1539–46) | Paul III | S. Stefano in Monte Celio | 1546 | St Andrews |
| 1801 | Charles Erskine | – | – | Pius VI | S. Maria in Portico in Campitelli | 1811 | Sainte-Geneviève, Paris |
| 1969 | Gordon Gray | – | St Andrews and Edinburgh (1951–85) | Paul VI | S. Chiara | 1993 | St Mary's Cathedral, Edinburgh |
| 1994 | Thomas Winning | – | Glasgow (1974– ) | John Paul II | S. Andrea delle Fratte | | |

*   Titular sees *in partibus infedelium* are not included in this list.

For Cardinals Stuart (d. 1807) and Heard (d. 1973) see Appendix I.

# Appendix III    *Irish Cardinals*

| Year created cardinal | Name of cardinal | Order | Bishoprics/archbishoprics (with dates)* | Promoted to Sacred College by | Titular church or suburbicarian bishopric (with dates) | Year of death | Where buried |
|---|---|---|---|---|---|---|---|
| 1866 | Paul Cullen | – | Armagh (1850–2) Dublin (1852–78) | Pius IX | S. Pietro in Montorio | 1878 | Clonliffe, Dublin |
| 1882 | Edward McCabe | – | Dublin (1879–85) | Leo XIII | S. Sabina | 1885 | Glasnevin, Dublin |
| 1885 | Patrick Francis Moran | – | Ossory (1872–84) Sydney (1884–1911) | Leo XIII | S. Susanna | 1911 | St Mary's Cathedral, Sydney |
| 1893 | Michael Logue | – | Raphoe (1879–87) Armagh (1887–1924) | Leo XIII | S. Maria della Pace | 1924 | St Patrick's Cemetery, Armagh |
| 1925 | Patrick O'Donnell | – | Armagh (1924–7) | Pius XI | S. Maria della Pace | 1927 | St Patrick's Cemetery, Armagh |
| 1929 | Joseph MacRory | – | Down and Connor (1915–28) Armagh (1928–45) | Pius XI | S. Giovanni a Porta Latina | 1945 | St Patrick's Cemetery, Armagh |

| Year created cardinal | Name of cardinal | Order | Bishoprics/archbishoprics (with dates)* | Promoted to Sacred College by | Titular church or suburbicarian bishopric (with dates) | Year of death | Where buried |
|---|---|---|---|---|---|---|---|
| 1953 | John D'Alton | – | Meath (1943–6) Armagh (1946–63) | Pius XII | S. Agata dei Goti | 1963 | St Patrick's Cathedral, Armagh |
| 1962 | Michael Browne | OP | – | John XXIII | S. Paolo Apostolo in Arenula | 1971 | St Mary's, Tallaght, Co. Dublin |
| 1965 | William Conway | – | Armagh (1963–77) | Paul VI | S. Patrizio | 1977 | St Patrick's Cathedral, Armagh |
| 1979 | Tómas O'Fiaich | – | Armagh (1977–90) | John Paul II | S. Patrizio | 1990 | St Patrick's Cathedral, Armagh |
| 1991 | Cahal Daly | – | Ardagh and Clonmacnoise (1967–82) Down and Connor (1982–90) Armagh (1990–6) | John Paul II | S. Patrizio | | |
| 2001 | Desmond Connell | – | Dublin (1988–) | John Paul II | S. Silvestro in Capite | | |

*  Titular sees *in partibus infedelium* are not included in this list.     OP    Order of Preachers/Dominican

# Notes

*(All books are published in London unless otherwise specified)*

## Introduction

1. S. Kuttner, '*Cardinalis*: The History of a Canonical Concept', *Traditio* 3 (1945), p. 176.
2. 'Cardinal', in *New Catholic Encyclopaedia* 3 (New York, 1967), p. 105.
3. I.S. Robinson, *The Papacy 1073–1198: Continuity and Innovation* (Cambridge, 1990), p. 120.
4. J.F. Broderick, 'The Sacred College of Cardinals: Size and Geographical Composition (1099–1986)', *Archivium historiae pontificiae* 25 (1987), pp. 7–71.
5. For the canon law and ceremonies associated with cardinals see James A. Coriden, Thomas J. Green and Donald E. Heintschel, *The Code of Canon Law: A Text and Commentary* (1985), pp. 286–94 and James-Charles Noonan, Jr, *The Church Visible: The Ceremonial Life and Protocol of the Roman Catholic Church* (New York, 1996), pp. 3–64. An atmospheric and colourful description of a conclave is provided by the old Harrovian convert Hartwell de la Garde Grissell (1839–1907), chamberlain of honour to the pope, in his *Sede Vacante* (London, 1903) which culminates in the coronation of Pius X.
6. For a discussion of cardinals' hats see H. Thurston, 'The Cardinal's Hat and its History', The *Month* 119 (1912), pp. 1–16. The number of tassels was not laid down until the pontificate of Pius VI (1775–99) and was made law by a decree of the Sacred Congregation of Ceremonies on 9 February 1832 (B.B. Heim, *Heraldry in the Catholic Church* (Gerrards Cross, 1978), p. 105.
7. Noonan, *Church Visible*, p. 18.
8. Thanks to Richard Sharp for information about bishop, cardinal, pope and similar alcoholic beverages. The recipes appear in *Oxford Nightcaps*, which went through numerous editions in the nineteenth century.

9. Noonan, *Church Visible*, p. 24.

10. H.D. Fernández, 'The Patrimony of St Peter: the Papal Court at Rome *c.* 1450–1700', in J. Adamson (ed.), *The Princely Courts of Europe* (1999), p. 152.

11. Ibid., p. 161. This study gives an excellent overview of the papal household, architectural setting, ceremonial and politics.

12. J.N.D. Kelly, *The Oxford Dictionary of Popes* (Oxford, 1986), pp. 329–30.

13. C.H. Lawrence (ed.), *The English Church and the Papacy in the Middle Ages*, new edn (Stroud, 1999), p. 66.

## One

1. A. Paravicini Bagliani, *The Pope's Body* (2000), pp. 13–14.

2. E. Kantorowicz, *The King's Two Bodies* (Princeton, 1957) and *Laudes Regiae: A Story in Liturgical Acclamations and Medieval Ruler Worship* (Berkeley, 1946).

3. A.B. Emden, *A Biographical Register of the University of Oxford to A.D. 1500*, 3 vols (Oxford 1957–9) is, along with the *Dictionary of National Biography*, the chief authority for this chapter. Variations on Pullen's name are found in vol. 3, p. 1525.

4. R.L. Poole, 'The Early Lives of Robert Pullen and Nicholas Breakspear', in *Studies in Chronology and History* (Oxford, 1934), pp. 287–98; F. Courtney, *Cardinal Robert Pullen: An English Theologian of the Twelfth Century* (Analecta Gregoriana 64, Rome, 1954).

5. Poole, *Studies in Chronology*, p. 288.

6. R.W. Southern, 'From Schools to University', in J.I. Catto (ed.), *The History of the University of Oxford: The Early Oxford Schools* (Oxford, 1984), pp. 6–8.

7. *The Letters of St Bernard of Clairvaux*, trans. B.S. James (1953; 2nd edn, Stroud, 1998), pp. 344–5.

8. Ibid., p. 387.

9. Poole, *Studies in Chronology*, p. 293.

10. Paravicini Bagliani, *The Pope's Body*, pp. 253–4. There are several biographies of Adrian IV. At present the most accessible account is M.F. Farley, 'Adrian IV England's Only Pope', *History Today* 28 (1978), pp. 530–6. Other 'lives' include E.M. Almedingen, *The English Pope (Adrian IV)* (1925); H.K. Mann, *Nicholas Breakspear* (1914), extracted from his multi-volume *History of the Popes*; F.M. Steele, *The Story of the English Pope* (1908) with its frontispiece showing a disconsolate Breakspear being turned away from St Albans by haughty monks; and the handsome tome of A.H. Tarleton, *Nicholas Breakspear (Adrian IV) Englishman and Pope* (1896).

11. Tarleton, *Nicholas Breakspear*, p. 270.

12. Robinson, *The Papacy*, p. 255.

13. Boso's *Life of Alexander III*, trans. G.M. Ellis (Oxford, 1973).

14. F. Barlow, *Thomas Becket* (1986), pp. 7–8 and *passim*.

15. For Langton see F.M. Powicke, *Stephen Langton* (Oxford, 1928) and the same author's 'Stephen Langton', in *The Christian Life in the Middle Ages* (Oxford 1935), pp. 130–46. Langton's *Commentary on the Book of Chronicles*, ed. A. Saltman, was published at Ramat-Gan in 1978.

16. F. Williams, *Lives of the English Cardinals*, vol. 1, p. 273.

17. A. Paravicini Bagliani, *Cardinali di Curia e 'Familiae' Cardinalizie dal 1227 and 1254* (Padua, 1972), pp. 228–55.

18. Williams, *Cardinals*, vol. 1, p. 344.

19. D. Knowles, *The Religious Orders in England*, vol. 1 (Cambridge, 1962), p. 167.

20. R. Kilwardby, *On Time and Imagination*, O. Lewry (ed.) (Oxford, 1987), p. xiii.

21. Ibid., p. xvi.

22. J.I. Catto, 'Theology and Theologians 1220–1320', in Catto (ed.), *The Early Oxford Schools* (Oxford, 1984).

23. Emden, pp. 2061.

24. C. Isaacson, *The Story of the Cardinals*, pp. 55–6.

## *Two*

1. Y. Renouard, *The Avignon Papacy 1305–1403* (Eng. trans., 1970) provides useful general coverage of the subject. L. von Pastor, *The History of the Popes from the Close of the Middle Ages*, 40 vols (Eng. trans., 1891–1953) begins its epic story with the Avignon period. The amount of detail increases as the narrative progresses and it remains a convenient basis for further study, even though many areas have been researched more thoroughly by twentieth-century historians.

2. See E.F. Jacob's *Essays in the Conciliar Epoch* (Manchester, 1943) and various essays by Margaret Harvey, details of which may be found in M. Harvey, *England, Rome and the Papacy 1417–1464: The Study of a Relationship* (Manchester, 1993), pp. 266–7.

3. In chronological order the cardinals dealt with in this chapter are Langham, Courtenay, Easton, Repyngdon, Langley, Hallum, Beaufort and Kemp. All are included in the *Dictionary of National Biography* (where the spelling 'Hallam' is preferred); see also A.B. Emden, *A Biographical Register of the University of Oxford to A.D. 1500*, 3 vols (Oxford, 1957–9) for all except Langley. For their appointments as cardinals and to major benefices, all details have been taken from K. Eubel, *Hierarchia Catholica*, vols 1–2 (Münster, 1913–14).

4. D. Knowles, *The Religious Orders in England*, vol. 2 (Cambridge, 1961), p. 56.

5. Pastor, *History of the Popes*, vol. 1, p. 260.

6. See n. 3 for Courtenay sources.

# Notes

7. Jacob, *Essays in the Conciliar Epoch*, p. 57.
8. In addition to the basic biographical sources provided in n. 3, see also D. Knowles, *The Religious Orders*, pp. 56–8.
9. M. Harvey, 'The Household of Cardinal Langham', *Journal of Ecclesiastical History*, 47, 1 (1996), p. 23.
10. See n. 3 for Repyngdon sources.
11. J.L. Kirby, *Henry IV of England* (1970), pp. 118–19.
12. *The Book of Margery Kempe*, S.B. Meech (ed.) (1940), pp. 43–6.
13. In addition to the sources detailed in n. 3, see also R.L. Storey, *Thomas Langley and the Bishopric of Durham, 1406–1437* (1961).
14. See n. 3 for Hallum sources.
15. The next pope to take the name Alexander was Rodrigo Borgia in 1492. That the Borgia pope was Alexander VI confirmed the papal status of Alexander V. Although elected by the same council, Baldassare Cossa's legitimacy as pope retained an element of doubt until Angelo Roncalli became Pope John XXIII in 1958.
16. For a survey of Henry V and ecclesiastical matters, including the Council of Constance and Lollardy, see C. Allmand, *Henry V* (1992).
17. That is, in conjunction with his new title.
18. G.L. Harriss, *Cardinal Beaufort: A Study of Lancastrian Ascendancy and Decline* (Oxford, 1988) is the only major biography of any of the cardinals dealt with in this chapter.
19. Henry Beaufort is known to have fathered one illegitimate daughter, Joan, whose mother was by Lady Alice Fitzalan, daughter of the Earl of Arundel: Harriss, *Cardinal Beaufort*, p. 16.
20. For details of all Beaufort's loans to the Crown between 1404 and 1446, see ibid., pp. 401–6.
21. Details of speeches and Beaufort's relations with Parliament are taken from Harriss, *Cardinal Beaufort*.
22. On this aspect of Anglo-papal relations see R.G. Davies, 'Martin V and the English Episcopate with Particular Reference to the Campaign for the Repeal of the Statutes of Provisors', *English Historical Review* 92 (1977), pp. 309–44; M.M. Harvey, 'Martin V and Henry V', *Archivium Historiae Pontificiae* 24 (1986), pp. 49–70.
23. Humphrey was the patron of Tito Livio Frulovisi's humanistic history of the life of Henry V. The duke's economic policies were also publicised in literary form, in the poem *The Libel of English Policy*. For Beaufort as a literary patron, albeit not a particularly effective one, see R. Weiss, *Humanism in England during the Fifteenth Century*, 3rd edn (Oxford, 1967). Employment as a papal scriptor had taken the distinguished Florentine humanist Poggio Bracciolini to the Council of Constance. When Beaufort returned home after his post-Constance pilgrimage to the Holy Land, Poggio accompanied him to

186

England, but was disappointed to discover that English libraries failed to yield the classical gems which had made Constance and its neighbourhood so popular with manuscript-hungry humanists.

24. K.B. McFarlane, 'Henry V, Bishop Beaufort and the Red Hat, 1417–21', *English Historical Review* 60 (1945), p. 322.
25. As archbishop of Canterbury Chichele was a *legatus natus*, as opposed to *legatus a latere*: see p. 2.
26. Harriss, *Cardinal Beaufort*, p. 173.
27. G. Holmes, 'Cardinal Beaufort and the Crusade against the Hussites', *English Historical Review* 88 (1973), pp. 721–50.
28. Kemp's role in the turbulent political life of mid-fifteenth-century England can be appreciated in R.A. Griffiths, *The Reign of Henry VI: The Exercise of Royal Authority 1422–1461* (1981) and P.B. Wolffe, *Henry VI* (1981).
29. See p. 50.

## Three

1. For Anglo-papal diplomacy in the period covered by this chapter see M. Harvey, *England, Rome and the Papacy* (Manchester, 1993) and W.E. Wilkie, *The Cardinal Protectors of England: Rome and the Tudors before the Reformation* (Cambridge, 1974).
2. Biographical information about all the cardinals in this chapter is found in A.B. Emden, *A Biographical Register of the University of Oxford to A.D. 1500*, 3 vols (Oxford, 1957–9), *A Biographical Register of the University of Oxford, A.D. 1501 to 1540* (Oxford, 1974) and *A Biographical Register of the University of Cambridge to 1500* (Cambridge, 1963). Bainbridge, Bourchier, Morton, Peto and Wolsey are included in the first three Oxford volumes, with Pole in the fourth; Fisher was the only Cambridge graduate among England's Renaissance cardinals. All seven are featured in the *Dictionary of National Biography*, with Bainbridge, Fisher, Pole and Wolsey also the subjects of monographs. Details of promotions to the Sacred College, as well as those to bishoprics and archbishoprics, are taken from K. Eubel, *Hierarchia Catholica*, vol. 2 (Regensburg, 1901).
3. Louis de Luxembourg's tomb is in Ely Cathedral; his heart was taken to Rouen.
4. C. Head, 'Pius II and the Wars of the Roses', *Archivium Historiae Pontificiae* 8 (1970), pp. 139–78.
5. D. Mancini, *The Usurpation of Richard III*, edited and translated by C.A.J. Armstrong (Gloucester, 1984): Dominic Mancini was writing to Angelo Cato.
6. *The History of King Richard the Third*, ed. R.S. Sylvester (New Haven and London, 1963).
7. Attainder: loss of estates, civil rights and other consequences of being sentenced to death or outlawry.

8. Margaret Harvey's study of the English diplomats in fifteenth-century Rome (n. 1) is a recent contribution to an already sizeable bibliography, which includes B. Behrens, 'Origins of the Office of English Resident Ambassador in Rome', *English Historical Review* 49 (1934), pp. 640–56. For the cultural dimension a convenient starting-point is R. Weiss, *Humanism in England during the Fifteenth Century*, 3rd edn (Oxford, 1967).

9. C.S.L. Davies, 'Bishop John Morton, the Holy See and the Accession of Henry VII', *English Historical Review* 102 (1987), pp. 2–30.

10. Morton's fork: 'If the persons applied to for benevolence live frugally, tell them that their parsimony must have enriched them, and that the King will therefore expect from them a liberal donation; if their method living on the contrary be extravagant, tell them that they can afford to give largely, since the proof of their opulence is evident from their expenditure.' This is the version quoted by E. Carpenter, *Cantuar: The Archbishops in their Office*, 2nd edn (Oxford, 1988), p. 76.

11. C. Ross, *Richard III* (1981), li: the character assassin in Ross's sights is Sir Clements Markham.

12. Thanks to D.S. Chambers, *Cardinal Bainbridge in the Court of Rome, 1509 to 1514* (Oxford, 1965), his Italian career can be appreciated in detail.

13. Ibid., pp. 131–40.

14. All Wolsey's modern biographers rely heavily on the memoirs of the cardinal's servant George Cavendish: *The Life and Death of Cardinal Wolsey*, ed. R.S. Sylvester (1959). A.F. Pollard, *Wolsey* (1929) is inevitably dated, but none the less readable. P. Gwyn, *The King's Cardinal: The Rise and Fall of Thomas Wolsey* (1990) is a monumental defence of its subject.

15. Quoted by J.J. Scarisbrick, *Henry VIII* (1968), p. 73.

16. For details, see J.G. Russell, *The Field of the Cloth of Gold* (1969).

17. Quoted by Chambers, *Cardinal Bainbridge*, p. 1.

18. Pastor, *History of the Popes*, vol. 7, p. 243.

19. Scarisbrick, *Henry VIII*, p. 85.

20. Quoted by Pastor, *History of the Popes*, vol. 9, p. 437.

21. S. Thurley, 'The Domestic Building Works of Cardinal Wolsey', in S.J. Gunn and P.G. Lindley (eds), *Cardinal Wolsey: Church, State and Art* (Cambridge, 1991), pp. 76–102.

22. J. Newman, 'Cardinal Wolsey's Collegiate Foundations', in Gunn and Lindley (eds), *Cardinal Wolsey*, pp. 103–15.

23. Ibid.

24. For Skelton see G. Walker, *John Skelton and the Politics of the 1520s* (Cambridge, 1988).

25. Scarisbrick, *Henry VIII*, p. 194, contains interesting observations on Wolsey's assessment of the divorce question.

26. Ibid., pp. 234–40.

27. In keeping with his princely air, Wolsey intended to be buried in an imposing Renaissance-style tomb. The tomb chest survives in the crypt of St Paul's Cathedral, housing the earthly remains of Lord Nelson: see P.G. Lindley, 'Playing Check-Mate with Royal Majesty? Wolsey's patronage of Italian Renaissance Sculpture', in Gunn and Lindley (eds), *Cardinal Wolsey*, pp. 261–85.

28. The principal source of information on Fisher employed here is B. Bradshaw and E. Duffy (eds), *Humanism, Reform and Reformation: The Career of Bishop John Fisher* (Cambridge, 1989).

29. For the relationship between Fisher and Lady Margaret Beaufort, see M.K. Jones and M.G. Underwood, *The King's Mother: Lady Margaret Beaufort, Countess of Richmond and Derby* (Cambridge, 1992).

30. Bradshaw and Duffy (eds), *Humanism*, pp. 235–49.

31. E. Duffy, 'The Spirituality of John Fisher', in ibid., pp. 205–31. See also R. Rex *The Theology of John Fisher* (Cambridge, 1991).

32. Jones and Underwood, *The King's Mother*, p. 249.

33. Quoted by Jones and Underwood, *The King's Mother*, p. 179.

34. Duffy, 'Spirituality', pp. 212–23.

35. See n. 2 for biographical information about Peto.

36. For a generation the most accessible study of Pole has been D. Fenlon, *Heresy and Obedience in Tridentine Italy: Cardinal Pole and the Counter Reformation* (Cambridge, 1972). T.F. Mayer, *Reginald Pole: Prince and Prophet* (Cambridge, 2000) is a major new biography to mark the 500th anniversary of the cardinal's birth.

37. D. Loades, *Mary Tudor: A Life* (Oxford, 1989), p. 304.

38. Fenlon, *Heresy and Obedience*, p. 283.

39. Ibid., p. 37.

40. For Contarini see E.G. Gleason, *Gasparo Contarini: Venice, Rome and Reform* (Berkeley, CA, 1993). In 1539 Contarini became the second successive non-resident non-English bishop of Salisbury, in succession to Campeggi. He retained the see until his death three years later.

41. Fenlon, *Heresy and Obedience*, p. 96.

42. In addition to Fenlon, *Heresy and Obedience*, see P. McNair, *Peter Martyr in Italy: An Anatomy of an Apostasy* (Oxford, 1967).

43. Quoted by Loades, *Mary Tudor*, p. 239. Loades provides valuable detailed coverage of Pole's brief English career.

44. For Pole and the Jesuits see T.M. McCoog, 'Ignatius Loyola and Reginald Pole: a Reconsideration', *Journal of Ecclesiastical History*, 47, 2 (1996), pp. 257–73.

45. Like his predecessors, Pole was buried in Canterbury Cathedral. Near his tomb is that of a French cardinal, Odet de Coligny (1515–71), bishop of Beauvais and archbishop of Toulouse, who had been created cardinal by Clement VII in

1533, but became sympathetic to Calvinism, was deprived of his ecclesiastical titles and married an ex-religious, Elisabeth de Kanteville. He died at Canterbury *en route* for France, allegedly poisoned by his valet.

## Four

1. J.F. Broderick, 'The Sacred College of Cardinals: Size and Geographical Composition (1099–1986); *Archivium Historiae Pontificiae* 25 (1987), pp. 7–71.
2. D.A. Bellenger, *English and Welsh Priests* (Bath, 1984), p. 246.
3. For an overview of the English Catholics see J. Bossy, *The English Catholic Community 1570–1850* (1975).
4. C. Hibbert, *Rome: The Biography of a City* (1985), p. 215.
5. For Allen see E. Duffy, 'William, Cardinal Allen, 1532–1594', *Recusant History* 22 (1995), pp. 265–90, and T.F. Fox (ed.), *The Letters and Memorials of William Allen* (1882).
6. See J. Loach, 'Reformation Controversies', in *The History of the University of Oxford*, vol. 3; J. McConica (ed.), *The Collegiate University* (Oxford, 1986), pp. 363–96.
7. Duffy, 'Allen', p. 269.
8. M.E. Williams, *The Venerable English College, Rome* (1979), p. 8.
9. Ibid., 'William Allen: The Sixteenth Century Spanish Connection', *Recusant History* 22 (1994), pp. 123–40.
10. Duffy, 'Allen', p. 288.
11. G. Albion, *Charles I and the Court of Rome: A Study in 17th century Diplomacy* (Louvain, 1935), p. 318.
12. Ibid., pp. 148–9. See also B. and M. Pawley, *Rome and Canterbury through Four Centuries* (1974), pp. 32–3.
13. For Philip Howard see G. Anstruther, *A Hundred Homeless Years: English Dominicans 1558–1658* (1958), especially pp. 194–221; B. Jarrett, 'Letters of Philip Howard', *Catholic Record Society* 25 (1925), pp. 1–94; J.M. Robinson, *The Dukes of Norfolk: A Quincentennial History* (Oxford, 1982), pp. 133–40, and B. Sewall, *Like Black Swans* (Padstow, 1982), pp. 1–30. The unpublished manuscript of a full biography by Anstruther is kept in the archives of the English Dominican Province.
14. T.S. Flynn, *The Irish Dominicans 1536–1642* (Dublin, 1993), pp. 118–19.
15. Anstruther, *Hundred Homeless Years*, pp. 203–4.
16. Robinson, *Dukes of Norfolk*, p. 133.
17. Williams, *Venerable English College*, p. 48.
18. Sewell, *Like Black Swans*, p. 27.
19. M.V. Hay, *The Enigma of James II* (1938), p. 158. For Petre, see Hay, pp. 154–67 and G. Holt, *The English Jesuits 1650–1829: A Biographical Dictionary* (1984).

20. J. Champ, *The English Pilgrimage to Rome* (Leominster, 2000), pp. 96–100.

21. Kelly, *Popes*, p. 298.

22. J. Lees-Milne, *The Last Stuarts* ( 1983), p. 143. Other books on the Cardinal of York include B. Fothergill, *The Cardinal King* (1958) and P. Bindelli, *Enrico Stuart Cardinale Duca di York* (Frascati, 1982), which is strong on his Frascati links and illustrates most of his surviving artefacts.

23. S. Gaselee, 'British Diplomatic Relations with the Holy See', *Dublin Review* 204 (1939), pp. 1–11, discusses Erskine at pp. 3–11. See also W.M. Brady, *Anglo-Roman Papers* (Paisley, 1890) and Pawley, *Rome and Canterbury*, pp. 80–6. Another high-placed English cleric in Rome at the end of the eighteenth century was Monsignor Christopher Stonor, head chamberlain of Clement XIV and Pius VI, a domestic prelate, but never a cardinal, who died in 1795 at the age of eighty (Champ, *English Pilgrimage*, p. 101). His kinsman, Archbishop Edmund Stonor, lived in Rome from 1861 until his death in 1912 (ibid., p. 200).

24. D.A. Bellenger, *The French Exiled Clergy* (Bath, 1986), pp. 3–4.

25. F. Hurtubis, 'Jean Lefebre de Cheverus, First Catholic Bishop of Boston', *The Bostinian Society* 2 (1965), pp. 51–77, and a fuller French biography, A.J.M. Hamon, *Vie de Cardinal de Cheverus* (Paris, 1858) with a portrait.

26. For Consalvi, see J.M. Robinson, *Cardinal Consalvi 1757–1824* (1987).

27. Ibid., p. 104.

28. N. Wiseman, *Recollections of the Last Four Popes* (1858), p. 207.

29. N. Davies, *The Isles: A History* (1999), pp. 510–17, and E. Jones, *The English Nation: The Great Myth* (Stroud, 1998), pp. 168–217.

30. M. Haile and E. Bowney, *Life and Letters of John Lingard, 1771–1851* (1911), pp. 220–9, for Lingard's cardinalate.

31. For Weld's biography see J. Berkeley, *Lulworth and the Welds* (Gillingham, 1971), pp. 209–36.

32. H. Clifford, *The House of Clifford* (Chichester, 1987), p. 159; Abbé Migne, *Dictionnaire des Cardinaux* (Paris, 1857), col. 1012.

33. Wiseman, *Recollections of the Last Four Popes* (1858), p. 242–7.

34. P. Gunn, *The Actons* (1978).

35. P. Cunich et al., *A History of Magdalene College Cambridge 1428–1988* (Cambridge, 1994), p. 208.

36. O. Chadwick, *A History of the Popes 1830–1914* (Oxford, 1998), p. 62.

37. D. Mathew, *Lord Acton and his Times* (1968), pp. 30–1.

## Five

1. E. Duffy, *Saints and Sinners* (1998), p. 224.

2. Ibid., p. 225. See also O. Chadwick, *A History of the Popes* (Oxford, 1998), especially pp. 61–272 and E.E.Y. Hales, *Pio Nono* (1954).

3. M. Murphy, *Blanco White: A Self-banished Spaniard* (1989), p. 7.

# Notes

4. R.J. Schiefen, *Nicholas Wiseman and the Transformation of English Catholicism* (Shepherdstown, 1984), p. 99.

5. Ibid., p. 128.

6. Ibid., p. 187.

7. Ibid., p. 189.

8. Quoted by B. Fothergill, *Nicholas Wiseman* (1963), pp. 294–5. W. Ward's two-volumed *Life and Times of Cardinal Wiseman* (1897) also contains much of interest.

9. Schiefen, *Wiseman*, p. 190.

10. L. Strachey, *Eminent Victorians* (1918), pp. 57–8.

11. J.D. Holmes, *More Roman than Rome: English Catholicism in the Nineteenth Century* (1978), p. 102.

12. V.A. McClelland, 'The Formative Years, 1850–92', in V.A. McClelland and M. Hodgetts (eds), *From Without the Flaminian Gate* (1999), p. 5.

13. Newsome, *The Convert Cardinals* (1993), p. 29.

14. Ibid., p. 180.

15. Ibid., p. 362.

16. Ibid., p. 360.

17. For a discussion of the biographical controversy see S. Gilley, 'New Light on an Old Scandal', in D.A. Bellenger (ed.), *Opening the Scrolls: Essays in Catholic History in Honour of Godfrey Anstruther* (Bath, 1987), pp. 166–95.

18. Newsome, *Convert Cardinals*, p. 3.

19. I. Ker, *John Henry Newman: A Biography* (Oxford, 1988).

20. S. Gilley, *Newman and his Age* (1990). M. Trevor's, two-volumed life, *Newman: the Pillar of Cloud* and *Newman: Light in Winter* (London, 1962) is readable but heavily Newmanophile. It reflects the rediscovery of Newman's importance by scholars such as John Coulson of Downside, Stephen Dessain of Birmingham, the first editor of the complete letters, and Owen Chadwick of Cambridge.

21. M. Bence-Jones, *The Catholic Families* (1992), pp. 224–5.

22. Isaacson, *Cardinals*, p. 286.

23. Robinson, *Dukes of Norfolk*, pp. 188–9.

24. M. Vaughan, *Courtfield and the Vaughans* (1989), p. 185.

25. R. O'Neil, *Cardinal Herbert Vaughan* (1995), p. 43.

26. Ibid., pp. 119–20.

27. Ibid., p. 154.

28. Ibid., p. 351.

29. R. Kollar, *Westminster Cathedral: From Dream to Reality* (Edinburgh, 1987).

30. O'Neil, *Vaughan*, p. 447.

31. Ibid., p. 498.

32. Holmes, *More Roman than Rome*, p. 32.

33. E. Norman, *The English Catholic Church in the Nineteenth Century* (Oxford, 1984), p. 373.

*Six*

1. H.R. Trevor Roper (ed.), *Macaulay's Essays* (1965), p. 276.
2. S. Leslie, *Cardinal Gasquet: a Memoir* (1953), pp. 81–90.
3. For Merry del Val, see among others P. Cenci, *Il Cardinale Raffaele Merry del Val* (Rome, 1933) which, at over 850 pages and 160 illustrations, provides an exhaustive survey full of *romanità*, and F.A. Forbes, *Rafael, Cardinal Merry del Val* (London, 1932) which emphasises his Englishness.
4. G. Lease, 'Vatican Foreign Policy and Origins of Modernism', in D. Jodock (ed.), *Catholicism Contending with Modernity* (Cambridge, 2000), pp. 50–1.
5. A. Hastings, *A History of English Christianity* (1986), p. 142.
6. D.A. Bellenger, 'Cardinal Gasquet (1846–1929): an English Roman', *Recusant History* 24 (1999), pp. 552–60.
7. D. Knowles, 'Cardinal Gasquet as an Historian', in D. Knowles, *The Historian and Character* (Cambridge, 1963), pp. 240–63.
8. E. Oldmeadow, *Francis Cardinal Bourne*, 2 vols (1940, 1944).
9. P. Caraman, *C.C. Martindale* (1967), p. 191.
10. T. Hooley, *A Seminary in the Making* (1927).
11. M. Clifton, *Amigo: Friend of the Poor* (Leominster, 1987).
12. T. Horwood, 'Public Opinion and the 1908 Eucharistic Congress', *Recusant History* 25 (2000) pp. 120–31.
13. E. Waugh, *Life of Ronald Knox* (1959).
14. G. Wheeler, 'The Archdiocese of Westminster', in G.A. Beck (ed.), *The English Catholics 1850–1950* (1950), p. 177.
15. Ibid., p. 178.
16. J.C. Heenan, *Cardinal Hinsley* (1944) and the *Dictionary of National Biography* provide a biographical framework for Hinsley and there is much of interest, especially on his public and political life, in T. Moloney, *Westminster, Whitehall and the Vatican* (1985).
17. G. Scott, *The RCs* (1967), p. 236.
18. C. Scott, *A Historian and his World: A Life of Christopher Dawson 1889–1970* (1984), p. 185.
19. Moloney, *Westminster*, p. 71.
20. S. Ball (ed.), *Parliament and Politics in the Age of Churchill and Attlee: The Headlam Diaries 1935–51* (Cambridge, 1999), p. 362.
21. M. de la Bedoyere, *Cardinal Bernard Griffin* (1955) is a hagiographical account, as is that of Derek Worlock in the *Dictionary of National Biography*.
22. C. Longley, *The Worlock Archives* (2000) is an essential introduction to Archbishop Worlock's *mentalité* and the Catholic Church in England in the second half of the twentieth century.
23. *Hierarchy Centenary Congress* (1950), p. 8.

24. Ibid., p. 56.
25. The *Dictionary of National Biography* remains the principal source for Godfrey, who has not attracted a biographer.
26. Longley, *Worlock*, p. 320.
27. Hastings, *Christianity*, p. 479.
28. C. Burns, 'His Eminence Cardinal William Theodore Heard', *The Venerabile* 26 (1974) pp. 7–14.
29. J.C. Heenan, *Not the Whole Truth* (1973) and *A Crown of Thorns* (1974) provide the most extensive autobiography of any English cardinal but there is, as yet, no biography. David Norris, one of his secretaries, provides a balanced *Dictionary of National Biography* entry.
30. O. Chadwick, *Michael Ramsay* (Oxford, 1990), p. 329.
31. Hastings, *Christianity*, p. 564.
32. Sermon for Cardinal Heenan, *The Venerabile* 25 (1978), p. 66.
33. Various congratulatory volumes on Basil Hume have appeared including the informative T. Castle (ed.), *Basil Hume: A Portrait* (1986). The *Ampleforth Journal* 104 (1999) for the autumn term has some perceptive observations, pp. 1–19.
34. J.F.S. Stephens, *Ampleforth Journal* 104 (1999), p. 13.
35. A. Hastings, 'Cardinal Basil Hume', *Priests and People* 14 (2000), p. 259.

# Bibliography

*(Published in London unless otherwise specified)*

## General works

Adamson, J. (ed.), *The Princely Courts of Europe* (1999)

Baxter, D., *England's Cardinals* (1903)

Blet, P., *Histoire de la Représentation Diplomatique du Saint Siège* (Rome, 1982)

Broderick, J.F., 'The Sacred College of Cardinals: Size and Geographical Composition (1099–1986)', *Archivium Historiae Pontificiae* 25 (1987), pp. 7–71

Carpenter, E., *Cantuar: The Archbishops in their Office* (2nd edn, Oxford, 1988)

Champ, J., *The English Pilgrimage to Rome: A Dwelling for the Soul* (Leominster, 2000)

Collinson, P., Ramsay, N. and Sparks, M. (eds), *A History of Canterbury Cathedral* (Oxford, 1995)

Coriden, A., Green, T.J. and Heintschel, D.E., *The Code of Canon Law: A Text and Commentary* (1985)

Davies, N., *The Isles: A History* (1999)

De la Garde Grissell, H., *Sede Vacante* (1903)

*Dictionary of National Biography*

*Dizionario biografico degli italiani*

Duffy, E., *Saints and Sinners* (1998)

Emden, A.B., *A Biographical Register of the University of Oxford to A.D. 1500*, 3 vols (Oxford, 1957–59)

——, *A Biographical Register of the University of Oxford, A.D. 1501 to 1540* (Oxford, 1974)

——, *A Biographical Register of the University of Cambridge to 1500* (Cambridge, 1963)

Eubel, K., et al., *Hierarchia Catholica Medii Aevi*, 8 vols (Münster and Padua, 1913–78)

Fernández, H.D., 'The Patrimony of St Peter: the Papal Court at Rome *c.* 1450–1700', in J. Adamson (ed.), *The Princely Courts of Europe* (1999)

Graham, R.A., *Vatican Diplomacy* (Princeton, NJ, 1959)

Heim, B.B., *Heraldry in the Catholic Church* (Gerrards Cross, 1978)

# Bibliography

Hibbert, C., *Rome: The Biography of a City* (1985)

Isaacson, C., *The Story of the English Cardinals* (1907)

Jones, E., *The English Nation: The Great Myth* (Stroud, 1998)

Kelly, J.N.D., *The Oxford Dictionary of the Popes* (Oxford, 1986)

Kuttner, S., '*Cardinalis*: The History of a Canonical Concept', *Traditio* 3 (1945), pp. 129–214

Lawrence, C.H. (ed.), *The English Church and the Papacy in the Middle Ages* (new edn, Stroud, 1999)

Mathew, D., *Catholicism in England 1535–1935* (1936)

Migne, Abbé, *Dictionnaire des Cardinaux* (Paris, 1857)

*New Catholic Encyclopaedia* (New York, 1967)

Noel, G., *The Anatomy of the Catholic Church* (1980)

Noonan, J.C., *The Church Visible: The Ceremonial Life and Protocol of the Roman Catholic Church* (New York, 1996)

Parks, G.B., *The English Traveler in Italy* (Rome, 1954)

Pastor, L. von, *History of the Popes*, 40 vols (Eng. trans., 1891–1953)

Pawley, B. and M., *Rome and Canterbury through Four Centuries* (1974)

Robinson, I.S., *The Papacy 1097–1198: Continuity and Innovation* (Cambridge, 1990)

Thurston, H., 'The Cardinal's Hat and its History', *The Month* 119 (1912), pp. 1–16

*Venerabile* 21 (sexcentenary issue): *The English Hospice in Rome* (1962)

Williams, F., *Lives of the English Cardinals including Historical Notices of the Papal Court from Nicholas Breakspear (Pope Adrian IV) to Thomas Wolsey, Cardinal Legate*, 2 vols (1868)

Williams, M.E., *The Venerable English College, Rome, 1579–1979: A History* (1979)

## Medieval Christendom

Almedingen, E.M., *The English Pope (Adrian IV)* (1925)

Barlow, F., *Thomas Becket* (1986)

Barraclough, G., *The Medieval Papacy* (1968)

*The Letters of St Bernard of Clairvaux*, trans. B.S. James (1953; 2nd edn, Stroud, 1998)

Birch, D., *Pilgrimage to Rome in the Middle Ages: Continuity and Change* (Woodbridge, 1998)

Boso, *Life of Alexander III*, trans. G.M. Ellis (Oxford, 1973)

Brentano, R., *Rome before Avignon: A Social History of Thirteenth Century Rome* (1990)

Catto, J.I. (ed.), 'Theology and Theologians 1220–1320', in J.I. Catto (ed.), *The History of the University of Oxford: The Early Oxford Schools* (Oxford, 1984)

Courtney, F., *Cardinal Robert Pullen: An English Theologian of the Twelfth Century* (Analecta Gregoriana 64, Rome, 1954)

Farley, M.F., 'Adrian IV: England's Only Pope', *History Today* 28 (1978), pp. 530–6

Kantorowicz, E., *Laudes Regiae: A Story in Liturgical Acclamations and Medieval Ruler Worship* (Berkeley, CA, 1946)

——, *The King's Two Bodies* (Princeton, NJ, 1957)

Kilwardby, R., *On Time and Imagination*, ed. O. Lewry (Oxford, 1987)

Knowles, D., *The Religious Orders in England*, 3 vols: vol. 1 (Cambridge, 1962 edn), vol. 2, *The End of the Middle Ages* (Cambridge, 1961 edn), vol. 3, *The Tudor Age* (Cambridge, 1971 edn)

# Bibliography

Langton, S., *Commentary on the Book of Chronicles*, ed. A. Saltman (Ramat-Gan, 1978)

Mann, H.K., *Nicholas Breakspear* (1914)

Morris, C., *The Papal Monarchy: The Western Church from 1050 to 1250* (Oxford, 1989)

Ortenberg, V., *The English Church and the Continent in the Tenth and Eleventh Centuries: Cultural, Spiritual and Artistic Exchanges* (Oxford, 1992)

Paravicini Baglioni, A., *Cardinali di Curia e 'Familiae' Cardinalizie dal 1227 al 1254* (Padua, 1972)

——, *The Pope's Body* (Eng. trans., 2000)

Poole, R.L., 'The Early Lives of Robert Pullen and Nicholas Breakspear', in *Studies in Chronology and History* (Oxford, 1934)

Powicke, F.M., *Stephen Langton* (Oxford, 1928)

——, 'Stephen Langton', in *The Christian Life in the Middle Ages* (Oxford, 1935), pp. 130–46

Sayers, J.E., *Papal Government and England during the Pontificate of Honorius III (1216–1227)* (Cambridge, 1984)

Southern, R.W., 'From Schools to University', in J.I. Catto (ed.), *The History of the University of Oxford: The Early Oxford Schools* (Oxford, 1984)

Steele, F.M., *The Story of the English Pope* (1908)

Tarleton, A.H., *Nicholas Breakspear (Adrian IV): Englishman and Pope* (1896)

Ullmann, W., *The Growth of Papal Government in the Middle Ages* (1955)

——, *A Short History of the Papacy in the Middle Ages* (1972)

## Avignon and Conciliarism

Allmand, C., *Henry V* (1992)

Davies, R.G., 'Martin V and the English Episcopate with Particular Reference to his Campaign for the Repeal of the Statutes of Provisors', *English Historical Review* 92 (1977), pp. 309–44

Griffiths, R.A., *The Reign of King Henry VI: The Exercise of Royal Authority 1422–1461* (1981)

Harriss, G.L., *Cardinal Beaufort: A Study of Lancastrian Ascendancy and Decline* (Oxford, 1988)

Harvey, M., *England, Rome and the Papacy, 1417–1464: The Study of a Relationship* (Manchester, 1993)

——, 'The Household of Cardinal Langham', *Journal of Ecclesiastical History*, 47, 1 (1996), pp. 18–44

Holmes, G., 'Cardinal Beaufort and the Crusade against the Hussites', *English Historical Review* 88 (1973), pp. 721–50

Jacob, E.F., *Archbishop Henry Chichele* (1967)

——, *Essays in the Conciliar Epoch* (Manchester, 1943)

Kemp, M., *Book of Margery Kempe*, ed. S.B. Meech, EETS 125 (1940)

Kirby, J.L., *Henry IV of England* (1970)

Krautheimer, R., *Rome: Profile of a City, 312–1308* (Princeton, NJ, 1980)

Lunt, W.E., *Financial relations of the Papacy with England, 1327–1534* (Cambridge, MA, 1962)

McFarlane, K.B., 'Henry V, Bishop Beaufort, and the Red Hat, 1417–21', *English Historical Review* 60 (1945), pp. 316–48

Mollat, G., *The Popes at Avignon 1305–1378* (Eng. trans., 1949)

Renouard, Y., *The Avignon Papacy 1305–1403* (Eng. trans., 1970)

# Bibliography

Saul, N., *Richard II* (New Haven and London, 1997)

Schofield, A.N.E.D., 'The First English Delegation to the Council of Basel', *Journal of Ecclesiastical History* 12 (1961), pp. 167–96

——, 'The Second English Delegation to the Council of Basel', *Journal of Ecclesiastical History* 17 (1966), pp. 29–64

Storey, R.L., *Thomas Langley and the Bishopric of Durham, 1406–1437* (1961)

Thomson, J.A.F., *Popes and Princes, 1417–1517* (1980)

Ullmann, W., 'Eugenius, Kemp and Chichele', in J.A. Watt et al. (eds), *Medieval Studies Presented to Aubrey S. Gwynn S.J.* (Dublin, 1961), pp. 359–83

Weiss, R., *Humanism in England during the Fifteenth Century* (3rd edn, Oxford, 1967)

Wolffe, P.B., *Henry VI* (1981)

## Renaissance and Reformation

Behrens, B., 'Origins of the Office of English Resident Ambassador in Rome', *English Historical Review* 49 (1934), pp. 640–56

Bireley, R., *The Refashioning of Catholicism, 1450–1700: A Reassessment of the Counter Reformation* (Basingstoke, 1999)

Bradshaw, B. and Duffy, E. (eds), *Humanism, Reform and Reformation: The Career of Bishop John Fisher* (Cambridge, 1989)

Cavendish, G., *The Life and Death of Cardinal Wolsey*, ed. R.S. Sylvester (1959)

Chambers, D.S., *Cardinal Bainbridge in the Court of Rome, 1509 to 1514* (Oxford, 1965)

——, *Renaissance Cardinals and their Worldly Problems* (Aldershot, 1997)

Chrimes, S.B., *Henry VII* (1972)

Davies, C.S.L., 'Bishop John Morton, the Holy See and the Accession of Henry VII', *English Historical Review* 102 (1987), pp. 2–30

Dickens, A.G., *The English Reformation* (1964)

Dobson, B. (ed.), *The Church, Politics and Patronage in the Fifteenth Century* (Gloucester, 1984)

Fenlon, D., *Heresy and Obedience in Tridentine Italy: Cardinal Pole and the Counter Reformation* (Cambridge, 1972)

Gleason, E.G., *Gasparo Contarini: Venice, Rome and Reform* (Berkeley, CA, 1993)

Gunn, S.J. and Lindley, P.G. (eds), *Cardinal Wolsey: Church, State and Art* (Cambridge, 1991)

Guy, J.A., *The Cardinal's Court: The Impact of Thomas Wolsey in Star Chamber* (Hassocks, 1977)

Gwyn, P., *The King's Cardinal: The Rise and Fall of Thomas Wolsey* (1990)

Hallman, B.M., *Italian Cardinals, Reform and the Church as Property, 1492–1563* (Berkeley and Los Angeles, 1985)

Harvey, M., *England, Rome and the Papacy, 1417–1464: The Study of a Relationship* (Manchester, 1993)

Head, C., 'Pius II and the Wars of the Roses', *Archivium Historiae Pontificiae* 8 (1970), pp. 139–78

Jones, M.K. and Underwood, M.G., *The King's Mother: Lady Margaret Beaufort, Countess of Richmond and Derby* (Cambridge, 1992)

Knecht, R.J., 'The Episcopate and the Wars of the Roses', *University of Birmingham Historical Journal* 6 (1957–8), pp. 108–31

# Bibliography

——, *Francis I* (Cambridge, 1982)

Lee, E., *Sixtus IV and Men of Letters* (Rome, 1978)

Lindley, P.G., 'Playing Check-Mate with Royal Majesty? Wolsey's Patronage of Italian Renaissance Sculpture', in S.J. Gunn and P.G. Lindley (eds), *Cardinal Wolsey: Church, State and Art* (Cambridge, 1991)

Loades, D.M., *Mary Tudor: A Life* (Oxford, 1989)

McCoog, T.M., 'Ignatius Loyola and Reginald Pole: A Reconsideration', *Journal of Ecclesiastical History*, 47, 2 (1996), pp. 257–73

McNair, P., *Peter Martyr in Italy: An Anatomy of an Apostasy* (Oxford, 1967)

Mallett, M.E., *The Borgias* (1969)

Mancini, D., *The Usurpation of Richard III*, ed. and trans. C.A.J. Armstrong (Gloucester, 1984)

Mayer, T.F., *Reginald Pole: Prince and Prophet* (Cambridge, 2000)

Mellano, M.F., *Rappresentanti Italiani della Corona Inglese a Rome ai Primi del Cinquecento* (Rome, 1970)

More, T., *The History of King Richard the Third*, ed. R.S. Sylvester (New Haven and London, 1963)

Newman, J., 'Cardinal Wolsey's Collegiate Foundations', in S.J. Gunn and P.G. Lindley (eds), *Cardinal Wolsey: Church, State and Art* (Cambridge, 1991), pp. 103–15

Pollard, A.F., *Wolsey* (1929)

Rex, R., *The Theology of John Fisher* (Cambridge, 1991)

Ridley, J., *The Statesman and the Fanatic: Thomas Wolsey and Thomas More* (1982)

Ross, C., *Edward IV* (1974)

——, *Richard III* (1981)

Russell, J.G., *The Field of the Cloth of Gold* (1969)

Sanderson, M.H.B., *Cardinal of Scotland: David Beaton, c. 1494–1546* (Edinburgh, 1986)

Scarisbrick, J.J., *Henry VIII* (1968)

Shaw, C., *Julius II: The Warrior Pope* (Oxford, 1993)

Starkey, T., *A Dialogue between Reginald Pole and Thomas Lupset*, ed. T.F. Mayer, Camden Fourth Series 37 (1989)

Stinger, C.L., *The Renaissance in Rome* (Bloomington, 1985)

Thurley, S., 'The Domestic Building Works of Cardinal Wolsey', in S.J. Gunn and P.G. Lindley (eds), *Cardinal Wolsey: Church, State and Art* (Cambridge, 1991), pp. 76–102

Walker, G., *John Skelton and the Politics of the 1520s* (Cambridge, 1988)

Weiss, R., *Humanism in England during the Fifteenth Century* (3rd edn, Oxford, 1967)

Wilkie, W.E., *The Cardinal Protectors of England: Rome and the Tudors before the Reformation* (Cambridge, 1974)

Woolfson, J., *Padua and the Tudors: English Students in Italy, 1485–1603* (Toronto, 1998)

## Exiles

Albion, G., *Charles I and the Court of Rome: A Study in Seventeenth Century Diplomacy* (Louvain, 1935)

Anstruther, G., *A Hundred Homeless Years: English Dominicans 1558–1658* (1958)

# Bibliography

Bellenger, D.A., *English and Welsh Priests* (Bath, 1984)

——, *The French Exiled Clergy* (Bath, 1986)

Berkeley, J., *Lulworth and the Welds* (Gillingham, 1971)

Bindelli, P., *Enrico Stuart Cardinale Duca di York* (Frascati, 1982)

Bossy, J., *The English Catholic Community 1570–1950* (1975)

Brady, W.M., *Anglo-Roman Papers* (Paisley, 1890)

Chadwick, O., *The Popes and European Revolution* (Oxford, 1981)

Clifford, H., *The House of Clifford* (Chichester, 1987)

Coppa, F.J., *The Modern Papacy since 1789* (1998)

Cunich, P. et al., *A History of Magdalene College Cambridge, 1428–1988* (Cambridge, 1994)

Duffy, E., 'William, Cardinal Allen, 1532–1594', *Recusant History* 22 (1995), pp. 295–90

Flynn, T.S., *The Irish Dominicans 1536–1642* (Dublin, 1993)

Fothergill, B., *The Cardinal King* (1958)

Fox, T.F. (ed.), *The Letters and Memorials of William Allen* (1882)

Gaselee, S., 'British Diplomatic Relations with the Holy See', *Dublin Review* 204 (1939), pp. 1–11

Gunn, P., *The Actons* (1978)

Haile, M. and Bowney, E., *Life and Letters of John Lingard, 1771–1851* (1911)

Hamon, A.J.M., *Vie de Cardinal de Cheverus* (Paris, 1858)

Hay, M.V., *The Enigma of James II* (1938)

Holt, G., *The English Jesuits 1650–1829: A Biographical Dictionary* (1984)

Hurtubis, F., 'Jean Lefèbre de Cheverus, First Catholic Bishop of Boston', *The Bostonian Society* 2 (1965), pp. 51–77

Ingamells, J., *A Dictionary of British and Irish Travellers in Italy, 1701–1800* (New Haven and London, 1997)

Jarrett, B., 'Letters of Philip Howard', *Catholic Record Society* 25 (1925), pp. 1–94

Lees-Milne, J., *The Last Stuarts* (1983)

Loach, J., 'Reformation Controversies', in *The History of the University of Oxford*, vol. 3, J. McConica (ed.), *The Collegiate University* (Oxford, 1986), pp. 363–96

McConica, J. (ed.), *The Collegiate University* (Oxford, 1986)

Mathew, D., *Lord Acton and his Times* (1968)

Robinson, J.M., *The Dukes of Norfolk: A Quincentennial History* (Oxford, 1982)

——, *Cardinal Consalvi 1757–1824* (1987)

Sewell, B., *Like Black Swans* (Padstow, 1982)

Shield, A., *Henry Stuart, Cardinal York, and his Times* (1908)

Williams, M.E., 'William Allen: The Sixteenth Century Spanish Connection', *Recusant History* 22 (1994), pp. 123–40

Wiseman, N., *Recollections of the Last Four Popes* (1858)

## Eminent Victorians

Bellenger, D.A. (ed.), *Opening the Scrolls: Essays in Catholic History in Honour of Godfrey Anstruther* (Bath, 1987)

Bence-Jone, M., *The Catholic Families* (1992)

# Bibliography

Bossy, J., *The English Catholic Community 1570–1950* (1975)

Chadwick, O., *The Secularization of the European Mind in the Nineteenth Century* (Cambridge, 1975)

——, *A History of the Popes 1830–1914* (Oxford, 1998)

Fothergill, B., *Nicholas Wiseman* (1963)

Gilley, S., 'New light on an Old Scandal', in Bellenger (ed.), *Opening the Scrolls*, pp. 166–95

——, *Newman and his Age* (1990)

Gorman, W.G., *Converts to Rome* (1910)

Gray, R., *Cardinal Manning: A Biography* (1985)

Hales, E.E.Y., *Pio Nono* (1954)

Holmes, J.D., *More Roman than Rome: English Catholicism in the Nineteenth Century* (1978)

Ker, I., *John Henry Newman: A Biography* (Oxford, 1988)

Kollar, R., *Westminster Cathedral: From Dream to Reality* (Edinburgh, 1987)

McClelland, V.A., *Cardinal Manning: His Public Life and Influence, 1865–1892* (1962)

—— (ed.), *By Whose Authority: Newman, Manning and the Magisterium* (Bath, 1996)

—— and M. Hodgetts (eds), *From Without the Flaminian Gate* (1999)

McIntire, C.T., *England Against the Papacy 1858–1861* (Cambridge, 1983)

Murphy, M., *Blanco White: A Self-exiled Spaniard* (1989)

Newsome, D., *The Convert Cardinals: John Henry Newman and Henry Edward Manning* (1993)

Norman, E.R., *The English Catholic Church in the Nineteenth Century* (Oxford, 1984)

O'Neil, R., *Cardinal Herbert Vaughan* (1989)

Pereiro, J., *Cardinal Manning: An Intellectual Biography* (Oxford, 1998)

Purcell, E.S., *Life of Cardinal Manning*, 2 vols (1895)

Schiefen, R.J., *Nicholas Wiseman and the Transformation of English Catholicism* (Shepherdstown, 1984)

Strachey, L., *Eminent Victorians* (1918)

Trevor, M., *Newman: The Pillar of Cloud* (1962)

——, *Newman: Light in Winter* (1962)

Vaughan, M., *Courtfield and the Vaughans* (1989)

Ward, W., *Life of John Henry Cardinal Newman*, 2 vols (1912)

——, *Life and Times of Cardinal Wiseman*, 2 vols (1897)

Weatherby, H.L., *Cardinal Newman in his Age: His Place in English Theology and Literature* (Nashville, 1973)

## Twentieth Century

Ball, S. (ed.), *Parliament and Politics in the Age of Churchill and Attlee: The Headlam Diaries 1935–51* (Cambridge, 1999)

Beck, G.A. (ed.), *The English Catholics 1850–1950* (1950)

Bellenger, D.A., 'Cardinal Gasquet (1846–1929): an English Roman', *Recusant History* 24 (1999), pp. 552–60

Burns, C., 'His Eminence Cardinal William Theodore Heard', *Venerabile* 26 (1974), pp. 7–14

Caraman, P., *C.C. Martindale* (1967)

# Bibliography

Castle, T. (ed.), *Basil Hume: A Portrait* (1986)

Cenci, P., *Il Cardinale Raffaele Merry del Val* (Rome and Turin, 1933)

Chadwick, O., *Michael Ramsey* (Oxford, 1990)

Clifton, M., *Amigo: Friend of the Poor* (Leominster, 1987)

De la Bedoyere, M., *Cardinal Bernard Griffin* (1955)

Forbes, F.A., *Rafael, Cardinal Merry del Val* (1932)

Hastings, A., *A History of English Christianity* (1986)

——, 'Cardinal Basil Hume', *Priests and People* 14 (2000), pp. 255–9

Heenan, J.C., *Cardinal Hinsley* (1944)

——, *Not the Whole Truth* (1973)

——, *A Crown of Thorns* (1974)

*Hierarchy Centenary Congress* (1950)

Hooley, T., *A Seminary in the Making* (1927)

Horwood, T., 'Public opinion and the 1908 Eucharistic Congress', *Recusant History* 25 (2000), pp. 120–31

Knowles, D., *The Historian and Character* (Cambridge, 1963)

Lease, G, 'Vatican Foreign Policy and Origins of Modernism', in D. Jodock (ed.), *Catholicism Contending with Modernity* (Cambridge, 2000)

Leslie, S. *Cardinal Gasquet: A Memoir* (1953)

Longley, C., *The Worlock Archives* (2000)

MacCormack, A., *Cardinal Vaughan* (1966)

Moloney, T., *Westminster, Whitehall and the Vatican* (1985)

Oldmeadow, E., *Cardinal Francis Bourne*, 2 vols (1940, 1944)

Rhodes, A., *The Power of Rome in the Twentieth Century* (1983)

Scott, C., *A Historian and His World: A Life of Christopher Dawson 1889–1970* (1984)

Scott, G., *The RCs* (1967)

Snead Cox, J.G., *Life of Cardinal Vaughan*, 2 vols (1910)

Stephens, J.F., *Ampleforth Journal* 104 (1999), pp. 1–19

Trevor Roper, H.R. (ed.), *Macaulay's Essays* (1965)

Waugh, E., *Life of Ronald Knox* (1959)

Wheeler, G., 'The Archdiocese of Westminster', in G.A. Beck (ed.), *The English Catholics 1850–1950* (1950)

# Index of People and Places

# Index